Marijuana Myths

Marijuana Facts

Marijuana Myths Marijuana Facts

a review of the scientific evidence

Lynn Zimmer
and
John P. Morgan

THE LINDESMITH CENTER
NEW YORK AND SAN FRANCISCO

ISBN 0-9641568-4-9

Published by the Lindesmith Center
888 Seventh Avenue
New York, NY 10106 USA

Cover design and graphics by Mark E. Phillips

Printed in the United States by Mirror Image Printing & Graphics

 182

For Lester Grinspoon

Contents

Foreword

Marijuana is by far the most commonly used illegal drug in the United States and in most other countries as well. More than seventy million Americans have tried marijuana, and more than twenty million have smoked it in the last year. The use of marijuana may decrease in years to come, as may the use of alcohol, tobacco, caffeine, and drugs such as Valium and Prozac. But the use of marijuana, like the use of these other psychoactive drugs, is here to stay.

Marijuana Myths, Marijuana Facts provides reliable information about marijuana's effects on people. This book is for everyone interested in the drug itself, and for everyone concerned about people who use it. It is for parents and adolescents, for school counselors and police officers, for drug treatment specialists and drug policy reformers. It is for people who love marijuana and people who hate it.

It seems obvious that marijuana policies, and the personal decisions people make about the use of marijuana, should be based on scientific evidence, factual information, and common sense. Unfortunately, that is frequently not the case. Instead, policies and personal decisions are often made on the basis of false information—on myths about marijuana. These myths abound in American society; they are reported in newspapers, magazines, on T.V. and in government publications. These myths are sometimes successful in scaring children and their parents, and they may deter some people from trying marijuana. But false information does not provide a sound basis for personal action or government policy. Telling the truth about marijuana can be risky, but those risks pale in comparison to the costs of lies and misinformation.

Professors Lynn Zimmer and John P. Morgan have systematically and thoroughly reviewed the many claims made about marijuana, and the latest scientific evidence about marijuana's effects. The scientific evidence shows that heavy marijuana use can be harmful, but that in general marijuana use is not nearly as harmful as the myths about marijuana claim. This is not surprising. In the last hundred years, more than a dozen blue-ribbon commissions in the United States and other countries have found that marijuana's dangers have been exaggerated and that moderate marijuana use is rarely harmful.

Perhaps the issue of greatest concern to most people is the use of psychoactive substances by children. Everyone agrees that children should not use marijuana. Among other things, marijuana possession is illegal and is likely to remain so for years, meaning that those who use it face both criminal punishment and what could be the lifelong stigma of a criminal record. Despite the criminalization of marijuana, and despite the massive efforts and huge costs of the War on Drugs, more adolescents have been trying marijuana in recent years. This is cause for concern by parents, educators, government officials and adolescents themselves. It is not, however, reason for panic or alarm, for spreading false information, or for demonizing marijuana and the people who use it. Rather, as Professors Zimmer and Morgan point out, it should encourage us to consider alternative policies and to learn from the experiences of other nations.

The Lindesmith Center is a drug policy research institute that seeks to stimulate more informed analysis and discussion of drugs and drug control policies. Lynn Zimmer and John P. Morgan are distinguished scholars and experts in the interdisciplinary study of drugs. *Marijuana Myths, Marijuana Facts* is one of a series of books that the Lindesmith Center will publish, reprint, or distribute. We at the Lindesmith Center are proud to be publishing this book. We strongly believe that it will contribute to more honest, accurate and productive discussions about marijuana use and marijuana policy.

Ethan A. Nadelmann
The Lindesmith Center

Acknowledgements

WE have dedicated this book to Lester Grinspoon because he has dedicated twenty-five years of scholarship to the topic of marijuana. In 1971, he wrote the first-ever comprehensive review of the scientific literature on marijuana, *Marihuana Reconsidered*. In 1997, with coauthor James B. Bakalar, Dr. Grinspoon revised and expanded *Marihuana, the Forbidden Medicine*, first published in 1993 by Yale University Press. The first edition was translated into eight languages and is recognized around the world as the authoritative text on marijuana's use as a medicine. We are enormously grateful to have had Lester Grinspoon as our guide.

Dr. Grinspoon was one of seven people who reviewed this manuscript from cover to cover and made many helpful suggestions. The six others are Louis Lasagna M.D., David Lewis M.D., sociologist Harry G. Levine, sociologist Marsha Rosenbaum, Aryeh Neier of the Open Society Institute, and Ethan Nadelmann of the Lindesmith Center. The following people read and commented on one or more chapters, at one or more stages in the book's development: Dan Abrahamson, Marianne Apostolides, Dan Baum, Wally

Bachman, Joel Brown, Gregory Chesher, Peter D.A. Cohen, Jeffery Fagan, JoAnn Gampel, Dale Gieringer, Jean-Paul Grund, Lana Harrison, Leo E. Hollister, Douglas Husak, Denise Kandel, Steven B. Karch, Claudia B. Morgan, Herbert Moscowitz, Laura Murphy, Sheigla Murphy, Rik Musty, Stanton Peele, Craig Reinarman, John K. Robinson, G. Alan Robison, Sidney Schnoll, Loren Siegel, Steven Sifanek, William S. Slikker, Keith Stroup, Donald Tashkin, Chuck Thomas, Andrew Weil, Charles Winick, and Kevin B. Zeese. We are grateful for the positive contribution each of these people made. We took seriously and responded to all of their comments and criticisms, even if not always to their liking. If there are mistakes in the final expression of ideas, evaluations, and conclusions, we are responsible for them.

Throughout this project, Harry G. Levine served as our chief editor, supporter, and critic. He convinced us we were wrong several times when we thought we were right. He encouraged us to work longer when we hoped we were finished. Later, when we wanted to work longer, he encouraged us to let the manuscript go. If we ever write another book, we want Harry to do exactly what he did with this one.

We owe special thanks to Ethan Nadelmann and the Smart Family Foundation for including us in the Princeton Working Group, an ensemble of drug scholars who met regularly from 1990 to 1994 to discuss past, current, and future drug policy. Every idea we have about drugs is influenced by the accumulated knowledge and wisdom expressed during those meetings, and from the conversations we have had since with many of its members. As director of the Lindesmith Center, Ethan Nadelmann continues to provide an intellectual and social environment conducive to serious scholarship on drugs and drug policy.

We could not have completed this project without the help of librarians Estelle Davis at the City College of New York and Leigh Hallingby at the Lindesmith Center. They found and delivered to us many of the articles, books, and reports cited in this book. Josef Filip-Ryan, Bethami Cooper, and Julie Cooper edited one or more versions of nearly every chapter. In a few weeks as our research assistant, Simon Rodberg gave months' worth of assistance. Brent Gardner was the most dependable typist we have ever encountered. Karynn Fish of the Lindesmith Center, who managed the entire production process, dazzled us with her common sense and efficiency. Ultimately, she is the person who made this book "happen."

A presidential research award and a sabbatical leave from Queens College, City University of New York, relieved Lynn Zimmer of teaching responsibilities for eighteen months, making this project possible. Financial support was provided by Peter Lewis. Production support was provided by the Lindesmith Center. Moral support was provided by family and friends. All gave us a free hand in creating this manuscript.

Indian Hemp Drugs Commission, 1894

The commission has come to the conclusion that the moderate use of hemp drugs is practically attended by no evil results at all.[1]

Panama Canal Zone Report, 1925

The influence of [marihuana] . . . has apparently been greatly exaggerated. . . . There is no evidence . . . that it has any appreciably deleterious influence on the individual using it.[2]

LaGuardia Commission Report, 1944

There [is] no direct relationship between the commission of crimes of violence and marihuana . . . and marihuana itself has no specific stimulant effect in regard to sexual desires. The use of marihuana does not lead to morphine or cocaine or heroin addiction.[3]

The British Wootten Report, 1969

[We] intended to present both sides of the controversy. . . . But once the myths were cleared, it became obvious that the case for and against was not evenly balanced. By any ordinary standards of objectivity, it is clear that cannabis is not a very harmful drug.[4]

The Canadian LeDain Commission Report, 1970

Physical dependence to cannabis has not been demonstrated and it would appear that there are normally no adverse physiological effects . . . occurring with abstinence from the drug, even in regular users.[5]

National Commission on Marihuana and Drug Abuse, 1972

There is little proven danger of physical or psychological harm from the experimental or intermittent use of natural preparations of cannabis. . . . Existing social and legal policy is out of proportion to the individual and social harm engendered by the drug.[6]

The Dutch Baan Commission, 1972

Cannabis does not produce tolerance or physical dependence. The physiological effects of the use of cannabis are of a relatively harmless nature.[7]

Commission of the Australian Government, 1977

One of the most striking facts concerning cannabis is that its acute toxicity is low compared with that of any other drugs. . . . No major health effects have manifested themselves in the community.[8]

National Academy of Sciences Report, 1982

Over the past 40 years, marijuana has been accused of causing an array of antisocial effects including . . . provoking crime and violence, . . . leading to heroin addiction, . . . and destroying the American work ethic in young people. [These] beliefs . . . have not been substantiated by scientific evidence.[9]

Report by the Dutch Government, 1995

Cannabis is not very physically toxic . . . . Everything that we now know . . . leads to the conclusion that the risks of cannabis use cannot. . . be described as "unacceptable."[10]

Introduction

DURING the past one hundred years, a number of independent commissions have investigated the effects of marijuana. In 1893, the British Parliament created the Indian Hemp Commission to determine the impact of marijuana consumption on "the social and moral condition" of the people of India. The commission concluded that "the moderate use of hemp drugs is practically attended by no evil results at all." In 1925, a committee investigating marijuana use by U.S. soldiers in the Panama Canal Zone said that marijuana's effects had "apparently been greatly exaggerated." Twenty years later, in 1944, a panel of medical experts commissioned by New York Mayor LaGuardia also found—as LaGuardia himself put it—that "the sociological, psychological, and medical ills commonly attributed to marihuana have been . . . exaggerated."

In response to increases in marijuana use in the 1960s and 1970s, governments in the United States, Canada, England, Australia, and the Netherlands appointed commissions to evaluate the scientific evidence on marijuana's dangers to individuals and society. In 1969, the British Wootten Report noted its agreement with the Indian

Hemp Commission and the LaGuardia Commission. It said that "the long term consumption of cannabis in moderate doses has no harmful effect." In 1972, a Dutch government commission concluded that "the physiological effects of the use of cannabis are of a relatively harmless nature." Also in 1972, the National Commission on Marihuana and Drug Abuse, appointed by President Richard Nixon, said, "The Commission is of the unanimous opinion that marihuana use is not such a grave problem that individuals who smoke marihuana, or possess it for that purpose, should be subject to criminal procedures."

Throughout the twentieth century, the findings of these expert commissions have been overshadowed by extreme claims of marijuana's dangers. State and federal laws against marijuana were enacted in the United States in the 1920s and 1930s, based mainly on reports by police chiefs, prosecutors, and federal drug enforcement officials that marijuana caused people to commit violent, heinous crimes. According to Federal Bureau of Narcotics director Harry Anslinger, "marihuana addicts" had become a "major police problem" in the United States. He claimed that "fifty per cent of the violent crimes commited ... by Mexicans, Turks, Filipinos, Greeks, Spaniards, Latin-Americans and Negroes" could be "traced to the abuse of marihuana." Organizations such as the World Narcotic Defense Association, the International Narcotic Education Association, and the Women's Christian Temperance Union joined the anti-marijuana crusade. They said that marijuana caused addiction, insanity, and sexual promiscuity. They also claimed that "marijuana peddlers" were selling marijuana to grammar school children, with the hope of turning them into addicts.[11]

In 1944, after an extensive investigation which included undercover surveillance at school yards in New York City, the LaGuardia committee concluded that the public had been needlessly frightened about marijuana's dangers. Yet, thirty years later, when the National Commission on Marihuana and Drug Abuse began its investigation, all of the claims from the 1920s and 1930s were still being made. Many new claims have since been added. In the 1950s, law enforcement officials said that marijuana was a "stepping stone" to heroin. They convinced Congress and state legislatures that harsher penalties for marijuana offenses—up to life imprisonment—were needed to reduce the number of heroin addicts. In the 1960s, opponents of marijuana use asserted that marijuana was dangerous because it caused cognitive impairment and an "amotivational syndrome," dooming a generation of young people to academic failure. In the early 1970s, some scientists began reporting serious biological damage from marijuana. They said, for example, that marijuana caused chromosomal abnormalities, immune impairment, and permanent brain damage.[12]

During the past thirty years, researchers funded by the federal government have studied every conceivable way that marijuana might be harmful to individual users and society. Researchers have looked for evidence of marijuana-induced crime, psychological damage, and amotivation. They have studied marijuana's effects on psychomotor ability, intellectual functioning, and behavior. They have looked for a link between marijuana use and other drugs. They have searched for evidence of biological damage from marijuana, often giving large doses of THC (marijuana's chief psychoactive ingredient) to animals or introducing THC into petri dishes containing human cells. Together, these researchers have produced a huge, highly technical body of literature on marijuana that spans many scientific disciplines.

Our goal in writing this book is to make the research on marijuana more accessible to journalists, policy makers, teachers, parents, physicians, marijuana users, and anyone else interested in knowing more about this widely-used drug. We began the project with a list of commonly-made claims about marijuana's harmful effects, all supposedly based on scientific studies. We found these claims in recent government reports, newsletters, and press releases. We found them in drug education pamphlets, Partnership for a Drug-Free America advertisements, and speeches by government officials. We saw them repeated frequently in newspaper and magazine articles about marijuana.

For each of these claims, we searched the scientific literature for relevant studies. Over and over, we discovered that government officials, journalists, and even many "drug experts" had misinterpreted, misrepresented, or distorted the scientific evidence. Indeed, there was so little scientific support for the twenty claims analyzed in this book that we have called them "myths." Like all myths, these may contain a kernel of truth, but never more than that.

Myths about marijuana today, as in the past, increase people's fear of marijuana and strengthen public support for criminal controls over its users. By presenting the facts about marijuana, we hope to promote discussion of less punitive policies. In addition, we hope to ease the fears of parents. Like most Americans, we believe that using psychoactive drugs is an activity for adults, not children. We also believe that lies and exaggerations about marijuana's dangers do little to discourage young people from trying marijuana, and may even have the opposite effect.

20 Myths About Marijuana

Marijuana's Harms Have Been Proved Scientifically

Marijuana Has No Medicinal Value

Marijuana Is Highly Addictive

Marijuana Is a Gateway Drug

Marijuana Offenses Are Not Severely Punished

Marijuana Policy in the Netherlands Is a Failure

Marijuana Kills Brain Cells

Marijuana Causes an Amotivational Syndrome

Marijuana Impairs Memory and Cognition

Marijuana Causes Psychological Impairment

Marijuana Causes Crime

Marijuana Interferes with Male and Female Sex Hormones

Marijuana Use During Pregnancy Damages the Fetus

Marijuana Impairs the Immune System

Marijuana Is More Damaging to the Lungs than Tobacco

Marijuana Gets Trapped in Body Fat

Marijuana Use Is a Major Cause of Highway Accidents

Marijuana-Related Hospital Emergencies Are Increasing

Marijuana Is More Potent Today than in the Past

Marijuana Use Can Be Prevented

MARIJUANA'S HARMS HAVE BEEN PROVED SCIENTIFICALLY. In the 1960s and 1970s, many people believed that marijuana was harmless. Today we know that marijuana is much more dangerous than previously believed.

> *"Every single scientific study that has been done in the last several years shows alarming increases in the toxicity and the danger of using marijuana."*[1]

> *"Parents ...who used marijuana a generation ago ...need to realize ...that research has shown the drug to be far more dangerous ...than was known in the 1960s and 1970s."*[2]

> *"New research tools, including sophisticated brain scanners and methods for studying the brain's system of chemical messengers ...provide new insights on the often subtle effects [of] marijuana."*[3]

> *"There are over ten thousand documented studies available that confirm the harmful physical and psychological effects of smoking marijuana."*[4]

> *"Whatever you may have heard or thought about marijuana in the '60s, '70s, and '80s, forget it."*[5]

IN 1972, AFTER REVIEWING THE SCIENTIFIC EVIDENCE, THE NATIONAL COMMISSION ON MARIHUANA AND DRUG ABUSE concluded that while marijuana was not entirely safe, its dangers had been grossly overstated. Since then, researchers have conducted thousands of studies of humans, animals, and cell cultures. None reveal any findings dramatically different from those described by the National Commission in 1972. In 1995, based on thirty years of scientific research, editors of the British medical journal *Lancet* concluded that "the smoking of cannabis, even long term, is not harmful to health."

1

Marijuana and Science

IN 1970, in response to marijuana's rapidly rising popularity, Congress authorized $1 million for a national commission to study marijuana.[6] The National Commission on Marihuana and Drug Abuse, generally referred to as the Shafer Commission, was headed by former Governor Raymond Shafer of Pennsylvania. Among its twelve other members were four physicians, two lawyers, and four members of Congress.

The Shafer Commission reviewed claims about marijuana's dangers dating back to the 1920s, some of which were still widely believed in the 1970s. The commission hired consultants to review the scientific evidence. Where important evidence was missing, the commission funded original studies. It also held hearings around the country at which lawyers, physicians, researchers, educators, students, and law enforcement officials presented their opinions about marijuana, its effects, and the laws prohibiting its sale and use.

The Shafer Commission found no convincing evidence that marijuana caused crime, insanity, sexual promiscuity, an amotivational syndrome, or that marijuana was a stepping stone to other drugs. Animal studies suggested that no dose of marijuana would be fatal to humans, and that even very large doses of marijuana did not damage tissues or organs. One of the commission's own studies, in which researchers gave men in a laboratory unlimited access to marijuana for twenty-one days, revealed no psychological or intellectual impairment following high-dose use. Research funded by the U.S. government in Jamaica and Greece found no physical or mental problems among men who had used marijuana heavily for many years. Numerous studies showed that marijuana did not produce physical dependence and withdrawal, even after long-term, high-dose use.

The Shafer Commission understood that no drug used by humans is ever completely safe. Given the known harmful effects of smoking tobacco, commission members assumed that smoking marijuana could damage the lungs of users. They worried that driving under the influence of marijuana might cause accidents. Like most other Americans, members of the commission thought kids should not use marijuana. Commission members also worried that long-term heavy marijuana use by adults could lead to social maladjustment. However, they felt that "marihuana related problems, which occur only in heavy, long-term users," had "been over-generalized and over-dramatized." Based on a substantial body of scientific research, the Shafer Commission concluded that "from what is now known about the effects of marihuana, its use . . . does not constitute a major threat to public health."[7]

The Shafer Commission hoped that its review of the scientific evidence would help resolve the social conflict over marijuana policy, a conflict that had been brewing in American society for more than a decade. By 1972, when the commission's report was issued, more than twenty-four million Americans had used marijuana. Among youth, marijuana had become a badge of rebellion. They were skeptical of earlier claims that marijuana caused crime and insanity. They also distrusted newer claims that marijuana caused psychological and biological damage. Large numbers of young people openly defied the law by smoking marijuana in public. Arrests for marijuana offenses had been increasing steadily. Youthful marijuana users with no previous criminal records were being sent to prison for possessing small amounts of marijuana. For all of these reasons and others, the Shafer Commission concluded that marijuana *policy* had become more damaging to American society than marijuana. "Recognizing the extensive degree of misinformation about marihuana," the commission "tried to *demythologize* it" so that a more rational discussion of marijuana policy could occur.[8]

The Shafer Commission's recommendation for marijuana policy, endorsed by all thirteen members, was to retain the prohibition against marijuana's cultivation and sale but to eliminate state and federal criminal penalties for marijuana possession and use. This recommendation was endorsed by mainstream organizations such as the American Bar Association, the American Medical Association, the American Public Health Association, the National Council of Churches, the National Education Association,[9] and the New York Academy of Medicine.[10] In separate reviews of the scientific evidence, several independent scholars agreed with the Shafer Commission that moderate marijuana use was not very dangerous.[11] Around the same time, government-appointed commissions in England, Canada, Australia, and the Netherlands also concluded that the risk of marijuana use was too small to justify harsh criminal sanctions.[12]

Columbia University anesthesiologist Gabriel Nahas, a longtime opponent of marijuana use in the United States and his native Egypt, publicly challenged the Shafer Commission.[13] In

1974, Nahas helped Senator James Eastland organize Judiciary Committee hearings explicitly for the purpose of refuting the commission's findings.[14] Only witnesses in favor of marijuana prohibition were invited. All complained that the Shafer Commission had ignored evidence of marijuana's social and moral dangers. Witnesses described marijuana's detrimental impact on motivation, personality, judgment, intellectual capacity, and the personal hygiene of users. They reported that marijuana molecules got trapped in the brain. As a result, they said, people who used marijuana only once a week were constantly intoxicated. Speakers testified about marijuana addiction and marijuana-induced violence. They claimed that marijuana diminished people's ability to resist homosexual advances, and made them more susceptible to communist propaganda. They said that marijuana use had already led many college students into heroin addiction.

Witnesses at the Eastland hearings also claimed that the Shafer Commission had ignored scientific evidence of marijuana's biological dangers. Many witnesses had themselves conducted studies looking for marijuana-related biological toxicity. One witness claimed to have found evidence of brain damage in young people who smoked marijuana. Another said he had found serious lung damage in U.S. soldiers who had smoked hashish for less than a year. Another said his study showed lowered testosterone levels and sperm counts in men who smoked marijuana. Some Eastland witnesses had given large doses of THC to animals. They claimed to have found hormone deficiencies, infertility, and fetal damage. One scientist reported that after forcing rhesus monkeys to inhale marijuana smoke, he found evidence of irreversible brain damage. Other researchers reported the results of cellular studies, in which they had exposed human cells to THC in laboratory petri dishes. They said THC produced chromosomal abnormalities and evidence of immune deficiency.

Every witness at the Eastland hearings warned that decriminalizing marijuana would be a social disaster. They predicted that marijuana use would skyrocket and that marijuana problems would reach epidemic proportions. Several witnesses warned that because more potent forms of marijuana had become available, all of marijuana's harmful effects would grow in prevalence and severity. Senator Eastland predicted that if marijuana use by youth continued, American society faced certain destruction:

> Our country has been caught up in a marihuana-hashish epidemic. . . . If the epidemic is not rolled back, our society may be largely taken over by a "marihuana culture"—a culture motivated . . . by a consuming lust for self-gratification, and lacking any higher moral guidance. Such a society could not long endure.[15]

During the past twenty-five years, the National Institute on Drug Abuse (NIDA) has funded research into nearly every claim made at the Eastland hearings. Researchers have compared sex hormone levels and brain-wave patterns in marijuana users and nonusers. They have looked for abnormalities in the sperm of men who use marijuana, and have looked for damage to the children of women who smoked marijuana during pregnancy. Medical scientists have examined lung cells taken from long-term marijuana smokers, and have given them repeated tests of pulmonary function. Social scientists have administered personality, social adjustment, and intelligence tests to marijuana users and nonusers. They have compared the grades of students who use marijuana with the grades of students who do not, and the wages of workers who use marijuana with the wages of workers who do not. Researchers have examined data on driving fatalities for evidence of a relationship between marijuana use and highway accidents. Epidemiologists have looked for a link between using marijuana and the use of other illegal drugs. In laboratory studies, researchers have given marijuana to people to evaluate marijuana's effects on memory, motivation, psychomotor skills, and social interaction. Other researchers have given large doses of THC to people, rats, mice, and monkeys every day for months, to see if physical dependence to marijuana develops. Scientists have exposed human cells to THC or marijuana smoke in the laboratory, then looked for cellular abnormalities under a microscope.

In 1982, committees of the Institute of Medicine (IOM) and the World Health Organization (WHO) reviewed the research on marijuana, including ten years of investigation subsequent to the Shafer Commission's review in 1972. Neither committee found convincing evidence of biological harm, psychological impairment, or social dysfunction among people who used marijuana moderately. Studies indicated that some long-term heavy marijuana smokers had problems, but no study indicated that marijuana had directly caused them. Instead, researchers consistently found that high-dose users with serious psychological and social adjustment problems usually had these problems before they began using marijuana.

Although studies of humans generally failed to find evidence of biological harm from marijuana, the IOM and WHO committees were troubled by the large number of animal and cellular studies suggesting *possible* biological toxicity. Although most of the research reported at the Eastland hearings had not been confirmed by other investigators, new claims had appeared, based on additional animal and cellular studies. Committee members were not convinced that animal and cellular studies were relevant to humans. Yet they were unwilling to dismiss them entirely. Neither report contained strong warnings about marijuana's dangers. However, the 1982 IOM and WHO reports[16] were more cautious than the Shafer Commission's report a decade earlier.

After 1982, government support for research into marijuana's effects increased steadily. In 1982, NIDA's marijuana research budget was about $3 million. By 1987 it was $15 million and by 1990 it was $26 million.[17] Much of this research has focused on the claims of biological toxicity first made in the early 1970s. In cellular studies, scientists show that large doses of THC or marijuana smoke regularly disrupt the function of cells in laboratory cultures. In animal studies, researchers are able to produce a variety of biological effects, particularly if they inject THC directly into the animals' veins, abdominal cavities, or brains. In animal and cellular studies, scientists have repeatedly found biological harms that have never been found in human marijuana users—for example, infertility, brain damage, immune impairment, and physical addiction.

Unlike in the 1970s, NIDA now funds few studies of human marijuana users. Early human studies, which often compared moderate marijuana users with nonusers, rarely found evidence of physiological or psychological harm, intellectual impairment, or social dysfunction related to marijuana. When differences were found, they were rarely confirmed by additional studies. Today, when researchers study people, they almost always compare long-term heavy marijuana users with occasional users or nonusers. Heavy marijuana users tend to differ from occasional users and nonusers in many ways other than their use of marijuana. For example, most heavy marijuana users are male, most have used many psychoactive drugs, and many have multiple problems that preceded their use of marijuana. As a result, these studies may identify adverse characteristics in marijuana users that are actually due to factors other than marijuana use.

By administering multiple tests, researchers increase the likelihood that some positive findings will occur by statistical chance. By using new technologies, researchers find subtle differences between marijuana users and nonusers that could not be detected previously. For example, using computer-generated quantitative analysis, researchers recently found "statistically significant" differences between the brain-wave patterns of heavy marijuana users and nonusers—differences that have not been associated with any real-life psychological or intellectual impairment.

In 1972, the Shafer Commission warned, "Science has become a weapon in a propaganda battle."[18] This statement is more true today than then. NIDA funds research to find harm from marijuana. NIDA and other government agencies then disseminate negative findings to Congress, the media, and the public through official reports, press releases, and drug education pamphlets. Findings from animal and cellular studies are used and cited as evidence of marijuana's biological harms, even when researchers have consistently found no such harm in humans. Very modest findings are presented as "significant." Statistical associations—for example, between heavy marijuana use and juvenile delinquency or heavy marijuana use and the use of cocaine—are used to imply a causal relationship. Studies showing no effect—or a positive effect related to marijuana—are ignored completely. In short, science is used selectively to support the claim that marijuana's dangers have been verified scientifically.

Our review of the scientific literature leads us to conclude that marijuana is no more dangerous to humans than the Shafer Commission believed in 1972. Indeed, the research shows that in some respects, marijuana is less dangerous than the Shafer Commission suspected. In 1995, a committee of the Dutch government said, "Everything we now know . . .leads to the conclusion that the risks of cannabis use cannot in themselves be described as 'unacceptable.' "[19] The same year, the editors of *Lancet,* a British medical journal, stated without equivocation that "the smoking of cannabis, even long term, is not harmful to health."[20] In the following chapters, we review the thirty years of scientific evidence on which the Dutch government and the *Lancet* based these conclusions.

MARIJUANA HAS NO MEDICINAL VALUE. Safer, more effective drugs are available. They include a synthetic version of THC, marijuana's primary active ingredient, which is marketed in the United States under the name Marinol.

> *"There is no evidence to prove marijuana's use in chemotherapy. There are numerous alternative drugs that obviate the need to even pursue research on the subject."[1]*

> *"Smoking pot does not qualify as a medicine. . . . The marijuana as medicine issue is a carefully orchestrated campaign . . . by aging hippies, lawyers, and marijuana users who are imposing a cruel hoax on sick and dying people."[2]*

> *"Considering the known effects of marijuana on short-term memory, it seems probable that marijuana would impair . . . the patient's ability to remember to take other lifesaving . . . medicines."[3]*

> *"The pro-drug lobby exploits the suffering of patients with chronic illness . . . as part of a strategy to legalize marijuana for general use."[4]*

> *"There could be no worse message to young people. . . . Just when the nation is trying its hardest to educate teenagers not to use psychoactive drugs, now they are being told that marijuana [is a] medicine."[5]*

FACT

MARIJUANA HAS BEEN SHOWN TO BE EFFECTIVE IN REDUCING NAUSEA INDUCED BY CANCER CHEMOTHERAPY, stimulating appetite in AIDS patients, and reducing intraocular pressure in people with glaucoma. There is also appreciable evidence that marijuana reduces muscle spasticity in patients with neurological disorders. A synthetic THC capsule is available by prescription, but it is not as effective as smoked marijuana for many patients. Pure THC may also produce more unpleasant psychoactive side effects than smoked marijuana. Many people use marijuana as a medicine today, despite its illegality. In doing so, they risk arrest and imprisonment.

2

Marijuana as a Medicine

MARIJUANA'S therapeutic uses are well documented in the modern scientific literature. Using either smoked marijuana or oral preparations of delta-9-THC (marijuana's main active ingredient), researchers have conducted controlled studies. These studies demonstrate marijuana's usefulness in reducing nausea and vomiting,[6] stimulating appetite, promoting weight gain,[7] and diminishing intraocular pressure from glaucoma.[8] There is also evidence that smoked marijuana and/or THC reduce muscle spasticity from spinal cord injuries[9] and multiple sclerosis,[10] and diminish tremors in multiple sclerosis patients.[11] Other therapeutic uses for marijuana have not been widely studied. However, patients and physicians have reported that smoked marijuana provides relief from migraine headaches, depression, seizures, insomnia, and chronic pain.[12] Delta-9-THC is probably responsible for most of marijuana's therapeutic effects, but one of marijuana's other cannabinoid constituents—cannabidiol—appears to be useful as an anticonvulsant.[13] Other cannabinoids may yet prove to have medicinal value.

In the United States, using marijuana for medical purposes is illegal because federal law includes marijuana in Schedule I, a category for drugs deemed unsafe, highly subject to abuse, and possessing no medicinal value.[14] Nonetheless, since the 1970s, thirty-five state legislatures have passed laws supporting marijuana's use as a medicine.[15] In 1996, voters in California and Arizona approved ballot initiatives to remove state criminal penalties for possessing marijuana for medicinal use.[16] However, federal law prevents states from making marijuana supplies legally available. Eight people receive marijuana through a federal "compassionate use" program which stopped admitting new patients in 1992 after the number of applications, mostly from AIDS patients, increased dramatically.[17] Thousands of Americans use marijuana as a medicine illegally, putting themselves at risk of arrest and prosecution.[18] Undoubtedly, others who might benefit from marijuana are deterred by its illegality.

Since 1986, synthetic THC (Marinol) has been available as a Schedule II drug, which allows physicians to prescribe it under highly regulated conditions. Marinol is labeled officially as an anti-nauseant and an appetite stimulant, but doctors can and do prescribe it for other conditions, such as depression and muscle spasticity. This oral preparation of THC, dissolved in sesame oil, works for some patients. However, many patients find that smoked marijuana is more effective. For people suffering from nausea and vomiting, who are unable to swallow and hold down a pill, smoking marijuana is often the only reliable way to deliver THC. For nauseated patients, smoking marijuana has the additional advantage of delivering THC quickly, providing relief in a few minutes, compared to an hour or more when THC is swallowed.[19]

Smoking marijuana not only delivers THC to the bloodstream more quickly than swallowing Marinol, but smoking delivers most of the THC inhaled. When Marinol is swallowed, it must move from the stomach to the small intestine before being absorbed into the bloodstream. After absorption, orally consumed THC passes immediately through the liver, where a significant proportion is biotransformed into other chemicals. Due to metabolism by the liver, 90 percent or more of swallowed THC never reaches sites of activity in the body.[20] Two hours after swallowing ten to fifteen milligrams of Marinol, 84 percent of subjects in a recent study had no measurable THC in their blood. After six hours, 57 percent still had none.[21] By contrast, two to five milligrams of THC consumed through smoking reliably produces blood concentrations above the effective level within a few minutes.[22]

When THC is swallowed, the effects vary considerably, both from one person to another and in the same person from one episode of use to another.[23] And because the onset of effect is an hour or more, patients using Marinol have difficulty achieving just the effective dose. When THC is swallowed, the effects last longer—up to six hours, compared to one or two hours when marijuana is smoked.[24] In other words, smoking marijuana is a more flexible route of administration than swallowing. Smoking allows patients to adjust their dose to coincide with the rise and fall of symptoms.[25] For people suffering from nausea and vomiting from AIDS or cancer chemotherapy, smoked marijuana provides rapid relief with lower overall doses of THC.

Another problem with swallowed THC is that the psychoactive side effects may be more intense than those that occur from smoking. When the liver biotransforms THC, one of the metabolites it produces is 11-hydroxy-THC, a compound of equal or greater psychoactivity.[26] Some 11-hydroxy-THC is produced when marijuana is smoked, but its concentration seldom reaches psychoactive levels.[27] With oral ingestion, patients experience psychoactive effects from THC *and* 11-hydroxy-THC,[28] increasing the likelihood of adverse psychological reactions (see chapter 10). There is also some evidence that one of marijuana's other cannabinoids—cannabidiol—modulates the psychoactive properties of marijuana.[29] In a study of elderly patients, the large dose of oral THC needed to reduce nausea and vomiting produced severe psychoactive effects, reducing its utility as a medicine.[30]

Given these problems, it is not surprising that physicians prescribe Marinol rarely. In one study, researchers asked oncologists (cancer specialists) to rank the effectiveness of available medications for the treatment of nausea and vomiting from cancer chemotherapy. They ranked THC (in natural or synthetic form) as ninth, accounting for only 2 percent of antiemetic prescriptions.[31] In another study, 49 percent of oncologists said they had prescribed Marinol, but only 5 percent had prescribed it more than ten times.[32] A 1990 survey asked oncologists to compare the effectiveness of Marinol and smoked marijuana. Only 28 percent felt familiar enough with both drugs to answer the question. Of these, only 13 percent thought Marinol was better; 43 percent believed the two forms of THC were equally effective, and 44 percent believed smoked marijuana was better. Four hundred and thirty-two oncologists (44 percent of those who returned the questionnaire) said they had recommended smoked marijuana to at least one of their cancer patients.[33] In a 1994 survey, 12 percent of oncologists said they had recommended smoked marijuana and 30 percent said they might prescribe it if it were legal.[34]

Smoking is a highly unusual way to administer a drug. Many drugs could be smoked, but there is no good reason to do so because oral preparations produce adequate blood concentrations. With THC this is not the case. Inhaling is a better route of administration than swallowing. Inhaling is about equal in efficiency to intravenous injection, and considerably more practical.[35]

Other than its illegality, the primary drawback of smoking marijuana is that it deposits irritants in the lungs. With prolonged high-dose use, this could cause pulmonary problems (see chapter 15). However, with short-term use, there is little risk of lung damage. For terminally ill patients, the potential harm from smoking is of little consequence. Other THC delivery systems—for example, suppositories[36] and aerosol sprays[37]—have not been proven effective, but should be studied further. Given currently available options, smoking marijuana is the most efficient and effective way to deliver THC. It is also potentially the cheapest. A patient taking twenty milligrams of Marinol per day would spend $600 or more per month for medication. With the "black market tax" on marijuana removed, plant preparations could be delivered to patients at a fraction of the cost of Marinol.

In the 1970s, the federal government funded research into marijuana's therapeutic uses[38] and provided marijuana supplies to qualified researchers.[39] It also established the "compassionate use" program, through which patients, on a case-by-case basis, could obtain marijuana from the government's marijuana farm in Mississippi.[40] In its 1976 *Marijuana and Health* reports to Congress, the National Institute on Drug Abuse (NIDA) recommended further exploration of marijuana's medicinal uses.[41] NIDA's next two reports, in 1977 and 1980, reiterated this position.[42]

Ronald Reagan's election as president in 1980 brought a renewed war on marijuana[43] and an end to the federal government's support for medical marijuana. NIDA's 1982 *Marijuana and Health* report to Congress reversed its earlier position. It warned that "the negative health effects of marijuana" diminished its therapeutic potential, and suggested that "synthetic analogs of marijuana derivatives" should be pursued instead.[44]

Opposition to medical marijuana continued under the Bush administration. In 1989 the head of the Drug Enforcement Administration (DEA), John Lawn, denied a petition by the National Organization for the Reform of Marijuana Laws (NORML) to reclassify marijuana as a Schedule II drug.[45] This change would have allowed physicians to prescribe marijuana under the strict regulations that now apply to amphetamine, morphine, and cocaine. Lawn denied the petition despite a recommendation for rescheduling by the DEA's own administrative law judge, Francis L. Young. After reviewing the evidence, Judge Young concluded not only that marijuana's medical utility had been adequately demonstrated, but that marijuana had been shown to be "one of the safest therapeutically active substances known to man."[46] The U.S. Court of Appeals upheld the legal authority of the DEA administrator to ignore Judge Young's decision.[47] Today, marijuana remains in Schedule I, a category for drugs deemed unsafe, highly subject to abuse, and possessing no medicinal value.[48]

In 1992, the Bush administration shut down the compassionate use program[49] and the Clinton administration, after some wavering, decided against reinstating it.[50] The DEA continues to oppose any legal change that would make marijuana available as a medicine[51] and even opposes further research on the topic.[52] There have been no government-funded studies of marijuana's medical utility in more than a decade. When California AIDS researcher Dr. Donald Abrams proposed to compare the effectiveness of Marinol to smoked marijuana in the treatment of AIDS-related wasting syndrome, NIDA denied him access to marijuana supplies—despite the fact that his study had received prior approval from the Food and Drug Administration (FDA).[53] In 1996, the Clinton administration opposed voter initiatives in California and Arizona to legalize marijuana for medical use.[54] After both initiatives passed, federal officials threatened to criminally prosecute physicians or revoke their licenses to prescribe controlled substances—simply for recommending smoked marijuana to their patients.[55]

A number of anti-drug organizations argued against legalizing the medical use of marijuana, claiming that any change in the law would send the "wrong message" to teenagers about marijuana's dangers.[56] Most formal associations of physicians have not taken an official position on medical marijuana.[57] However, the federal government's strict prohibitionist position is opposed by the American Public Health Association,[58] the Federation of American Scientists,[59] the Physicians Association for AIDS Care, the Lymphoma Foundation of America,[60] and former U.S. Surgeon General Joycelyn Elders,[61] as well as national associations of prosecutors[62] and criminal defense attorneys.[63] The *New England Journal of Medicine* has taken a stand in support of allowing marijuana's use as medicine,[64] and the *Journal of the American Medical Association* published an invited editorial with the same message.[65] The editorial boards of numerous newspapers have urged the Clinton administration to loosen current restrictions[66]—a view that recent opinion polls show is supported by a majority of Americans.[67]

In defiance of existing law, people across the country use marijuana for medical purposes. Some do so with the knowledge and approval of their physicians.[68] Because the practice is illegal, most patients use marijuana medicinally without medical supervision.[69] Marijuana's illegality means that patients cannot be sure of obtaining standardized products that are free of fungal spores—a critical problem for AIDS patients who have suppressed immune systems (see chapter 14). In some cities, "cannabis buyers' clubs" have formed to supply uncontaminated products to patients.[70] However, in most parts of the country patients must rely on criminal markets that deliver marijuana of unknown potency and purity. Reclassifying marijuana as a Schedule II drug and creating a legal system for its distribution would guarantee that all patients have access to pure, standardized marijuana.

For new drug approval, the FDA requires "substantial evidence" of efficacy, based on "adequate and well-controlled clinical investigations," plus evidence of the drug's limited toxicity when used in therapeutic doses.[71] Smoked marijuana meets this standard. Based on a review of twenty-five years of research, pharmacologist Roger Pertwee concluded that "there is no evidence to suggest that psychotropic cannabinoids (or cannabis) are particularly unsafe or that their adverse effects are any more severe or unacceptable than those of many drugs now used clinically."[72]

In an important sense, the FDA's prior approval of oral THC *is* evidence of marijuana's effectiveness in treating nausea, vomiting, and AIDS-related wasting. The few studies that have directly compared the two forms of THC delivery show smoked marijuana to be more effective than oral administration.[73] In any case, the question is not whether marijuana is *better* than existing medication. For many medical conditions, there are numerous medications available, some which work better in some patients and some which work better in others. Having the maximum number of effective medications available allows physicians to deliver the best possible medical care to individual patients.

Politics, not medical science, has stood in the way of marijuana's approval as a legal medication. In a 1982 letter to the *Journal of the American Medical Association*, Congressman Newt Gingrich wrote that the "outdated federal prohibition" of medical marijuana was "corrupting the intent of state laws and depriving thousands of glaucoma and cancer patients of the medical care promised them by their state legislatures." According to Gingrich, "the hysteria . . . over marijuana's social abuse" and "bureaucratic interference" by the federal government had prevented "a factual [and] balanced assessment of marijuana's use as a medicant."[74] Fifteen years later, that observation is still accurate.

MYTH

MARIJUANA IS HIGHLY ADDICTIVE. Long-term marijuana users experience physical dependence and withdrawal, and often need professional drug treatment to break their marijuana habits.

> *"There is a demand for marijuana-specific treatment that is currently unmet. Marijuana dependence is a challenge that does not pale in comparison to other dependencies, as many people think."[1]*

> *"Marijuana can put a serious chokehold on long-term users who try to quit."[2]*

> *"Studies show that after abruptly stopping marijuana use, the long-term heavy pot user may develop signs and symptoms of withdrawal."[3]*

> *"In 1993, over 100,000 people entering drug treatment programs reported marijuana as their primary drug of abuse, showing they need help to stop."[4]*

FACT

MOST PEOPLE WHO SMOKE MARIJUANA SMOKE IT ONLY OCCASIONALLY. A small minority of Americans—less than 1 percent—smoke marijuana on a daily or near daily basis. An even smaller minority develop dependence on marijuana. Some people who smoke marijuana heavily and frequently stop without difficulty. Others seek help from drug treatment professionals. Marijuana does not cause physical dependence. If people experience withdrawal symptoms at all, they are remarkably mild.

3

Marijuana and Addiction

EPIDEMIOLOGICAL surveys indicate that the large majority
of people who try marijuana do not become long-term frequent
users. A study of adults in their thirties, who were first surveyed in
high school, found a high "discontinuation rate" for marijuana. Of
those who had tried marijuana, 75 percent had not used it in the
past year and 85 percent had not used it in the past month.[5] In
1994, among Americans age twelve years and older, 31 percent had
used marijuana sometime in their lives. Eleven percent had used it
in the past year and 2.5 percent had used it an average of once a
week or more. Only 0.8 percent of Americans currently smoke
marijuana on a daily or near daily basis.[6]

Some people smoke marijuana regularly for years without experiencing adverse physical, psychological, or social consequences.[7]
At some point, many high-dose frequent users decide to reduce
their intake or cease using marijuana altogether. For most, this
appears to be a relatively simple process. For example, one study
looked at twenty-eight- and twenty-nine-year-old men who had been
daily marijuana users sometime during the previous decade. At the

time of the survey, 85 percent were no longer using marijuana on a daily basis, although most continued to use it occasionally.[8]

Some people who use marijuana heavily and frequently find the process of reduction or cessation more difficult, and some seek assistance from drug treatment providers.[9] There has been a recent increase in the number of people entering treatment programs with a primary diagnosis of marijuana dependence.[10] However, most marijuana users enrolled in drug treatment programs are poly-drug abusers who also report problems with alcohol, cocaine, amphetamine, tranquilizers, or heroin.[11]

Studies conducted over several decades in a variety of settings have found that when high-dose marijuana users stop using the drug, withdrawal symptoms rarely occur.[12] When withdrawal symptoms do occur, they tend to be "mild and transitory."[13] In a study conducted at the Federal Narcotics Hospital in Lexington, Kentucky in the 1960s, ten men were kept constantly "high" with at least one marijuana cigarette during every waking hour for thirty days. Upon the abrupt cessation of smoking, no withdrawal symptoms were evident.[14] In another study, huge oral doses of THC were given daily to people for thirty days. When drug administration was ended, subjects had modest complaints of restlessness, sleep disturbance, nausea, decreased appetite, and sweating.[15] In a recent survey, 16 percent of high-dose marijuana users reported some withdrawal symptoms upon quitting, most commonly nervousness and sleep disturbance.[16]

In some animal studies, high doses of THC given intravenously, then stopped abruptly, produce behavioral alteration, including increases in aggressiveness and motor activity. However, no matter how much THC is administered to animals, when it is stopped, animals do not self-administer THC.[17] In a recent study, researchers precipitated more pronounced physical withdrawal symptoms in mice. They did this by infusing the mice with large doses of THC continuously for four days, and then administering a cannabinoid "blocker drug" which immediately strips THC from receptors.[18] This NIDA-funded rodent study of "precipitated withdrawal" is now cited as evidence that marijuana causes physical dependence.[19] In fact, it has no relevance to human marijuana users who, upon ceasing use, always experience a gradual separation of THC from receptors.

Although people develop dependence on marijuana, a 1991 U.S. Department of Health and Human Services report to Congress states that:

> Given the large population of marijuana users and the infrequent reports of medical problems from stopping use, tolerance and dependence are not major issues at present.[20]

Recently, pharmacologists Jack Henningfield and Neal Benowitz independently ranked the dependence potential of six psychoactive drugs: caffeine, nicotine, alcohol, heroin, cocaine, and marijuana. Both ranked caffeine and marijuana as the two least addictive. Henningfield gave the two drugs identical scores and Benowitz ranked marijuana as slightly less addicting than caffeine.[21]

Nonetheless, the number of people diagnosed as marijuana dependent and the number of marijuana users enrolled in drug treatment programs have been rising steadily. Using the American Psychiatric Association's (APA) list of criteria for drug dependence, researchers evaluating marijuana users in community samples have diagnosed as many as 25 percent as marijuana dependent.[22] Drug treatment providers Norman Miller and Mark Gold claim that because the symptoms of marijuana addiction are "often subtle and difficult to identify," marijuana users should be diagnosed as dependent even when they do *not* meet APA's standard.[23] Gold maintains that "it is important to treat all cases of marijuana use as potentially addictive."[24]

Most of the recent articles and books claiming a growing problem of marijuana dependence have been written by drug treatment providers.[25] This group has also benefited enormously from the expansion of treatment services to marijuana users, many of whom are pressured or forced into treatment by parents or other relatives, the courts, or employers.[26] Most workers who test positive in workplace drug testing programs are marijuana users,[27] and many use marijuana only occasionally. Employers typically require workers to participate in drug treatment as a condition of continued employment.[28] Drug treatment programs diagnose marijuana users as "marijuana dependent" even when they do not meet official criteria of drug dependence.

MYTH

MARIJUANA IS A GATEWAY DRUG. Even if marijuana itself causes minimal harm, it is a dangerous substance because it leads to the use of "harder drugs" like heroin, LSD, and cocaine.

> *"Marijuana use is on the rise. . . . These findings are especially alarming since the use of marijuana—the most widely used drug often leads to the use of other, more dangerous drugs."[1]*

> *"Children who have used marijuana are 85 times likelier to use cocaine than children who have not used marijuana."[2]*

> *"It appears that the biochemical changes induced by marijuana in the brain result in a drug-seeking, drug-taking behavior, which in many instances will lead the user to experiment with other pleasurable substances."[3]*

> *"Since marijuana use, harmful as it is in its own right, is often a prelude to the use of other drugs . . . [it is] doubly disastrous."[4]*

> *"Although marijuana is not as addictive or toxic as cocaine, . . . smoking marijuana—or seeing others smoke marijuana— might make some individuals more disposed to use other drugs."[5]*

FACT

MARIJUANA DOES NOT CAUSE PEOPLE TO USE HARD DRUGS. What the gateway theory presents as a causal explanation is a statistical association between common and uncommon drugs, an association that changes over time as different drugs increase and decrease in prevalence. Marijuana is the most popular illegal drug in the United States today. Therefore, people who have used less popular drugs, such as heroin, cocaine, and LSD, are likely to have also used marijuana. Most marijuana users never use any other illegal drug. Indeed, for the large majority of people, marijuana is a *terminus* rather than a *gateway* drug.

4

Marijuana, Hard Drugs and the Gateway Theory

PROPONENTS of the gateway theory, formerly known as the "stepping-stone hypothesis," argue that even if marijuana itself is not very dangerous, marijuana leads people to use other more dangerous drugs.[6] In the 1950s, marijuana was said to be a gateway to heroin,[7] and in the 1960s, a gateway to LSD.[8] Today, marijuana is discussed primarily as a gateway to cocaine.[9]

People who use cocaine, a relatively unpopular drug, are likely to have used the more popular drug, marijuana. Marijuana users are also more likely than nonusers to have had previous experience with legal drugs, such as alcohol, tobacco, and caffeine.[10] Alcohol, tobacco, and caffeine do not cause people to use marijuana. Marijuana does not cause people to use heroin, LSD, or cocaine.

The relationship between marijuana and other drugs varies across societies.[11] Within the United States, the relationship varies across age groups and substances,[12] and from one social group to another.[13] Over time, as any particular drug increases or decreases in popularity, its relationship to marijuana changes. While marijuana use was increasing in the 1960s and 1970s, heroin use was declining. During the past twenty years, as marijuana use rates fluctuated, rates for LSD remained constant. Cocaine became popular in the early 1980s as marijuana use was declining; later, both marijuana and cocaine use declined. Recently, marijuana use has increased while the decline in cocaine use has continued.[14]

Figure 4-1 illustrates the changing relationship between marijuana use and cocaine use over time. At the height of cocaine's popularity in 1986, 33 percent of high school seniors who had used marijuana had also tried cocaine. By 1995, only 14 percent of marijuana users had tried cocaine. Even when marijuana users try cocaine, they do not necessarily become regular users. In fact, very few do. As shown in figure 4-2, of the seventy-two million Americans who have used marijuana, about twenty million have tried cocaine. Of this twenty million, about 30 percent used cocaine only once or twice. Only 17 percent used cocaine more than one hundred times. In other words, for every one hundred people who have used marijuana, *only one* is a current regular user of cocaine.

The probability of trying cocaine is not distributed equally across

FIGURE 4-1

PROPORTION OF MARIJUANA USERS EVER TRYING COCAINE
High School Seniors, 1975-1996

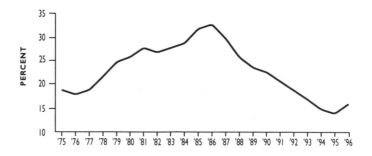

Based on data from *National Survey Results on Drug Use from The Monitoring the Future Study, 1975-1996* (National Institute on Drug Abuse).

the population of marijuana users. Teens who use marijuana occasionally, and use no illicit drugs other than marijuana, are unlikely to ever try cocaine. Indeed, most teens who try marijuana never even become regular users of marijuana. In 1994, among twelve- to seventeen-year-olds who had tried marijuana, 60 percent had used it fewer than twelve times and about 40 percent had tried it only once or twice.[15]

Studies show that most teens who try cocaine have had many previous drug experiences. Most began using alcohol and marijuana at an earlier age than their peers, and most continue to use both alcohol and marijuana frequently.[16] Most also tried numerous other illicit drugs before trying cocaine.[17] One study, looking at adults who had been marijuana users in high school, found that over 80 percent of those who eventually tried cocaine were already multiple-drug users. They regularly used alcohol, tobacco, and marijuana, and had also tried stimulants, sedatives, and psychedelics.[18]

Few adolescents become early multiple-drug users, and those who do differ from their peers in a number of ways. They are more likely to be poor, more likely to live in neighborhoods where illicit drug use is prevalent, less likely to come from stable homes, less likely to be successful at school, and more likely to have psychological problems.[19] Most multiple-drug users engage in a variety of deviant and delinquent activities prior to using legal or illegal drugs.[20] In other words, within the general population of adolescent marijuana users, there is a deviant minority who become multiple-drug users.

A report by the Center on Addiction and Substance Abuse (CASA) says that youthful marijuana users are eighty-five times more likely than nonusers to use cocaine.[21] CASA's calculation is based on marijuana and cocaine prevalence data from 1991. To obtain the eighty-five times "risk factor," CASA divided the proportion of marijuana users who had ever tried cocaine (17 percent) by the propor-

FIGURE 4-2

VERY FEW MARIJUANA USERS BECOME
REGULAR USERS OF COCAINE

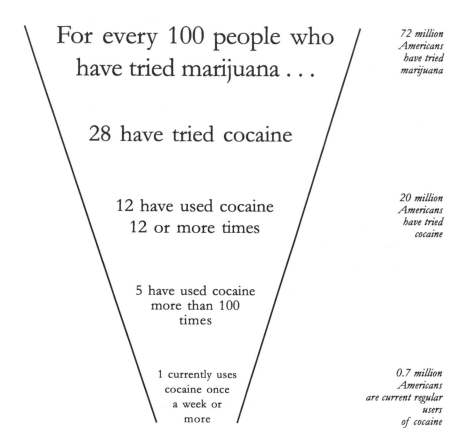

For every 100 people who
have tried marijuana . . .

*72 million
Americans
have tried
marijuana*

28 have tried cocaine

12 have used cocaine
12 or more times

*20 million
Americans
have tried
cocaine*

5 have used cocaine
more than 100
times

1 currently uses
cocaine once
a week or
more

*0.7 million
Americans
are current regular
users
of cocaine*

Based on data from *National Household Survey on Drug Abuse: Population Estimates 1994*,
Rockville, MD: U.S. Department of Health and Human Services (1995); *National Household Survey on Drug Abuse: Main Findings 1994*, Rockville, MD: U.S. Department of Health
and Human Services (1996).

tion of cocaine users who had never used marijuana (0.2 percent). The "risk factor" is large not because so many marijuana users experiment with cocaine, but because very few people try cocaine without trying marijuana first.

Recent animal studies showing that THC increases the availability of dopamine in the brain's "pleasure-reward substrate"[22] are used to claim that marijuana "primes" the brain for heroin and cocaine,[23] drugs which also affect dopamine's availability in this system. Other researchers have failed to find a dopamine effect from THC.[24] More importantly, there are no studies showing that "priming" animals with injections of THC increases their willingness to self-administer heroin or cocaine. After injections of THC, animals will not even self-administer THC. In short, pharmacological explanations for a gateway effect from marijuana have no foundation.

In the end, the gateway theory is not a theory at all. It is a description of the typical sequence in which multiple-drug users initiate the use of high-prevalence and low-prevalence drugs. A similar statistical relationship exists between other kinds of common and uncommon related activities. For example, most people who ride a motorcycle (a fairly rare activity) have ridden a bicycle (a fairly common activity). Indeed, the prevalence of motorcycle riding among people who have never ridden a bicycle is probably extremely low. However, bicycle riding does not cause motorcycle riding, and increases in the former will not lead automatically to increases in the latter. Nor will increases in marijuana use lead automatically to increases in the use of cocaine or other drugs.

MYTH

MARIJUANA OFFENSES ARE NOT SEVERELY PUNISHED. Few marijuana law violators are arrested and hardly anyone goes to prison. This lenient treatment is responsible for marijuana's continued availability and use.

> *"Marijuana enforcement has become far too lax. . . . Marijuana felons must face greater odds of arrest and incarceration."[1]*

> *"The lax treatment has allowed criminals to use and traffic in marijuana with impunity."[2]*

> *"There have to be meaningful consequences when people pollute our young people with marijuana. Right now, we are not doing a good job."[3]*

> *"Marijuana is how this country got into this [drug] problem in the first place. . . . Possession of less than one ounce of marijuana . . . [is often] classed a minor infraction. . . . I believe this is far too lenient."[4]*

> *"It's time to get tough with those who sell marijuana to our most vulnerable citizens—children. . . . Clearly, we should be as tough on marijuana dealers as we are on heroin and cocaine pushers."[5]*

FACT

MARIJUANA ARRESTS IN THE UNITED STATES DOUBLED BETWEEN 1991 AND 1995. In 1995, more than one-half-million people were arrested for marijuana offenses. Eighty-six percent of them were arrested for marijuana possession. Tens of thousands of people are now in prison for marijuana offenses. An even greater number are punished with probation, fines, and civil sanctions, including having their property seized, their driver's licenses revoked, and their employment terminated. Despite these civil and criminal sanctions, marijuana continues to be readily available and widely used.

5

Marijuana Law and Punishment

IN 1972, President Nixon's Shafer Commission concluded that for marijuana users, the harm of an arrest was significantly greater than the harm from using marijuana. It recommended that state and federal laws be changed to remove criminal penalties for "possession of marihuana for personal use" and for the "casual distribution of small amounts of marihuana for no remuneration, or insignificant remuneration not involving profit."[6] In 1982, a National Academy of Sciences report on marijuana also concluded that criminal justice approaches were inappropriate and harmful. It recommended not only that marijuana possession be decriminalized, but that lawmakers give serious consideration to creating a system of regulated distribution and sale.[7]

Since the Shafer Commission's report in 1972, ten million people have been arrested for marijuana offenses in the United States. Federal law enforcement officials—from the DEA, the FBI, the U.S. Customs, the U.S. Forest Service, and the National Park Service—focus mainly on growers, distributors, and large-scale sellers.[8] For example, in 1994, about two-thirds of the marijuana offenders sentenced in federal court possessed two hundred pounds or more of marijuana.[9]

These federal marijuana arrests account for only a fraction of marijuana arrests in the United States—less than 5 percent. At the state and local level, where most marijuana arrests occur, the vast majority are for simple possession, not cultivation, trafficking, or sale. An all-time high was reached in 1995, when state and local police officers arrested nearly 589,000 people for marijuana offenses. Most—86 percent—were arrested for possessing marijuana (see table 5-1). Because of plea bargaining, some people *convicted* of marijuana possession may be marijuana sellers. However, most people *arrested* for possessing marijuana are users, who possess small amounts for personal use.

The increase in marijuana arrests has occurred nationwide. In Georgia, marijuana arrests doubled from 1990 to 1995, from about nine thousand to about eighteen thousand. Juvenile marijuana arrests increased from less than 4 percent of the total in 1990 to about 13 percent in 1995.[10] In Wisconsin, 12,408 people were arrested for possessing marijuana in 1996—more than double the number in 1992.[11] In New York City, arrests for smoking marijuana in public increased from roughly six thousand in 1992 to more than fourteen thousand in 1994.[12]

Ethnic minorities are overrepresented among those arrested for marijuana offenses. Although Blacks and Hispanics constitute approximately 20 percent of marijuana users in the United States,[13] they were 58 percent of the marijuana offenders sentenced under federal law in 1995.[14] In Illinois, 57 percent of those sent to prison for marijuana offense were Black or Hispanic.[15] In California, 49 percent of those arrested for marijuana offenses were Black or Hispanic.[16] In 1995, in New York State, 71 percent of those arrested

TABLE 5-1

MARIJUANA ARRESTS IN THE UNITED STATES
STATE AND LOCAL LEVEL, 1970-1995

	Total Arrests	% Possession
1970:	188,903	*
1971:	225,828	*
1972:	292,179	*
1973:	420,700	*
1974:	445,600	*
1975:	416,100	*
1976:	441,100	*
1977:	457,600	86%
1978:	445,800	86%
1979:	391,600	87%
1980:	401,982	84%
1981:	400,329	86%
1982:	452,244	85%
1983:	403,454	83%
1984:	415,831	82%
1985:	451,138	81%
1986:	361,779	82%
1987:	378,709	83%
1988:	391,612	83%
1989:	398,977	79%
1990:	327,860	80%
1991:	283,700	79%
1992:	340,890	79%
1993:	380,399	82%
1994:	481,098	84%
1995:	588,963	86%

*Data not available

Source: Uniform Crime Reports, 1970-1995 (Federal Bureau of Investigation).

on misdemeanor marijuana possession charges were non-white.[17]

Criminal penalties for marijuana offenses vary across the country. In ten states, possessing small amounts of marijuana (usually less than one ounce) is punishable by a fine. In other states, incarceration is possible, although probation and fines are often given. Under federal law, possessing a single joint (or less) of marijuana is punishable by a fine of from $1,000 to $10,000 and up to one year in prison—the same penalty as for possessing small amounts of heroin, powder cocaine, and crack cocaine. State penalties for possessing a few ounces or more of marijuana range from a low of six months' imprisonment in some states to possible life imprisonment in others.

Penalties for marijuana sale also vary from state to state. Ten states have a maximum sentence of five years or less and eleven states have a maximum penalty of thirty years or more. Under federal law and in six states, marijuana importers and traffickers can be punished with life in prison. In some states, cultivation of a few marijuana plants for personal use is punished as severely as large-scale trafficking and sale.[18]

There has been no systematic compilation of imprisonment rates for marijuana offenses in the United States. However, data from the federal prison system and from a number of states indicate that substantial numbers of marijuana law violators are being incarcerated. The trend is toward increased incarceration, not only for marijuana sale, but also for possession. For example:

- An average of 3,677 marijuana offenders have been put in federal prison each year since 1990. This compares to an average of about 1,900 per year in the 1980s, and about 1,200 per year in the 1970s.[19] Given a current average sentence of about four years, as many as sixteen thousand marijuana offenders may now be in federal prison, comprising about 17 percent of the federal prison population.[20]

- In Michigan, in 1995, 22 percent of those sentenced for marijuana offenses were sent to prison.[21] The same year, in New York State, 34 percent of the people convicted of marijuana offenses were incarcerated.[22]

- In Texas, 33 percent of those convicted of marijuana possession were sent to prison. A slightly higher proportion of sellers and distributors (43 percent) were imprisoned, and half of them possessed two ounces or less of marijuana at the time of arrest.[23]

- In Georgia, where marijuana arrests have doubled since 1990, about four hundred marijuana offenders were sent to prison in 1995, more than half of them for possession.[24]

- Of more than 1,500 people now in prison for a marijuana offense in California, half were convicted of possession.[25] Under California's "three strikes" law, more people have been sent to prison for possessing marijuana than for all violent offenses combined.[26]

- In addition to tens of thousands of inmates sentenced to state and federal prisons for one year or more, tens of thousands of marijuana offenders are serving sentences of less than a year in local jails around the country.

Marijuana violators who avoid incarceration are often punished with probation, community service, or fines, which can be as high as $10 million.[27] The courts can also deny marijuana defendants access to state and federal benefits, including college loans, small business loans, farm subsidies, occupational licenses, and government grants, contracts, and fellowships.[28] More than half the states have enacted "possess a joint, lose your license" laws. Unlike driving-while-intoxicated laws, which link the loss of driving privileges to impaired driving, these laws automatically revoke the driver's license of anyone convicted of any marijuana offense, even if it was not driving related.[29]

Being arrested for a marijuana offense is itself a form of punishment. After an arrest, people may spend hours or days in jail awaiting the first court appearance. An arrest can be costly—not only in lawyer's fees, but, for some people, in lost wages due to absence from work.[30] In some parts of the country, police notify the employers of people who are arrested. As a result, workers may be fired.[31] For people on probation or parole for any criminal offense, a marijuana arrest can result in their immediate incarceration.[32] For people who live in public housing, the arrest of any family member for a drug offense can cause eviction of the entire family—even if there is never a criminal conviction.[33] At least twenty-one state legislatures have enacted laws that require the possessor of illegal drugs to pay for tax stamps upon arrest. The tax on a single ounce of marijuana ranges from $100 to $2800, and for larger amounts, the tax escalates infinitely.[34]

Under state and federal law, mere investigation for a marijuana offense can result in the forfeiture of property, including cash, cars, boats, land, and houses.[35] Government officials seize homes for a few marijuana plants growing on the premises. They seize vehicles that are used to purchase or transport small amounts of marijuana. In some places, the police use undercover sting operations, selling drugs to customers for the purpose of confiscating their cars.[36]

Once the property of suspected drug violators is seized, the government can keep it, even if formal criminal charges are never brought. There are legal means through which innocent owners can seek the return of their property, but the proceedings are time-consuming and costly. And because they take place in civil court rather than criminal court, there is no presumption of innocence—meaning citizens have to *prove* they are innocent of the drug offense to get their property back.[37] Even a formal acquittal on criminal charges does not guarantee that seized property will revert to its owners. For example, after a Kentucky man was found not guilty of marijuana cultivation, state officials kept his thirty-seven-acre farm until he agreed to pay $12,500 in processing fees.[38] From 1992 to 1995, the DEA alone seized over $217 million in assets related to alleged marijuana offenses.[39] Low-level drug offenders are often targeted. For example, the average value of homes seized by Michigan law enforcement officials in 1992 was under $16,000,[40] indicating the owners were not people who had grown wealthy from growing or selling marijuana.

Increasingly, businesses, schools, and social service agencies impose civil sanctions for marijuana use—which may occur instead of, or in addition to, criminal penalties. In the workplace, where urine testing programs are common, job applicants who test positive for drugs are usually denied employment. Current workers who test positive may be fired without evidence of drug use at work or of impaired performance.[41] In fact, because inert marijuana metabolites can be detected for days or weeks following use, drug testing programs mainly catch marijuana users, many of whom use marijuana only occasionally.[42] Public and private schools monitor students for marijuana use, and can impose a variety of sanctions, including exclusion from extracurricular activities, suspension, and expulsion.[43] In some states, drug users are denied medical assistance and welfare benefits,[44] and can be expelled from homeless shelters.[45]

There is no evidence that this escalation of penalties has reduced marijuana's availability or marijuana use. Surveys of high school students since 1975 indicate little change in the proportion who report that marijuana is easy to obtain, ranging only from 83 to 90 percent.[46] Over time, there has been no detectable relationship between marijuana use rates and the degree of enforcement or the severity of punishment. Since 1990, despite the increase in civil and criminal sanctions—and higher rates of arrest and imprisonment for marijuana offenses than ever before in American history— adolescent marijuana use has been rising,[47] and adult marijuana use has remained steady.[48]

MYTH

MARIJUANA POLICY IN THE NETHERLANDS IS A FAILURE. Dutch law, which allows marijuana to be bought, sold, and used openly, has resulted in increasing rates of marijuana use, particularly among youth.

> *"Foreign experiments in . . . permissiveness have failed. In the Netherlands . . . adolescent marijuana use has increased 250 percent."[1]*

> *"In Holland, anyone more than fifteen years old can buy marijuana as easily as different . . . flavors of ice cream. Those who sing the praises of this policy skip over the 250 percent increase in adolescent marijuana use."[2]*

> *"The Netherlands has a tolerant attitude toward . . . marijuana and hashish. . . . I've visited their parks. Their children walk about like zombies."[3]*

> *"The Netherlands has Europe's highest crime rate and crime there has increased as the number of drug 'coffee shops' and drug users expanded."[4]*

FACT

THE NETHERLANDS' DRUG POLICY IS THE MOST NONPUNITIVE IN EUROPE. For more than twenty years, Dutch citizens over age eighteen have been permitted to buy and use cannabis (marijuana and hashish) in government-regulated coffee shops. This policy has not resulted in dramatically escalating cannabis use. For most age groups, rates of marijuana use in the Netherlands are similar to those in the United States. However, for young adolescents, rates of marijuana use are lower in the Netherlands than in the United States. The Dutch people overwhelmingly approve of current cannabis policy which seeks to *normalize* rather than *dramatize* cannabis use. The Dutch government occasionally revises existing policy, but it remains committed to decriminalization.

6

Dutch Marijuana Policy

IN the 1970s, the United States and some other countries reduced penalties for marijuana offenses. In some places criminal penalties for personal possession were eliminated altogether. A second wave of marijuana law reform is now occurring today in Europe and Australia.[5] Leading the way, in the 1970s and today, is the Netherlands. Following the recommendations of two national commissions, the Dutch Parliament decriminalized cannabis possession and retail sale in 1976. Even before this date the police seldom made arrests for possession or small-volume sales.[6] While not officially legalizing marijuana, the 1976 law allowed the Dutch government to create a set of guidelines under which coffee shops could sell marijuana and hashish without fear of criminal prosecution.

Guidelines for the coffee shops have changed somewhat over time and vary slightly from community to community. The basic rules in place today include a ban on advertising, a minimum purchase age of eighteen, and a five-gram limit on individual transactions. The sale of any other illicit drug on the premises is strictly prohibited, and is grounds for immediate closure. Local government officials may limit the number of coffee shops concentrated in one area, and they can close an establishment if it creates a public nuisance. In the Netherlands, there are now over one thousand coffee shops where adults can purchase marijuana and hashish to be used there or carried away for use later.[7]

The decision of Dutch legislators to permit the regulated sale and use of cannabis was based on a number of practical considerations.[8] By allowing marijuana to be sold indoors rather than on the streets, the Dutch sought to improve public order. By separating the retail market for marijuana from the retail market for "hard drugs," they sought to reduce the likelihood of marijuana users being exposed to heroin and cocaine. By providing a nondeviant environment in which cannabis could be consumed, they sought to diminish the drug's utility as a symbol of youthful rebellion. Dutch officials have little faith in the capacity of the criminal law to stop people from using marijuana. They fear that arresting and punishing marijuana users—particularly youthful marijuana users—will alienate them from society's mainstream institutions and values.

These principles of normalization also guide the Dutch approach to drug education and prevention. Programs are specifically designed to be low-key and minimalist, to avoid provoking young people's interest in drugs. There are no mass media campaigns against drugs, and school-based programs do not use scare tactics or moralistic "just say no" messages. Instead, in the context of general health education, young people in the Netherlands are given information about drugs and cautionary warnings about their potential dangers.[9] In leaflets distributed through the coffee shops, current users of cannabis are advised to be "sensible and responsible."[10]

TABLE 6-1

PERCENTAGE OF PEOPLE WHO HAVE EVER USED MARIJUANA

	United States	The Netherlands
Total Population	31.1[1]	28.5[2]
Young Adults	47.3[3]	45.5[4]
Older Teens	38.2[5]	29.5[6]
Younger Teens	13.5[7]	7.2[8]

1   U.S. population, age 12 and over (*National Household Survey on Drug Abuse: Population Estimates 1994*).

2   Amsterdam residents, age 12 and over (Sandwijk, J.P. et al., *Licit and Illicit Drug Use in Amsterdam II*, 1994).

3   Ages 18-34 (see note 1 above).

4   Ages 20-34 (see note 2 above).

5   Twelfth graders, average of 1992, 1993, and 1994 data (*The Monitoring the Future Study, 1975-1994*).

6   Ages 16-19, average of data from 1994 Amsterdam survey (see note 2 above) and 1992 national school-based survey (De Zwart, W.M. et al., *Key Data: Smoking, Drinking, Drug Use and Gambling Among Pupils Aged 10 Years and Older*, Netherlands Institute on Alcohol and Drugs).

7   Eighth graders, average of 1992, 1993, and 1994 data (see note 5 above).

8   Ages 12-15, average of 1994 Amsterdam data (see note 2 above) and 1992 national data (see note 6 above).

This pragmatic cannabis policy has not resulted in an explosion of marijuana use. During the 1970s, marijuana use increased in the Netherlands,[11] as it did in the United States. Today, as shown in table 6-1, marijuana prevalence rates in the United States and the Netherlands are similar for most age groups. However, among young adolescents, marijuana use is lower in the Netherlands—about 7 percent compared to about 13 percent in the United States. A 1994 survey in the city of Amsterdam, where marijuana is more available than almost anywhere else in the world, found that the average age of initiation into cannabis use was twenty,[12] compared to an average age of initiation in the United States of 16.3.[13]

In the last few years, marijuana use has increased in the Netherlands, as it has in the United States and other Western countries.[14] Based on surveys of Dutch students from 1984, 1988, and 1992, American critics of Dutch policy claim that lenient policies caused a 250 percent increase in marijuana use. However, because new sampling techniques were adopted in 1992, the Dutch researchers who conducted the study caution against this interpretation.[15] Another survey conducted in Amsterdam found no increase in cannabis use among youth from 1987 to 1994.[16] Cannabis prevalence in the Netherlands today is similar to that in other European countries, including those with much harsher prohibition policies.[17]

Fewer adolescents in the Netherlands than in the United States use other illegal drugs. In 1994, only 0.3 percent of twelve- to nineteen-year-olds in Amsterdam had ever tried cocaine.[18] The rate among American twelve- to seventeen-year-olds was 1.7 percent.[19] Most cocaine users in the Netherlands, as in the United States, have had previous experience with cannabis. However, youthful Dutch cannabis users today, who grew up under liberal policies, are less likely than older Dutch cannabis users to try cocaine.[20] This may be due to the Netherlands' success in socially separating cannabis from "hard drugs," as well as separating its retail sale.[21] According to a recent government report:

> If young adults wish to use soft drugs—and experience has shown that many do—they should . . . not [be] exposed to the criminal subculture surrounding hard drugs. Tolerating relatively easy access to quantities of soft drugs for personal use is intended to keep the consumer markets for soft and hard drugs separate, thus creating a social barrier to the transition from soft to hard drugs.[22]

Although there are individuals in the Netherlands who oppose the current cannabis policy,[23] it has widespread public and political support. This is because, by all objective measures, it has accomplished what its creators intended. Without threatening citizens with criminal sanctions, marijuana-prevalence rates in the Netherlands are similar to those in the United States where, by contrast, more than ten million people have been arrested for marijuana law violations since 1970 (see chapter 5).

Wholesale distribution of cannabis is still illegal in the Netherlands. As a result, coffee shops obtain cannabis supplies from criminal organizations of the same sort as exist in strict prohibitionist countries. Dutch officials have discussed full legalization as a solution to the problem.[24] However, at present, opposition from prohibitionist governments in other countries[25] and the requirements of international treaties make it politically impossible for the Netherlands to formally legalize cannabis.[26]

Recently, in response to complaints from political leaders in some neighboring countries, the Dutch government reduced the amount of marijuana that coffee shops can sell to an individual. This was done to discourage foreigners from coming into the Netherlands to purchase marijuana for resale across the borders.[27] This change does not mean that Dutch support for decriminalization is waning. Police officials, public health officials, and representatives of all major political parties remain steadfastly committed to the reforms begun in the 1970s.[28] Those policies were based on expert opinions that cannabis, although not entirely safe, posed "an acceptable risk" to users and society.[29] Since then, thousands of additional studies of marijuana's effects have been conducted. Taking their findings into account, a 1995 Dutch government report concluded that no major change in cannabis policy was warranted:

> Cannabis is not very physically toxic. . . . It mainly affects mood, consciousness, and memory and its effect is dependent on the amount used. . . . Neither fatal overdoses nor physical dependency can occur. . . . Cannabis use generates less aggression than drinking alcohol and it is certainly not an automatic step on the road to the use of hard drugs. . . . Everything that we now know . . . leads to the conclusion that the risks of cannabis use cannot in themselves be described as "unacceptable."[30]

MYTH

MARIJUANA KILLS BRAIN CELLS. Used over time, marijuana permanently alters brain structure and function, causing memory loss, cognitive impairment, personality deterioration, and reduced productivity.

> *"When the cell walls in brain tissue become completely saturated with THC, the brain cells die. They cannot be replaced."[1]*

> *"Regular use of marijuana produces cerebral atrophy in young adults."[2]*

> *"Chronic marijuana use can cause brain damage and changes in the brain similar to those that occur during aging."[3]*

> *"Delta-9-THC, the psychoactive ingredient of marijuana ...produces permanent changes in brain function and structure of monkeys, a subhuman primate close to man."[4]*

FACTS

NONE OF THE MEDICAL TESTS CURRENTLY USED TO DETECT BRAIN DAMAGE IN HUMANS HAVE FOUND HARM FROM MARIJUANA, EVEN FROM LONG-TERM HIGH-DOSE USE. An early study reported brain damage in rhesus monkeys after six months' exposure to high concentrations of marijuana smoke. In a recent, more carefully conducted study, researchers found no evidence of brain abnormality in monkeys that were forced to inhale the equivalent of four to five marijuana cigarettes every day for a year. The claim that marijuana kills brain cells is based on a speculative report dating back a quarter of a century that has never been supported by any scientific study.

7

Marijuana and the Brain

THE search for brain damage from marijuana began in the early 1970s, fueled by descriptions of marijuana users as lazy, dull, apathetic, unproductive, irrational, delusional, and intellectually impaired. To marijuana's opponents, these observations constituted prima facie evidence of brain damage.[5] They accepted, without reservation,[6] an early report by British physicians who claimed to have found irreversible brain damage in ten male marijuana users—all of whom had been referred for medical treatment because of psychiatric illness, neurological symptoms, or drug abuse problems. Using a brain imaging technology called pneumoencephalography, Dr. A.M.G. Campbell and his associates forced air into these patients' brains through the spinal column. Campbell reported seeing abnormalities consistent with cerebral atrophy—actual brain tissue shrinkage.[7] Psychiatrists and neuroscientists criticized Campbell's methods and conclusions[8] and, within a few years, this brain imaging technique was abandoned as medically risky and unreliable.

Employing more modern brain imaging technologies, such as the CAT scan, researchers have found no evidence of brain damage in human marijuana users,[9] even in subjects smoking an average of nine marijuana cigarettes per day.[10] Brain-wave patterns of chronic marijuana users and nonusers, produced by standard electro-encephalographic (EEG) tests, cannot be distinguished by visual examination.[11] Using computer-generated quantitative analysis, however, one group of researchers found differences in the distribution of certain brain-wave frequencies between heavy marijuana users and occasional users[12]—differences of unknown significance. With a specialized EEG technique, researchers have also measured the amplitude of a particular brain wave (the P300) in response to auditory and visual stimuli. One study found minor abnormalities in this "event-related potential" (ERP) of chronic marijuana users.[13] However, in the only ERP study to use medically and psychiatrically healthy subjects—and to institute controls for age—researchers found no difference in the ERP responses of chronic marijuana users and nonusers.[14]

With massive doses of THC—one hundred times or more the psychoactive dose in humans—researchers have produced structural brain damage in laboratory animals.[15] Most of these studies have employed rodents. Few studies of primates have been conducted, and until recently, all were done by psychiatrist Robert Heath at the Tulane School of Medicine. In the early 1970s, Heath implanted electrodes in the brains of rhesus monkeys to obtain "deep" EEG readings before and after they inhaled marijuana smoke. Heath reported that marijuana produced profound changes.[16] Despite the fact that the monkeys' EEG readings returned to normal within one hour of drug administration, Heath predicted that with long-term exposure, marijuana would produce permanent brain-wave abnormalities and structural damage.[17]

To test this hypothesis, Heath conducted a six-month study using thirteen rhesus monkeys. Two monkeys were injected with THC, nine monkeys were administered marijuana smoke (in high, moderate, or light doses), and two monkeys were administered smoke from inactive marijuana (containing no THC). All but four of the thirteen monkeys were implanted with electrodes, to allow deep EEG recordings. According to Heath, after three months, monkeys exposed to marijuana or THC showed significant brain-wave abnormalities suggestive of "irreversible changes in brain function." Heath also claimed that the changes persisted throughout the eight-month post-drug period, even though by this point in the study two of the implanted monkeys had died and the electrodes in three others had become dysfunctional. In fact, only one marijuana-smoke-exposed monkey was available for the eight-month analysis.[18]

Heath and his colleagues conducted postmortem examinations of three monkeys' brains. Of these three monkeys, one had received THC injections, one had received placebo smoke, and one had received marijuana. For comparison, the brains of two monkeys not involved in the experiment were also examined. Based on these five brains, the researchers reported marijuana-related structural damage to cells in the brain's septal region.[19] Heath later reexamined these five brains, along with the brain from one of six monkeys used in a second marijuana-smoke-exposure experiment. From this second examination, involving brains from only four of the nineteen experimental animals used in the two studies, Heath reported damage to the brain's hippocampus, a region associated with intellectual function in humans.[20] Even prior to their publication, many people heralded Heath's findings as definitive proof that marijuana caused brain damage.[21]

Heath's studies had numerous problems, including medical complications from the implanted electrodes, difficulty in delivering the marijuana smoke, and inadequate measures of marijuana doses. For years, no additional brain studies with primates were conducted. Recently, scientists at the National Center for Toxicological Research in Arkansas did a rhesus monkey study which effectively repudiated all of Heath's findings.

In the Arkansas study, sixteen rhesus monkeys were dosed, via face-mask inhalation, with the equivalent of four to five marijuana cigarettes every day for a year. Seven months after the yearlong exposure, researchers killed the monkeys and conducted microscopic examinations of their brains. The sixteen high-dose monkeys were compared to sixteen monkeys given lower doses of marijuana, sixteen monkeys given placebo smoke, and sixteen monkeys that had inhaled no smoke at all. The researchers found no marijuana-related differences in neurochemical concentrations,[22] receptor-site configurations,[23] hippocampal architecture, cell size, cell number, or synaptic structure.[24] Indeed, this study found no marijuana-related brain abnormalities at all.

Based on current scientific evidence, the claim of marijuana-induced brain damage is unfounded. Yet it continues to be made. A television ad by the Partnership for a Drug-Free America—evidently inspired by Campbell's long-discredited claim of cerebral atrophy—warns viewers that marijuana "accelerates the aging process." A National Institute on Drug Abuse (NIDA) newsletter reports that "NIDA-supported animal studies do show structural damage to the hippocampus, a structure critical to learning and memory from the principal psychoactive ingredient in marijuana."[25] Government reports and drug education pamphlets still include the warning that "marijuana kills brain cells."[26]

All of the claimed manifestations of brain damage—memory loss, apathy, personality deterioration, and the like—continue to be discussed and studied. In chapter 8, we review the research on motivation and productivity. Chapter 9 examines marijuana's alleged impact on memory and cognition, and chapter 10 explores the claim that marijuana produces psychological impairment and mental illness.

MYTH

MARIJUANA CAUSES AN AMOTIVATIONAL SYNDROME. Marijuana makes users passive, apathetic, and disinterested in the future. Students who use marijuana become underachievers and workers who use marijuana become unproductive.

> *"Young marijuana users . . . are less likely to achieve their academic potential, which detracts from national productivity."*[1]

> *"An amotivational syndrome has been reported in heavy, chronic marijuana users. It is characterized by decreased drive and ambition."*[2]

> *"Marijuana keeps a person from functioning at full potential. It makes an above average student average, and an average student below average."*[3]

> *"The . . . amotivational syndrome . . . is easily recognized. There is a loss of ambition and initiation, a withdrawal from customary activity, and a regression to a simpler kind of life."*[4]

FACT

FOR TWENTY-FIVE YEARS, RESEARCHERS HAVE SEARCHED FOR A MARIJUANA-INDUCED AMOTIVATIONAL SYNDROME AND HAVE FAILED TO FIND IT. People who are intoxicated constantly, regardless of the drug, are unlikely to be productive members of society. There is nothing about marijuana specifically that causes people to lose drive and ambition. In laboratory studies, subjects given high doses of marijuana for several days or several weeks exhibit no decrease in work motivation or productivity. Among working adults, marijuana users tend to earn higher wages than nonusers. College students who use marijuana have the same grades as nonusers. Among high school students, heavy marijuana use is associated with school failure, but school failure usually comes first.

8

Marijuana, Motivation and Performance

IN the late 1960s and early 1970s, as marijuana became increasingly popular among middle-class youth, old claims about marijuana-induced crime and insanity lost credibility. A new set of claims emerged, focusing specifically on marijuana's dangers to adolescents. Among them was the claim that marijuana causes an "amotivational syndrome."[5] For decades, marijuana's critics in India, Morocco, and Egypt had described marijuana users as lethargic, apathetic, and unproductive.[6] Beginning in the late 1960s, some physicians in the United States reported similar characteristics in adolescent patients who admitted using marijuana.[7] In response, researchers conducted various kinds of studies to evaluate marijuana's impact on motivation, work performance, and academic achievement.

Studies of Students

Studies of college students have found few differences between marijuana users and nonusers. Marijuana users and nonusers are equally inclined to participate in sports and extracurricular activities,[8] and place equal value on achievement and success.[9] Some researchers in the 1970s found that marijuana users were less likely than nonusers to have specific plans for the future,[10] and more likely to take temporary leaves of absence from college.[11] No studies have found that using marijuana interferes with college students' academic performance. Most researchers have found that marijuana users have the same grades as nonusers.[12] A few have found higher grades among marijuana users.[13]

Studies of high school students show that heavy marijuana use is associated with academic failure. Heavy marijuana users have lower grades and lower career aspirations than occasional users or nonusers. Heavy marijuana users are also more likely than occasional users or nonusers to drop out of school before graduation.[14] However, most high school students who use marijuana heavily were performing poorly in school before they began using marijuana.[15] Most have a number of emotional, psychological, and behavioral problems, often dating back to early childhood.[16] In addition, heavy marijuana users are more likely than occasional marijuana users or nonusers to use other illegal drugs and to use alcohol heavily.[17] When studies control for these other factors, marijuana use makes no significant contribution to high school students' academic performance.[18]

In the late 1970s, researchers conducted an in-depth study of seventeen adolescents who were heavy marijuana users. All had academic problems. None were motivated to resolve them. However, researchers found no evidence of a generalized lack of motivation or ambition among these adolescents. Many had rejected traditional standards of educational and occupational success, but they had typically done so long before they began using marijuana.[19] In a more recent study, researchers found that as a group, heavy marijuana users were less "achievement oriented" than occasional marijuana users. However, after controlling for symptoms of depression, the researchers concluded that marijuana had not caused diminished motivation. They argued instead that some depressed persons with low motivation became heavy marijuana users.[20]

Studies of Workers

Researchers have looked for evidence of a marijuana-related amotivational syndrome in adults by examining occupational achievement and work performance in marijuana users and nonusers. In the 1970s, researchers conducted studies of working-class men in Jamaica,[21] Costa Rica,[22] and Greece[23]—countries where high-dose marijuana use was common. In all three countries, researchers found little difference in the educational and employment records of high-dose marijuana users, moderate users, and nonusers. In Costa Rica, marijuana users were more frequently unemployed—which the authors attributed to their higher rates of arrest and imprisonment for marijuana offenses. Still, the heaviest marijuana users in Costa Rica had higher-status, higher-wage jobs than either moderate users or nonusers. In Jamaica, where farm laborers often smoked marijuana while they worked, heavy users worked harder than moderate users or nonusers. The researchers concluded that, in this setting at least, marijuana increased workers' productivity.[24]

Recently, a number of researchers have examined labor-force participation and wages among marijuana users and nonusers in the United States. Most have used data from two long-term studies. The first is a survey of four hundred young men in New York State. The second is the National Longitudinal Survey of Youth, with a sample of twelve thousand young adults from across the country. There is nothing in these data to suggest that marijuana reduces people's motivation to work, their employability, or their capacity to earn wages. Studies have consistently found that marijuana users earn wages similar to or higher than nonusers.[25] One study found that marijuana users had longer and more frequent episodes of unemployment.[26] However, another researcher who examined these same data for a greater number of years found no difference in the number of hours worked by frequent marijuana users, occasional users, and nonusers.[27]

Laboratory Studies

A final group of studies, conducted in closed laboratories, have examined marijuana's effects on motivation during and immediately following marijuana smoking. In one study, a group of men volunteered to live on a hospital ward for ninety-four days. During this time, they worked for tokens which they could use to purchase marijuana cigarettes or, at the study's completion, exchange for cash. After an initial twelve-day abstinence period, subjects were required to smoke at least one marijuana cigarette per day. In addition, they could use earned tokens to purchase more marijuana. Some of the men smoked a little, others smoked a lot. At no point in the study did cannabis consumption affect the amount of time men spent working, or the accuracy with which they performed physical and cognitive tasks.[28]

In a second laboratory study, lasting thirty-one days, researchers recruited heavy and moderate marijuana users. During the first few days, when no marijuana smoking was permitted, the heavy users worked harder and earned more tokens than the moderate users. Later, when tokens could be exchanged for marijuana, prior heavy users purchased more marijuana, but they also continued to work harder. On the days following their heaviest smoking, subjects were somewhat less productive than they had been previously. Still, heavy marijuana smokers had a higher total work output than moderate smokers. The heavy smokers spent more tokens on marijuana. However, because they had earned more tokens than moderate users, they turned in the same number of tokens for cash at the study's completion.[29]

Canadian researchers designed a similar token-economy study to evaluate marijuana's impact on motivation. They found that subjects worked less efficiently in the period immediately after they were allowed to smoke marijuana. However, productivity quickly increased and surpassed levels achieved during the abstinence period. Although subjects consuming the most marijuana spent the least amount of time working, overall, they were no less productive. This is because when they worked, they worked harder. In addition, during the period of highest marijuana consumption, subjects organized a strike and successfully negotiated with researchers for increased wages. After that, they worked even harder.[30]

In 1990, NIDA-funded researchers, led by Richard Foltin at the Johns Hopkins School of Medicine, conducted an additional residential laboratory study lasting fifteen days. Unlike the token-economy studies of the 1970s, which motivated subjects with marijuana and money, the Foltin study required subjects to perform extremely boring tasks to earn permission to perform slightly less boring tasks. After establishing individual preferences for four highly undesirable tasks (for example, sorting baskets of plastic chips by color and size or putting five hundred seven-character "nonsense words" into alphabetical order), researchers permitted each subject to work at his most preferred task only after he had worked many more hours at his least preferred task. The researchers expected that during periods of marijuana smoking, subjects would be less willing to work for permission to shift to preferred activities. They found the opposite. Marijuana smoking actually increased subjects' willingness to perform highly boring tasks in return for modest improvements in their work conditions.[31]

• • •

Despite these consistently negative findings, from studies using many different methods, researchers continue to investigate the claim that marijuana causes an amotivational syndrome. Denise Kandel and her colleagues have found that marijuana users, on average, earn higher wages than nonusers. Nonetheless, because the wage benefit decreases as marijuana users get older, these researchers predict that future studies will find marijuana-related wage deficits.[32] Unconvinced by the results of their own laboratory study, Foltin and his associates conclude that "the complicated effects of smoked marijuana on the motivational aspects of human performance" need to be studied more rigorously, under a wider "range of clinical, epidemiological, and experimental conditions."[33] Perhaps, these researchers or others may yet conduct a study—in some population in some setting—that links marijuana use to diminished motivation. Twenty-five years of research already provides convincing evidence that marijuana's pharmacological action does not cause an amotivational syndrome.

MARIJUANA IMPAIRS MEMORY AND COGNITION. Under the influence of marijuana, people are unable to think rationally and intelligently. Chronic marijuana use causes permanent mental impairment.

> *"Marijuana savages short-term memory and the ability to concentrate."[1]*

> *"Marijuana can cause difficulty speaking, listening effectively, thinking, retaining knowledge, problem solving, and forming concepts."[2]*

> *"Cannabis use may lead to acute episodes of mental confusion, and, in the long run, to general mental deterioration."[3]*

> *"Former marijuana users who . . . engage in intellectual activities report they are not able to perform at pre-exposure levels months or even years after having stopped smoking."[4]*

> *"THC suppresses the neurons in the information-processing system of the hippocampus, the part of the brain that is crucial for learning, memory, and the integration of sensory experiences."[5]*

FACT

MARIJUANA PRODUCES IMMEDIATE, TEMPORARY CHANGES IN THOUGHTS, PERCEPTIONS, AND INFORMATION PROCESSING. The cognitive process most clearly affected by marijuana is short-term memory. In laboratory studies, subjects under the influence of marijuana have no trouble remembering things they learned previously. However, they display diminished capacity to learn and recall new information. This diminishment only lasts for the duration of intoxication. There is no convincing evidence that heavy long-term marijuana use permanently impairs memory or other cognitive functions.

9

Marijuana, Memory and Cognition

THERE are two kinds of studies that, in different ways, evaluate marijuana's effects on cognition and intellectual functioning. One examines people while they are "high" on marijuana. The other examines marijuana users while they are sober, looking for long-lasting or permanent effects of marijuana on cognition. In both kinds of studies, researchers administer one or more standardized tests, measuring memory, intelligence, attention, information processing, problem solving, abstract thinking, or learning ability.

The "While High" Studies

Since the late 1960s, dozens of studies have evaluated intellectual performance during the hour or two after people have smoked marijuana.[6] These studies take place in a laboratory, using experienced marijuana users as subjects. Researchers give marijuana to some subjects and a placebo to others. Or, researchers give high doses of marijuana to some subjects and low doses to others. Then one or more cognitive tests are administered to both groups.

The only cognitive tests that fairly consistently show a short-term effect from marijuana are tests of short-term memory. Some memory tests are unaffected by marijuana. While high, people are able to remember things they learned prior to becoming high.[7] Also, when people are given things to remember while they are high, they are able to *recognize* them later.[8] For example, when asked whether a specific word was included on a list of words presented earlier, subjects in the marijuana group and placebo group recognize about the same number of words. However, marijuana does diminish people's ability to freely *recall* words, pictures, stories, or sounds that were presented earlier in the intoxication period. A delay or distraction between the original presentation and the recall task further diminishes the ability of intoxicated subjects to recall the original presentation. In these studies, subjects err mainly by adding extraneous material rather than excluding presented material. That is, while high on marijuana, subjects are especially inclined to "recall" information that was not part of the earlier presentation.[9]

No other cognitive test is consistently affected by marijuana. Many researchers have found that marijuana does not affect people's performance on tests of attention, perceptions, information processing, and problem solving.[10] Some researchers have found minor differences on such tests, and the results are inconsistent from one study to another.[11] These contrary findings may be due to statistical chance. Or they may occur because individual responses to marijuana vary considerably—a factor that is particularly important in studies such as these, which typically use a few dozen subjects.

Findings from these laboratory studies probably do not accurately reflect marijuana's cognitive effects in real-world settings. In fact, such studies may miss some of marijuana's effects on cognition and exaggerate others. Outside the laboratory, people report that marijuana intoxication makes it harder for them to concentrate on one thing, and harder to sustain linear trains of thought.[12] These reports are consistent with laboratory studies showing impairment of short-term memory. Other effects reported by marijuana users—for example, that marijuana enhances problem solving and creative thinking[13]—have not been produced in the laboratory, and probably cannot be replicated in this setting. Ultimately, marijuana's effects on cognition in the real world depend on the time and place people chose to use marijuana and the tasks they are performing.[14] In the laboratory, marijuana temporarily impairs short-term memory and learning. In real-world structured settings, such as the classroom, marijuana is very likely to have similar effects.

The Long-Term Effect Studies

Psychologist M.I. Soueif was the first researcher to report long-term cognitive harm from marijuana. In articles published in the early 1970s, he described significant cognitive deficits in Egyptian prisoners with a history of cannabis use.[15] Other researchers criticized Soueif's findings, saying they were biased by class and educational differences between the cannabis users and nonusers in his sample.[16] Since then, researchers have matched subjects for such factors as age, education, and socioeconomic status. Doing so reduces the potential for bias, but does not eliminate it. Marijuana users and nonusers—particularly high-dose marijuana users and nonusers—often differ in other ways that can affect their scores on tests of cognition. This is especially true in the United States, where high-dose long-term marijuana users are rare, where they tend to be deviant in numerous ways, and where they tend to use many other psychoactive drugs in addition to marijuana.[17] As a consequence, differences between marijuana users and nonusers cannot be attributed automatically to marijuana.

In the 1970s, the U.S. government funded studies of cognition in Jamaica, Greece, and Costa Rica—all countries with long traditions of cannabis use, and where researchers could identify fairly comparable groups of heavy cannabis users, moderate users, and nonusers. The findings from all three countries contrast dramatically with Soueif's reports on Egyptian prisoners. On most cognitive measures, researchers in Jamaica, Greece, and Costa Rica found no difference between long-term cannabis users and nonusers.[18] In a separate Jamaican study, Canadian researchers also found no evidence of permanent cognitive impairment related to frequent high-dose marijuana use.[19]

In 1985 and 1990, researchers conducted two follow-up studies of the Costa Rican sample—twelve and seventeen years after the original study. At both follow-ups, researchers administered the eight original cognitive tests and nine new cognitive tests. Most of these seventeen tests had several subscales, which allowed researchers to conduct over one hundred separate analyses.

In neither follow-up study were there differences between cannabis users and nonusers on any of the original cognitive measures. In 1985, the new cognitive tests produced three statistically significant findings. Long-term cannabis users were slower to complete one subtest (out of fourteen) on a test that had them underline the one symbol in a group of symbols that was different from the others. However, when subjects were instructed to perform the task as quickly as possible, there were no differences between marijuana users and nonusers. On another test, marijuana users were somewhat slower to push the button in response to the sudden appearance of an airplane on a computer screen. Finally, on one section of the Selective Reminding Test, cannabis users remembered fewer words from a list of words presented earlier.[20]

The second follow-up study, in 1990, identified four statistically significant differences between cannabis users and nonusers. However, only one of these findings was consistent with a finding from 1985, and it appeared only after researchers divided the cannabis users into older and younger cohorts. In 1990, on the Selective Reminding Test, older cannabis users (average age forty-five) remembered 10.5 words, compared to 10.9 for older non-cannabis users.[21] This difference was actually *smaller* than the difference found in the entire sample of cannabis users in 1985—a difference the earlier researchers identified as "not particularly robust."[22]

Research in other countries has also found relatively minor differences between marijuana users and nonusers, and they vary considerably from study to study. In India, some researchers have found lower cognitive scores among long-term cannabis users,[23] but other researchers have not,[24] even when employing similar measures. In the United States, two studies in the 1970s found memory deficits among long-term high-dose marijuana users,[25] but three other researchers found that marijuana use had no permanent effect on memory.[26] On cognitive tests measuring problem-solving ability, verbal reasoning, and abstract thinking, most researchers have found no differences between marijuana users and nonusers.[27] In a study of ten American Rastafarians who smoked marijuana (mixed with tobacco) several times each day for an average of 7.4 years, researchers found nothing unusual in the group's cognitive test scores compared to national samples.[28] In a few studies, researchers have even found that heavy marijuana users have higher scores than nonusers on some cognitive measures.[29]

During the past decade, three studies in the United States have reported evidence of long-lasting cognitive impairment from marijuana. In one, Robert Block and M. Ghoneim, from the Department of Anesthesia at the University of Iowa, gave adult marijuana users and nonusers a standard intelligence (IQ) test and a series of computerized tests measuring memory, concept formation, and learning. The study found that heavy marijuana users—who reported seven or more uses per week for an average of 6.5 years— scored lower on two subscales of the IQ test (mathematical skill and verbal expression) and lower on one computerized test of memory. The researchers concluded that because marijuana users and nonusers had been matched for fourth-grade IQ test scores and other factors, marijuana was the probable cause of the detected impairment.[30]

There are reasons to question Block and Ghoneim's conclusions. Their "intermediate" marijuana users—who used marijuana almost as frequently as heavy users (five to six times per week compared to seven times or more)—showed no cognitive deficits at all. In an early analysis of the data, Block and Ghoneim defined heavy use as five or more uses per week. Using this definition, they found that heavy users differed from nonusers on only one subscale of the IQ test.[31] The fact that the researchers later reconceptualized the drug-use categories in a way that created more significant findings raises questions about the entire study's validity. Casting further doubt on Block and Ghoneim's findings is that there was no supervised period of abstinence prior to the tests' administration. Subjects were asked not to use marijuana during the previous twenty-four hours, but there is no guarantee that subjects in the heavy use category—who reported having used marijuana every day during the previous six years—did not smoke marijuana on the day of the study. As a result, some of the detected differences may have been due to marijuana's short-term effects rather than marijuana's long-term effects.

A second recent study was conducted by Harrison Pope and Deborah Yurgelun-Todd of the Department of Psychiatry at Harvard Medical School. They administered a series of cognitive tests to sixty-five heavy marijuana users (who had smoked an average of twenty-nine days during the previous month) and sixty-four light users (who had smoked up to nine times during the previous month). The researchers found no differences between heavy users and light users on tests of attention, verbal fluency, and complex drawing. They found differences on one of two memory tests, and on a card-sorting task designed to measure "mental flexibility." Although the differences were statistically significant, they were not large. For example, in the first (but not the second) trial of the card-sorting task, heavy marijuana users sorted fewer items correctly. Their average score was 51.3, compared to 53.3 for light users. In the memory test, subjects were given five chances to recall words from a list of words presented earlier. At the test's completion, the average number of words recalled by light users was 15.3 and the average for heavy users was 14.9.[32]

Pope and Yurgelun-Todd conclude that the cognitive deficits they found in heavy marijuana users were caused by marijuana. However, gender differences in the data argue against a pharmacological explanation. Together, all of the memory and card-sorting subtests produced eight statistically significant findings. When women were analyzed separately, however, there was only one statistically significant finding. Since there is no other evidence that marijuana affects men and women differently, the cognitive impairments found in male subjects were probably due to factors other than marijuana use.

A final recent report of prolonged cognitive harm from marijuana is based on a study of ten adolescent marijuana users who were committed by their parents to a therapeutic community. The program's medical director, Richard Schwartz, gave a battery of neuropsychological tests (including seven tests of short-term memory) to these youthful marijuana users and two control groups of adolescents. One control group consisted of nine drug-free adolescents from the surrounding community. The other control group consisted of eight adolescents who had been admitted to the treatment program for other reasons, and had used little or no marijuana. According to the authors, the second control group was required "to control for the possible confounding effect on cognitive processing and concentration ability by emotional states of fear, anxiety, or depression possibly experienced by all adolescents immediately after entry into a treatment program."[33] Tests were administered to both treatment samples within five days of their admittance to the program and, again, six weeks later.

At the initial examination, Schwartz et al. report "significant differences between the cannabis-dependent group and the two control groups" on two tests of short-term memory. They also report that, after six weeks, a statistically significant difference remained on one of these two tests. In the paper's abstract the authors say "that cannabis-dependent adolescents have selective short-term memory deficits that continue for at least six weeks after the last use of marijuana."[34] Other researchers now cite the Schwartz study as a "well-controlled" study showing long-term memory impairment from marijuana.[35]

This conclusion is not supported by data presented in the paper. In fact, on the Wechsler Memory Prose Passages Test—the only test showing a six-week difference—marijuana users and other program participants had identical scores. In the discussion section of the paper, the authors write that "the failure to obtain significant differences between the cannabis-dependent group and the control group in the sample may have been due to small sample sizes." Alternatively, they suggest "that the common environment of the two groups (both appearing in the treatment program) may act to commonly alter scores on these tests."[36] The only statistically significant finding at six weeks actually came from comparing the cannabis users to adolescents in the community sample.[37] If this study shows anything, it shows no long-term memory deficit related directly to marijuana use by adolescents.

During the past thirty years, researchers have found, at most, minor cognitive differences between chronic marijuana users and nonusers, and the results differ substantially from one study to another. Based on this evidence, it does not appear that long-term marijuana use causes any significant permanent harm to intellectual ability. Even animal studies, which show short-term memory and learning impairment with high doses of THC, have not produced evidence of permanent damage.[38]

MYTH

MARIJUANA CAN CAUSE PERMANENT MENTAL ILLNESS. Among adolescents, even occasional marijuana use may cause psychological damage. During intoxication, marijuana users become irrational and often behave erratically.

> *"Marijuana causes many mental disorders, including toxic psychosis, panic attacks, flashbacks, delusions, depersonalization, hallucinations, paranoia, and uncontrollable feelings of aggression."[1]*

> *"Marijuana has been known to trigger attacks of mental illnesses such as manic depression and schizophrenia."[2]*

> *"Marijuana . . . impairs development of healthy social relationships. . . . It also appears to impair a young person's ability to make good decisions."[3]*

> *"THC can permanently impair the basic biochemical neural mechanisms which control coherent behaviour."[4]*

FACT

THERE IS NO CONVINCING SCIENTIFIC EVIDENCE THAT MARIJUANA CAUSES PSYCHOLOGICAL DAMAGE OR MENTAL ILLNESS IN EITHER TEENAGERS OR ADULTS. Some marijuana users experience psychological distress following marijuana ingestion, which may include feelings of panic, anxiety, and paranoia. Such experiences can be frightening, but the effects are temporary. With very large doses, marijuana can cause a temporary toxic psychosis. This occurs rarely, and almost always when marijuana is eaten rather than smoked. Marijuana does not cause profound changes in people's behavior.

10

Marijuana, Psychology and Insanity

EARLY advocates of marijuana prohibition in the United States said that marijuana needed to be controlled because it caused insanity.[5] They offered reports from India and Egypt, where a large proportion of institutionalized mental patients, mostly from the lower classes, were known to be cannabis users.[6] In the 1970s, American psychiatrists, scholars, and government commissions criticized these data, pointing out that in Western societies, where more middle-class people used marijuana, there was no apparent association between marijuana use and mental illness. They also noted that a statistical association, even if it were found, would not prove that cannabis *caused* mental illness.[7]

Since the 1970s, numerous researchers have examined the relationship between marijuana and mental illness in Western societies. Most have studied populations of psychiatric patients, looking for a link between marijuana use and the onset or severity of symptoms. Based on retrospective reports from patients' files, one group of researchers found that among people diagnosed with both schizophrenia and cannabis dependence, cannabis use preceded the first psychotic episode in 69 percent of the cases.[8] However, other studies have found that marijuana use is much more likely to follow than precede the onset of psychiatric symptoms—eliminating it as a causal factor in most cases.[9] Some researchers have reported that using marijuana can exacerbate symptoms in people with existing psychiatric disorders.[10] However, others have found less severe symptoms and fewer hospital admissions among psychiatric patients who use marijuana.[11]

A recent study of Swedish military conscripts has prompted renewed claims that marijuana causes mental illness—schizophrenia, in particular. This study assessed the risk of a later diagnosis of schizophrenia based on cannabis use at age eighteen. It found that the prevalence of schizophrenia in men who had used marijuana fifty or more times was 2.8 percent, compared to 1.4 percent in men who had used marijuana less than fifty, but more than ten times. Heavy cannabis use was only one of many factors present at age eighteen that was associated with a later diagnosis of schizo-phrenia. In fact, all of the later schizophrenics had been given a psychiatric diagnosis of some sort by military psychiatrists at the point of conscription. All had previously been prescribed medication for "nervous problems." All had come from broken homes and all had, at some point in their lives, been in trouble at school and in trouble with the police.[12] In other words, in this sample, heavy can-nabis use was associated with a variety of psychological and social problems, all of which were also associated with a later diagnosis of schizophrenia.

This Swedish conscript study did not include data on subjects' cannabis use after age eighteen, or data on their use of other illegal drugs. However, in a more in-depth analysis of a smaller subsample of the original cohort, researchers found that half had used amphetamine,[13] a drug that may precipitate schizophrenia in predisposed persons.[14] Given that the incidence of schizophrenia declined substantially in Western societies in the 1970s, at the same time cannabis use was rising,[15] it seems highly unlikely that marijuana causes schizophrenia in otherwise healthy people.

The claim that marijuana causes subtle psychological damage, particularly among adolescents, first emerged in the 1960s.[16] Studies found that adolescents with psychological and behavioral problems were more likely than other adolescents to use marijuana heavily.[17] Parents, physicians, and drug abuse counselors may identify marijuana as the primary problem—the one causing all the others.[18] Researchers, however, have consistently found that most teens who use marijuana heavily had preexisting psychological and behavioral problems.[19] Heavy marijuana use may exacerbate teens' other problems,[20] but it seems more of a symptom than a cause of social and psychological maladjustment.

Well-adjusted and well-behaved teens who try marijuana are unlikely to become frequent heavy users; and using marijuana occasionally appears to have no significant effect on young people's personalities, psychological status, or behavior. Marijuana users are more likely than nonusers to have personality traits reflecting unconventionality, nonconformity, and sensation-seeking.[21] However, longitudinal surveys, which examine the same subjects over time, find that these traits typically precede rather than follow marijuana experimentation.[22] On measures of social and psychological adjustment, teenagers who use marijuana occasionally are remarkably similar to nonusers.[23] In fact, researchers who followed a group of kids from early childhood through adolescence found that teens who used marijuana occasionally were better adjusted, socially and psychologically, than non-marijuana-using teens.[24] Like other studies showing a statistical association, this one does not demonstrate a causal effect.

Short-Term Psychological Effects

Marijuana temporarily alters mood, perceptions, thoughts, and feelings. For the most part, users perceive these alterations as positive. Occasionally, marijuana intoxication is accompanied by adverse psychological reactions. For example, when smoking marijuana, some people experience a "panic reaction" that may include feelings of loss of control, anxiety, fear, and paranoia. Novice marijuana users, particularly adults, are prone to having panic reactions. They may worry that marijuana's acute physical effects (for example, increased heart rate) are life-threatening, or worry that marijuana's psychoactive effects will escalate or be permanent. Panic episodes vary in intensity and can last anywhere from a few minutes to a few hours. People who repeatedly experience panic from marijuana are unlikely to keep using marijuana.[25]

High doses of THC may increase the likelihood of panic attacks, particularly if the drug is eaten—for example, by swallowing hashish, pure THC, or food containing marijuana. It is difficult to consume extremely large doses of THC by smoking, but it is easy to do so by eating. When swallowing large doses of THC, people experience not only the effects of THC, but also the effects of 11-hydroxy-THC, a distinct psychoactive compound produced by the liver as it metabolizes THC.[26] 11-hydroxy-THC is present following cannabis smoking, but at levels too low to be psychoactive. When a large dose of cannabis is eaten, the dose of 11-hydroxy-THC is pushed into the psychoactive range. The higher incidence of adverse reactions following eating cannabis products is probably due to the combined effects of THC and 11-hydroxy-THC.[27]

Cultural attitudes about marijuana, the setting in which it is used, and individual predispositions appear to play a more important role in panic attacks than dose. High-dose oral consumption does not inevitably produce a panic reaction,[28] and smoking low-potency marijuana does not necessarily prevent it.[29] Some people report never experiencing panic from marijuana. Others seem constitutionally inclined toward having a panic reaction. In fact, just knowing that marijuana can produce panic increases the likelihood of panic occurring. In a double-blind study of marijuana's therapeutic uses, subjects were given a list of possible adverse reactions. Some of the subjects who received the active drug reported the side effects of anxiety and panic. So did some of those who had received a placebo.[30]

A more severe adverse consequence of cannabis use is a "toxic psychosis" in which people experience disorientation, mental confusion, and distorted visual and auditory perceptions.[31] The symptoms can be quite dramatic, and medical personnel sometimes misdiagnose the condition as a nondrug psychosis. Cannabis psychosis is self-limiting, disappearing in a few days with or without medical treatment. Toxic psychosis probably occurs more commonly in individuals with preexisting psychiatric disorders, but by eating high enough doses of THC, presumably anyone can experience psychotic symptoms. Most reports of toxic psychosis come from cultures where people eat hashish or drink potent cannabis beverages.[32] In the United States, where cannabis is consumed mainly through smoking, toxic psychosis rarely occurs.[33]

Some marijuana users report having "flashbacks." This is a state of altered consciousness that resembles being high, but occurs while sober.[34] Flashbacks are of short duration—lasting from a few seconds to a few minutes—and are much less intense than actual drug experiences. Most marijuana users never have flashbacks. Those who do typically report one or two episodes, with no lasting effects. There has never been a cogent pharmacological theory of drug flashbacks. In *The Natural Mind*, Andrew Weil offers a non-pharmacological explanation. He says that what people identify as flashbacks are similar to the transitory déjà vu episodes that nearly everyone experiences at one time or another. Weil suggests that when people have a déjà vu episode soon after using a drug, it may provoke a vivid flash-memory of the drug experience.[35] Reports of marijuana flashbacks are less common today than in the 1960s and 1970s— probably because when the media pay less attention to the topic, people are less likely to interpret their déjà vu experiences as related to prior marijuana use.

Marijuana temporarily alters mood, thought, emotions, and perception, sometimes quite dramatically. None of marijuana's effects cause people to behave in any particular manner. In the midst of a toxic psychosis, people may become agitated and frightened. In response to acute panic, people may become withdrawn and inactive. Neither of these states eliminates the social and moral restraints that guide human behavior. Marijuana does not cause people to become crazed or violent (see chapter 11). In the many laboratory studies that have been conducted, there has never been a report of dramatic behavioral change following cannabis ingestion, even in subjects given very high doses.

Marijuana causes crime. Marijuana users commit more property offenses than nonusers. Under the influence of marijuana, people become irrational, aggressive, and violent.

> *"Young marijuana users are more likely than nonusers . . . to be arrested. [Marijuana] . . . is clearly associated with increased truancy and crime."*[1]

> *"Another issue is the strong link between marijuana use and violence. . . . Sixty-six percent of high school students who carried guns to school also used marijuana. So another important message to our youngsters is that if you use marijuana, you could end up in a violent fight."*[2]

> *"Chronic effects of frequent marijuana use may include . . . pervasive anger with easy provocation to hostile aggression, even against loved ones."*[3]

Every serious scholar and government commission examining the relationship between marijuana use and crime has reached the same conclusion: marijuana does not cause crime. The vast majority of marijuana users do not commit crimes other than the crime of possessing marijuana. Among marijuana users who do commit crimes, marijuana plays no causal role. Almost all human and animal studies show that marijuana *decreases* rather than *increases* aggression.

11

Marijuana, Deviance and Crime

W HEN most Americans first heard about marijuana in the
1920s and 1930s, they learned that it turned people into violent
criminals.[4] Advocates of marijuana prohibition, such as Bureau
of Narcotics director Harry Anslinger, promoted the idea that
marijuana caused crime. For example, in a 1937 article in *American
Magazine*, Anslinger warned readers about the "many murders,
suicides, robberies, criminal assaults, holdups, burglaries and deeds
of maniacal insanity" that marijuana "causes each year."[5] Newspapers across the country provided lurid details of heinous violent crimes
that were allegedly committed under the influence of marijuana.

In 1972, after the Shafer Commission reviewed the evidence
on marijuana and crime, it said:

> Some users commit crimes more frequently than non-users
> not because they use marihuana but because they happen
> to be the kinds of people who would be expected to have
> a higher crime rate, wholly apart from the use of
> marihuana. In most cases, the differences in crime rates
> between users and non-users are dependent not on
> marihuana use per se but on these other factors.[6]

Research conducted since 1972 confirms the Shafer Commission's conclusions. Juvenile delinquents and adult criminals tend to have higher rates of marijuana use than the general population.[7] However, this is because both marijuana use and crime are related to a set of preexisting factors in offenders' social environments, life histories, and personalities. When researchers control for these factors,[8] and control for the use of other drugs,[9] the association between marijuana use and crime diminishes or disappears. Most criminals who smoke marijuana began committing crimes before they began smoking marijuana.[10]

Undoubtedly, there are violent people who smoke marijuana, but marijuana does not make people violent. Marijuana users are more likely to report that marijuana has a "calming effect."[11] Indeed, some people report this effect as an important motivation for their use of marijuana.[12] Many studies show that marijuana users are substantially underrepresented among violent criminals.[13] In a recent study of prisoners in New York State, eighteen of 268 homicide offenders said marijuana had contributed to their committing the murder. However, fifteen of the eighteen also reported they were under the influence of alcohol and/or other drugs at the time of the murder. In none of the eighteen cases did the researchers conclude that marijuana actually contributed to the crime.[14]

A single laboratory study is sometimes cited as evidence that marijuana makes people more aggressive. In this study, eight inner-city men, all with multiple drug problems, were paired in a strategy game. They played the game before and after smoking marijuana. After smoking marijuana, subjects became somewhat more likely to use offensive, as opposed to defensive, strategies against their opponents.[15] In other laboratory experiments, researchers have consistently shown that marijuana decreases hostility and aggression,[16] even when subjects are provoked.[17] Indeed, researchers cannot even produce aggression in laboratory animals[18] unless they subject the animals to extreme stress conditions—such as starvation—before administering THC.[19]

MARIJUANA INTERFERES WITH MALE AND FEMALE SEX HORMONES. In both men and women, marijuana can cause infertility. Marijuana retards sexual development in adolescents. It produces feminine characteristics in males and masculine characteristics in females.

"Marijuana causes a drop in testosterone production, which sometimes leads to deficient puberty in adolescent males."[1]

"Female adolescents who become regular marijuana smokers face . . . raised testosterone levels, which can result in increased facial and body hair and acne."[2]

"Marijuana . . . [causes] lower sperm counts and difficulty having children in men."[3]

"Smoking a single marijuana cigarette suppresses production of the female hormone essential for implantation of a fertilized egg in the uterus."[4]

"Every . . . scientific study that has been done . . . shows . . . the danger of using marijuana, especially to young women, and what might happen to their child-bearing capacity in the future."[5]

FACT

THERE IS NO EVIDENCE THAT MARIJUANA CAUSES INFERTILITY IN MEN OR WOMEN. In animal studies, high doses of THC diminish the production of some sex hormones and can impair reproduction. However, most studies of humans have found that marijuana has no impact on sex hormones. In those studies showing an impact, it is modest, temporary, and of no apparent consequence for reproduction. There is no scientific evidence that marijuana delays adolescent sexual development, has a feminizing effect on males, or a masculinizing effect on females.

12

Marijuana, Sex Hormones and Reproduction

A letter to the *New England Journal of Medicine* in 1972 described gynecomastia (breast enlargement in males) in three marijuana users.[6] This report seems to have initiated the search for a marijuana effect on the hormones that control sexual development and reproduction. The later publication of a study showing no higher prevalence of gynecomastia in marijuana users than nonusers[7] did not deter additional research.

Researchers in the 1970s compared blood testosterone levels in male marijuana users with nonusers. One of the first researchers to do this was Robert Kolodny, who had previously examined testosterone levels in homosexual men.[8] In 1974, Kolodny and his associates reported that frequent marijuana users had lower testosterone levels than occasional marijuana users.[9] Later, these researchers reported temporary reductions in testosterone immediately after men smoked marijuana.[10] In numerous other studies, however, researchers have found no reduction in testosterone after men smoked marijuana, even very high doses.[11] Studies of men in the general population have also failed to find differences in the testosterone levels of marijuana users and nonusers.[12]

Researchers have also examined marijuana's impact on the quantity and quality of sperm. In his 1974 study, Kolodny reported that frequent marijuana users had lower sperm counts than occasional users.[13] However, this study failed to control for sexual activity in the days prior to examination, a factor known to affect sperm concentrations.[14] In another study, men spent thirty days in a closed laboratory where they smoked up to twenty cigarettes per day before researchers examined their sperm. This study found some decrease in sperm concentrations and sperm motility. However, on neither of these tests were the values outside normal ranges. The slight differences that did occur were reversed when the experiment was ended.[15]

Much less research has been conducted with women. One study in the 1970s reported more menstrual cycle abnormalities among marijuana users than nonusers.[16] However, because the sample size was small, the researchers were not able to control for potentially confounding variables. Since then, no one has replicated these findings. In one laboratory study researchers measured female sex hormones following marijuana administration. Some subjects displayed lowered prolactin levels, but the effect was of short duration and concentrations were never below normal.[17] More recently, a study of women in the general population found no effect of marijuana on any hormones, even among high-dose frequent users.[18]

By giving large doses of THC to animals, researchers have produced appreciable effects on sex hormone levels.[19] However, the effects vary from one study to another, depending on the dose and timing of drug administration. When effects occur, they are temporary. In both male and female animals, a single large dose of

THC has more impact on sex hormones than repeated administration. When animals are exposed to THC for weeks or months, tolerance develops, and marijuana loses its impact. For example, in one study of female primates, hormone levels and ovulation cycles were suppressed initially, but after continual daily dosing with THC, they returned to normal.[20] These animal studies suggest that naturally occurring cannabinoid-like compounds play some role in regulating sex hormone secretions. A large dose of THC may alter the system temporarily. With repeated doses, the system adjusts to THC's presence and returns to normal.

In neither male nor female animals have researchers produced permanent harm to reproductive function from either acute or chronic marijuana administration. Recently, researchers added anandamide—a cannabinoid-like compound that occurs naturally in humans—to petri dishes containing two-cell mouse embryos that had been removed from their mothers. In 60 percent of the cases, anandamide halted the embryo's development.[21] Although this study has appeared in government reports as evidence of "the serious and harmful effects of marijuana" on pregnancy,[22] it has no obvious relevance to humans.

There is no convincing evidence of infertility related to marijuana consumption in humans. In one survey, women who were seeking professional help for infertility reported higher rates of marijuana use than a matched sample of fertile women. However, the difference was slight (61 percent versus 53 percent), and was even lower when researchers controlled for lifestyle factors associated with infertility.[23] In a recent study, researchers found no association between marijuana use and early pregnancy loss.[24]

There are no epidemiological studies showing that men who use marijuana have higher rates of infertility than men who do not. Nor is there evidence of diminished reproductive capacity among men in countries where marijuana use is common.[25] It is possible that marijuana could cause infertility in men who already have low sperm counts. However, it is likely that regular marijuana users develop tolerance to marijuana's hormonal effects.

A single case report of a sixteen-year-old marijuana smoker who failed to progress to puberty[26] continues to be cited as evidence that marijuana retards adolescent sexual development. In animal studies, THC has been shown to alter the onset and character of puberty in both sexes—although even with extremely large doses, the results are inconsistent from one study to another.[27] More importantly, there are no systematic clinical data showing delayed sexual maturation in adolescents who use marijuana.

Marijuana has neither a masculinizing effect in females nor a feminizing effect in males. One study reported elevated testosterone levels in female marijuana users, but it was based on a very small sample.[28] A larger, more recent study of women found no differences in the testosterone levels of female marijuana users and nonusers.[29] Numerous studies show that marijuana does not increase female hormones in men[30]—even when high doses are administered in the laboratory.[31]

MARIJUANA USE DURING PREGNANCY DAMAGES THE FETUS. Prenatal marijuana exposure causes birth defects in babies and, as they grow older, developmental problems. The health and well-being of the next generation is threatened by marijuana use by pregnant women.

"Pot smokers have many cells with 10 or 8 or 5 chromo-somes—far fewer than a frog! . . . This can affect the health of the baby the pot smoker may have one day."[1]

"They're not retarded. . . . But it's possible that [marijuana-exposed babies] won't achieve their full potential."[2]

"Marijuana babies . . . may have trouble learning in school because the marijuana has affected their central nervous system."[3]

"An unexpected recent finding has linked heavy cannabis use by pregnant women with a rare form of cancer in their children."[4]

"Children born to marijuana-using mothers [may] have learning disabilities, attention deficits, and hormonal irregularities as they grow older, even if there are no apparent signs of damage at birth."[5]

STUDIES OF NEWBORNS, INFANTS, AND CHILDREN SHOW NO CONSISTENT PHYSICAL, DEVELOPMENTAL, OR COGNITIVE DEFICITS RELATED TO PRE-NATAL MARIJUANA EXPOSURE. Marijuana has no reliable impact on birth size, length of gestation, neurological development, or the occur-rence of physical abnormalities. The administration of hundreds of tests to older children has revealed only minor differences between the offspring of marijuana users and nonusers, and some are positive rather than negative. Two unconfirmed case-control studies identified prenatal marijuana exposure as one of many factors statistically associated with childhood cancer. Given other available evidence, it is highly unlikely that marijuana causes cancer in children.

13

Marijuana Use During Pregnancy

W<small>ARNINGS</small> that marijuana causes birth defects date back to the late 1960s.[6] Some researchers claimed to have found chromosomal abnormalities in blood cells taken from marijuana users. They predicted that young men and women who used marijuana would produce deformed babies.[7] Although later studies disproved this theory,[8] some current drug education materials still claim that genetic damage is passed on by marijuana users to their children.[9]

Today, researchers look for a direct effect of THC on the fetus. In animal studies, THC has been shown to produce spontaneous abortion, low birth weight, and physical deformities—but only with extremely large doses, only in some species of rodents, and only when THC is given at specific times during pregnancy.[10] Because the effects of drugs on fetal development differ substantially across species,[11] these studies have little or no relevance to humans. Studies with primates show little evidence of fetal harm from THC.[12] In one study, researchers exposed chimpanzees to high doses of THC for up to 152 days and found no change in the sexual behavior, fertility, or health of their offspring.[13]

Dozens of studies have compared the newborn babies of women who used marijuana during pregnancy with the babies of women who did not. Mainly, they have looked for differences in birth weight, birth length, head circumference, chest circumference, gestational age, neurological development, and physical abnormalities. Most of these studies, including the largest study to date with a sample of over twelve thousand women,[14] have found no differences between babies exposed to marijuana prenatally and babies not exposed.[15] Given the large number of studies and the large number of measures, some differences are likely to occur by chance. Indeed, researchers have found differences in both directions. In some studies, the babies of marijuana users appear healthier and hardier.[16] In others, researchers have found more adverse outcomes in the babies of marijuana users.[17]

When adverse outcomes are found, they are inconsistent from one study to another, always relatively minor, and appear to have no impact on infant health or mortality.[18] For example, in one recent study, researchers reported a statistically significant effect of marijuana on birth length. The marijuana-exposed babies, on average, were *less than two-tenths of one inch shorter* than babies not exposed to marijuana.[19] Another study found a negative effect of marijuana on birth weight, but only for White women in the sample.[20] In a third study, marijuana exposure had no effect on birth weight, but a small negative effect on gestational age.[21] Overall, this research indicates no adverse effect of prenatal marijuana exposure on the physical health of newborns.

Researchers have also examined older children for the effects of prenatal exposure to marijuana. A study of one-year-olds found no differences between marijuana-exposed and nonexposed babies on measures of health, temperament, personality, sleeping patterns, eating habits, psychomotor ability, physical development, or mental functioning.[22] In two studies, one of three-year-olds,[23] the other of four-year-olds,[24] there was no effect of prenatal marijuana exposure on children's overall IQ test scores. However, in the first study, when researchers looked at Black and White children separately, they found, among Black children only, slightly lower scores on two subscales of the IQ test. On one subscale, it was children exposed to marijuana only during the first trimester who scored lower. On the other subscale, it was children exposed during the second trimester who scored lower.[25] In neither case did the frequency or quantity of mothers' marijuana use affect the outcomes. This makes it highly unlikely they were actually caused by marijuana. Nonetheless, this study is now cited as evidence that using marijuana during pregnancy impairs the intellectual capacity of children.[26]

Also widely cited are two recent case-control studies describing a relationship between marijuana use by pregnant women and two rare forms of cancer in their children. A case-control study compares people with a specific disease (the case sample) to people without the disease (the control sample). Using this method, researchers identify group differences in background, environment, lifestyle, drug use, diet, and the like that are *possible* causes of the disease.

A study of children with non-lymphoblastic leukemia reported a tenfold greater risk related to their mothers' use of marijuana during pregnancy.[27] A second study reported a threefold greater risk of rhabdomyosarcoma.[28] These calculations were based on women's reports that they used marijuana at some point during pregnancy. In the first study, ten out of the 204 case-group mothers (5 percent) reported marijuana use, compared to one out of the 204 control-group mothers (0.5 percent). In the second study, 8 percent of case-group mothers reported using marijuana, compared to 4.3 percent of controls.

These studies do not prove that marijuana use by pregnant women causes cancer in their children. They report a statistical association based solely on women's self-reports of marijuana use. It is likely that both groups of mothers underreported marijuana use; in other studies, researchers have found that marijuana use by pregnant women typically ranges from 10 to 30 percent.[29] There is reason to suspect greater underreporting by control-group mothers, who were randomly selected and questioned about their marijuana use on the telephone. Because the mothers of the sick children were trying to help researchers identify the cause of their children's disease, they had more reason to be honest about their illegal drug use.

Like all case-control studies, these two studies identified many differences between case-group mothers and control-group mothers, all of which could possibly lead scientists to discover the cause of these rare forms of cancer. Other factors associated with childhood rhabdomyosarcoma include low socioeconomic status, fathers' cigarette smoking, a family history of allergies, children's exposure to environmental chemicals, childhood diets that include organ meats, mothers' use of antibiotics during pregnancy, mothers being over age thirty at the time of the child's birth, overdue delivery, and the child having had fewer immunizations.[30] Without additional research, none of the factors that are statistically associated with childhood cancer can be identified as *causes* of childhood cancer. At this time, there is no corroborative evidence to link marijuana with cancer. In fact, in a recent study, researchers found significantly lower rates of cancer in rats and mice following two years of exposure to extremely large doses of THC.[31]

Since 1978, psychologist Peter Fried and his colleagues have collected longitudinal data on prenatal marijuana exposure as part of the Ottawa Prenatal Prospective Study (OPPS). Over the years, these researchers have administered hundreds of tests to the same group of children, assessing their physical development, psychomotor ability, emotional and psychological adjustment, cognitive functioning, intellectual capacity, and behavior.

Out of all the OPPS studies and all the tests given, researchers have found very few differences between marijuana-exposed and nonexposed children. At age one, researchers found that marijuana-exposed infants scored higher on one set of cognitive tests.[32] At age three, the children of moderate marijuana users (one to five joints per week during pregnancy) had higher scores on one test of psychomotor ability.[33] At age four, the children of women who smoked marijuana heavily during pregnancy (an average of nineteen joints per week) scored lower on one subscale of one cognitive test.[34] However, at ages five and six, this difference was no longer present.[35] When the children were six, the researchers added several new measures of "attentional behavior." The children of heavy marijuana users scored lower on one computer-based test of "vigilance."[36] Eleven new psychological and cognitive tests, administered to six- to nine-year-olds, showed no statistically significant differences between the children of marijuana users and nonusers. Parents rated marijuana-exposed children as having more "conduct problems," but this difference disappeared after the researchers controlled for confounding variables.[37]

Despite the overwhelming similarities in the children of marijuana users and nonusers, in their published reports OPPS researchers consistently highlight the occasional negative finding. Fried believes that these findings underestimate the harms of prenatal marijuana exposure. He suggests that "more sensitive measures" are needed because:

> instruments that provide a general description of cognitive abilities may not be capable of identifying nuances in neurobehaviour that may discriminate between the marijuana-exposed and non-marijuana exposed children. . . . Tests that examine specific characteristics that may underlie cognitive performance may be more appropriate and successful.[38]

Recently, Fried predicted that a new test of "executive function" would reveal marijuana-related deficits in preteen youngsters.[39] A short time later, Fried announced that preliminary analysis of his data showed this effect was present.[40] Almost immediately, his announcement appeared in U.S. government reports as evidence of marijuana's harm to the fetus.[41] Additional reports of harm based on the OPPS sample, which now includes fewer than thirty marijuana-exposed children, may be forthcoming—despite the fact that, according to Fried, the consequences of prenatal drug exposure typically diminish as children get older.[42]

After controlling for known confounding variables, Fried estimates that prenatal drug exposure accounts for 8 percent or less of the variance in children's scores on developmental and cognitive tests—and this estimate is for alcohol, tobacco, and marijuana combined.[43] In essentially all studies, marijuana contributes less than alcohol or tobacco.[44] In addition, the findings differ from one study to another, and show no consistent relationship of fetal harm to either the timing or degree of marijuana exposure. While it is sensible to advise women to abstain from all drugs during pregnancy, the weight of current scientific evidence suggests that marijuana does not directly harm the human fetus.

MARIJUANA USE IMPAIRS THE IMMUNE SYSTEM. Marijuana users are at increased risk of infection, including from HIV. AIDS patients are particularly vulnerable to marijuana's immunopathic effects because their immune systems are already suppressed.

> *"Marijuana impairs the immune system and increases susceptibility to sexually transmitted diseases such as genital herpes and AIDS."[1]*

> *"Research has shown that the THC in marijuana has a damaging effect on white blood cells. . . . Marijuana use may increase a person's susceptibility to colds."[2]*

> *"Because marijuana weakens the immune system, marijuana users are vulnerable to all kinds of infections. A weakened immune system has great difficulty fighting diseases such as bronchitis and aspergillosis."[3]*

> *"Cellular immunity is impaired [by marijuana] . . . and impaired ability to fight infection is now documented in humans."[4]*

> *"Smoking marijuana compromises the immune system and puts AIDS patients at significant risk for infections and respiratory problems."[5]*

THERE IS NO EVIDENCE THAT MARIJUANA USERS ARE MORE SUSCEPTIBLE TO INFECTIONS THAN NONUSERS. Nor is there evidence that marijuana lowers users' resistance to sexually transmitted diseases. Early studies which showed decreased immune function in cells taken from marijuana users have since been disproved. Animals given extremely large doses of THC and exposed to a virus have higher rates of infection. Such studies have little relevance to humans. Even among people with existing immune disorders, such as AIDS, marijuana use appears to be relatively safe. However, the recent finding of an association between tobacco smoking and lung infection in AIDS patients warrants further research into possible harm from marijuana smoking in immune-suppressed persons.

14

Marijuana and the Immune System

THE human immune system is a complex set of structures, cells, and mechanisms that protects the body against foreign materials and organisms. Many researchers have looked for evidence of marijuana-related immune impairment in humans, animals, and cell cultures. One of the first was Gabriel Nahas, a long-time opponent of marijuana use who believed that this "deceptive weed" had made "a land once known as 'the fertile crescent' ... stagnant and destitute."[6] Around 1970, in response to the increase in marijuana use by American youth, Nahas became "determined to look into the possibility of physical, even cellular damage" from marijuana.[7]

Nahas's first study employed a standard test of immune function, using human lymphocytes (T-cells) that had been extracted from the blood of marijuana users and nonusers. After exposing the T-cells to known immune activators, Nahas measured their rate of transformation.[8] He predicted the marijuana users would display *enhanced* immune responses, proving that the human body worked diligently to eliminate marijuana's presence. When the research instead showed *diminished* immune response in cells from marijuana users, Nahas argued that marijuana was dangerous because it weakened the immune system and made marijuana users susceptible to infectious disease.[9]

Employing the same method as Nahas, other scientists have consistently found no difference in the transformation in T-cells from marijuana users and nonusers.[10] Even Nahas was unable to replicate his earlier finding using cells taken from heavy marijuana users who had been further exposed to marijuana in his laboratory.[11] Using other tests of cell-mediated immunity, researchers have also found no consistent difference in the immune responses of cells taken from people who use marijuana and those who do not.[12]

When extracted lymphocytes are exposed to THC or marijuana smoke in a petri dish, they typically display diminished response to immune-activating chemicals.[13] In large doses, many drugs (including Valium, Librium, caffeine, aspirin, and alcohol) also decrease lymphocyte transformation in laboratory experiments.[14] Such experiments do not prove that when humans consume these substances their immune systems become suppressed. All drug effects depend on dose, and all drug effects depend on a chain of cellular reactions that cannot be duplicated in laboratory petri dishes. In short, knowing marijuana's direct effect on isolated T-cells reveals nothing about its impact on immune-system functioning in living organisms.

In animals, researchers are able to produce evidence of immune impairment by administering very high doses of THC.[15] For example, researchers can increase infection rates in female guinea pigs and mice by pretreating the animals with THC and applying herpes virus directly to the vagina. To get these results researchers had to administer doses of THC that are forty[16] to one thousand[17] times the psychoactive dose in humans. Although these studies are often cited as evidence that marijuana causes immune impairment, they have no relevance to humans. Using the skin reaction tests that physicians commonly employ to assess immune competence in patients, researchers have found no differences between high-dose marijuana users and nonusers.[18]

At a 1981 conference on marijuana sponsored by the World Health Organization and Canada's Addiction Research Foundation, reviewers of the research literature on immunity reported, "There is no conclusive evidence that cannabis predisposes man to immune dysfunction."[19] A few years later, in approving oral THC (Marinol) for use as a medicine, the FDA found no convincing evidence that THC caused immune impairment. The *Physician's Desk Reference* does not even mention suppressed immunity among the warnings of possible adverse effects from Marinol.[20] In 1992, the FDA approved Marinol as an appetite stimulant specifically for AIDS patients, who have serious immunosuppression.[21]

Another set of researchers has studied the impact of marijuana smoke on alveolar macrophages—cells that help clear the lungs of particulate matter and microorganisms. After exposing macrophages from humans to marijuana smoke in laboratory cultures, researchers have found alterations in macrophage structure and function.[22] Other researchers have found macrophage abnormalities in monkeys that have been forced to inhale marijuana smoke.[23] Macrophage abnormalities have also been found in long-term heavy marijuana smokers.[24] Even in this group, the effects are much less pronounced than typically found in tobacco smokers.[25] Since the effect of smoking on macrophages is dose-dependent, moderate marijuana smoking may produce no actual dysfunction or clinical impairment.

In recent studies of persons testing positive for HIV, researchers have found that tobacco smokers get more lung infections than nonsmokers.[26] One study found more lung infections among HIV-positive persons who report smoking marijuana, cocaine, or crack. All patients in the sample were intravenous drug users. Most smoked *all three* illicit drugs and the vast majority also smoked tobacco.[27] This study does not show immune impairment related specifically to marijuana. In a number of other studies, researchers have found no relationship between marijuana use and the onset or intensity of AIDS symptoms.[28]

Since large numbers of AIDS patients now smoke marijuana to diminish nausea, increase appetite, and promote weight gain (see chapter 2), further research into possible smoking-related infection in immune-suppressed persons is warranted. However, at this point, there is no basis for the dire warnings of immune damage that anti-marijuana activists often make as part of their opposition to marijuana's use as a medicine.[29]

AIDS patients who use marijuana do face an increased risk of contracting aspergillosis. This pulmonary disease, caused by fungal spores that sometimes contaminate improperly stored marijuana,[30] has only been reported in smokers with immune-suppression disorders.[31] Careful screening of marijuana supplies for aspergillus spores and other contaminants would make marijuana safer for AIDS patients, whether they use marijuana medicinally or recreationally.

MYTH

MARIJUANA IS MORE DAMAGING TO THE LUNGS THAN TOBACCO.
Marijuana smokers are at high risk of developing lung cancer, bronchitis, and emphysema.

> *"The effects of one marijuana joint on the lungs are equivalent to four [tobacco] cigarettes, placing the user at increased risk of bronchitis, emphysema, and bronchial asthma."[1]*

> *"Benzopyrene, a known cancer-causing chemical produced in the burning process, is 70 percent more abundant in marijuana smoke than in [tobacco] smoke."[2]*

> *"Damaging effects . . . caused by prolonged exposure to marijuana smoking that have been reported include emphysema-like symptoms [and] cancer of the lung."[3]*

> *"A single joint contains the same amount of tar and other noxious substances as approximately fourteen to sixteen filtered cigarettes."[4]*

FACT

MODERATE SMOKING OF MARIJUANA APPEARS TO POSE MINIMAL DANGER TO THE LUNGS. Like tobacco smoke, marijuana smoke contains a number of irritants and carcinogens. But marijuana users typically smoke much less often than tobacco smokers and, over time, inhale much less smoke. As a result, the risk of serious lung damage should be lower in marijuana smokers. There have been no reports of lung cancer related solely to marijuana. However, because researchers have found precancerous changes in cells taken from the lungs of heavy marijuana smokers, the possibility of lung cancer from marijuana cannot be ruled out. Unlike heavy tobacco smokers, heavy marijuana smokers exhibit no obstruction of the lung's small airways. This indicates that people will not develop emphysema from smoking marijuana.

15

Marijuana Smoking and the Lungs

TOBACCO smoking causes a number of lung diseases, including chronic bronchitis, emphysema, and cancer.[5] Except for their active ingredients—nicotine and cannabinoids—tobacco smoke and marijuana smoke are similar.[6] Marijuana smokers typically inhale more deeply and retain smoke in their lungs longer than tobacco smokers. As a result, marijuana smokers deposit more dangerous material in the lungs each time they smoke.[7] Still, it is the total volume of inhaled toxic material over time that matters—not the amount inhaled per cigarette. Even heavy marijuana smokers never reach the smoke consumption levels of heavy tobacco smokers.

Research conducted over the past thirty years indicates that marijuana smokers are much less likely than tobacco smokers to develop serious lung disease. Heavy marijuana smokers and heavy tobacco smokers both report more adverse respiratory symptoms than nonsmokers. These include chronic cough, phlegm, wheezing, and episodes of bronchitis. However, marijuana-only smokers report fewer of these symptoms than tobacco smokers.[8] In a recent review of records from the Kaiser Permanente Medical Care

Program, researchers found that people who smoked marijuana daily, and did not smoke tobacco, were only slightly more likely than non-smokers to make outpatient visits for respiratory illnesses. During a six-year period, 36 percent of daily marijuana smokers sought treatment for colds, flu, and bronchitis. The rate among nonsmokers was slightly lower, 33 percent.[9]

After years of study, researchers at UCLA report that "marijuana smokers probably will not develop emphysema."[10] Since 1983, these investigators, led by Donald Tashkin, have been examining pulmonary function in the same groups of tobacco smokers, marijuana smokers, smokers of both substances, and nonsmokers. All of the marijuana-only smokers in the sample are heavy users. At the most recent examination, they had been smoking an average of three to four marijuana cigarettes per day for about fifteen years.

At each evaluation, the researchers have looked for small airway obstruction by measuring the volume of air that people can expel from their lungs in one second. Over time, most tobacco smokers have shown increasing obstruction of the lung's small airways. Heavy marijuana smokers have not. In a 1997 paper reporting their latest findings, the researchers conclude that "in contrast to the accelerated annual rate of decline in lung function that occurs in regular tobacco smokers of comparable age . . . findings in the present study do not support an association between even heavy, regular marijuana smoking and the development of chronic obstructive lung disease." In this paper, Tashkin et al. also report that in smokers of both tobacco and cannabis, there was no additive effect on airway obstruction. Indeed, smokers of both substances had less obstruction, probably because they smoked fewer tobacco cigarettes than tobacco-only smokers.[11] A recent study of 268 marijuana smokers in Australia supports the UCLA finding. After smoking cannabis on a daily or weekly basis for an average of nineteen years, the cannabis users had a lower prevalence of emphysema and asthma than the general population.[12]

There are no epidemiological or aggregate clinical data showing higher rates of lung cancer in people who smoke marijuana. THC does not appear to be carcinogenic. In laboratory petri dishes, THC does not cause cellular changes of the sort associated with cancer.[13] However, marijuana smoke—like tobacco smoke—does.[14] In the 1970s, some chemists reported that, compared to tobacco, marijuana had higher levels of one cancer-causing chemical, benzopyrene.[15] However, other chemists have found more benzopyrene in tobacco.[16] Probably neither form of smoke is inherently safer or more dangerous than the other.

For all smoking-related diseases, what matters most is the dose of smoke inhaled over time.[17] Researchers at UCLA have detected precancerous changes in bronchial cells taken from heavy long-term marijuana smokers.[18] Other researchers have found greater cell pathology in people who smoke both marijuana and tobacco than in people who smoke only one or the other.[19] In a recent study of lung cancer patients, all thirteen patients who were under age forty-five had smoked marijuana at some point in their lives. However, twelve of the thirteen were also current smokers of tobacco.[20] It is possible that people who smoke both marijuana and tobacco heavily have an increased risk of lung cancer. A case-control comparison of marijuana prevalence among lung cancer patients—currently planned by UCLA researchers—should produce a better assessment of marijuana smokers' cancer risk.

Most marijuana-only smokers in the United States probably do not ingest enough smoke to cause serious lung damage. Most people who smoke marijuana smoke far less than the marijuana smokers studied at UCLA. For example, in 1994, of adults who said they had used marijuana during the previous year, nearly half said they had not used it at all during the previous month. Among past-month marijuana users, 55 percent said that they had used it on four or fewer occasions. Only 0.8 percent of Americans reported using marijuana on a daily or near daily basis.[21]

Heavy frequent marijuana users might reduce the pulmonary risk by smoking higher-potency marijuana, which can produce desired psychoactive effects with less smoking. However, as we discuss in chapter 19, a substantial increase in potency is required to produce greater psychoactivity. Some people have speculated that inhaling marijuana smoke through a water pipe delivers less tar and particulate matter. However, a recent study found this to be untrue.[22] Putting filters on marijuana cigarettes might reduce tar delivery, but it is unclear how much this will reduce pulmonary risk. Heavy smokers, in particular, are advised to stop inhaling marijuana deeply and holding their breath. These rituals increase the deposit of dangerous material in the lungs, but increase psychoactive effects marginally, if at all.[23]

MARIJUANA'S ACTIVE INGREDIENT, THC, GETS TRAPPED IN BODY FAT. Because THC is released from fat cells slowly, psychoactive effects may last for days or weeks following use. THC's long persistence in the body damages organs that are high in fat content, the brain in particular.

> *"THC molecules are very busy, and they are up to no good seeping through the fatty membrane wall of the cell and its core, creating havoc with the chemical process of cell division."[1]*

> *"Cannabinoids accumulate in the fatty cells, and the three-pound brain is one-third fat. . . . Therefore, in the brain of the chronic pot-smoker, millions of . . . axons are continually surrounded by THC."[2]*

> *"Cannabinoids, which are soluble only in fat, are stored in bodily tissues. . . . Anyone using marijuana more than once a week . . . cannot be drug-free."[3]*

> *"Even people using marijuana only once each month are continually exposing their brain, lungs, liver, and other vital tissues to the poisonous effects of THC."[4]*

MANY ACTIVE DRUGS ENTER THE BODY'S FAT CELLS. What is different (but not unique) about THC is that it *exits* fat cells slowly. As a result, traces of marijuana can be found in the body for days or weeks following ingestion. However, within a few hours of smoking marijuana, the amount of THC in the brain falls below the concentration required for detectable psychoactivity. The fat cells in which THC lingers are not harmed by the drug's presence, nor is the brain or other organs. The most important consequence of marijuana's slow excretion is that it can be detected in blood, urine, and tissue long after it is used, and long after its psychoactivity has ended.

16

Marijuana's Persistence in the Body

THE body processes THC much as it processes other psychoactive drugs. After THC enters the bloodstream—most commonly via the lungs through smoking—a small proportion (about 1 percent of the dose) is delivered to the brain where it binds to a specific set of receptors.[5] If the amount of drug in the brain exceeds the threshold dose, psychoactive effects occur. Maximum psychoactive effects are typically achieved within fifteen to thirty minutes after the onset of smoking.

While THC is being delivered by the bloodstream to the brain, it is also being distributed to all other parts of the body. As this process of distribution continues, THC concentrations in the blood fall, reducing the amount of drug available for binding to brain receptors. Within two to four hours, THC levels in the brain typically fall below those necessary for psychoactivity.[6] As shown in figure 16-1, when blood concentrations are below a range of two to twenty-five nanograms per milliliter (ng/ml), psychoactive effects have usually ended.[7]

Many drugs, including THC, are *lipid soluble*. This allows them to easily enter cells throughout the body by dissolving into cell

119

FIGURE 16-1

SINGLE EPISODE OF MARIJUANA SMOKING
TYPICAL DISAPPEARANCE OF EFFECT

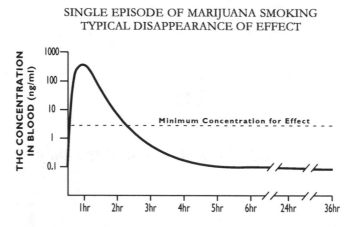

membranes, which are themselves largely lipid (fatty) in character. Drugs move rather quickly out of most cells—either in their original form or, due to *biotransformation* within the cell, as water-soluble *metabolites*. After reentering the bloodstream, drugs may be biotransformed further, particularly as they pass through the liver. Eventually, all of the drug and its metabolites are excreted from the body in sweat, feces, and urine.[8]

THC enters and leaves most cells in the body at about the same rate as other psychoactive drugs. However, certain characteristics of THC—in particular, its high lipid-solubility—delay its exit from fat cells.[9] THC does not preferentially seek out fatty tissue. Like some other drugs that humans consume—for example, Valium, Pentothal, and Thorazine—THC is released from fat cells slowly.[10] Since little or no biotransformation occurs in fat cells, some active THC reenters the bloodstream. However, the amount released from fat cells is too small to be psychoactive. Indeed, none of marijuana's effects last beyond a few hours. A few researchers have reported subtle marijuana effects persisting up to twenty-four hours.[11] However, in dozens of other studies measuring psychomotor ability and intellectual performance, researchers have found that all marijuana effects disappear within a few hours of smoking.[12]

FIGURE 16-2

MULTIPLE EPISODES OF MARIJUANA SMOKING
TYPICAL DISAPPEARANCE OF EFFECT

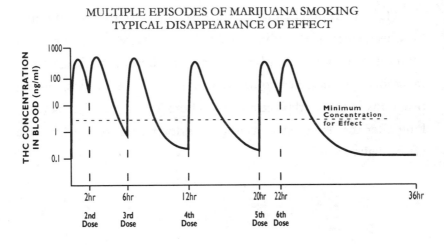

Even for frequent marijuana users, amounts of THC in the blood fall below the psychoactive level within a few hours of each episode of smoking. Figure 16-2 shows blood concentrations when people smoke several times within a thirty-six-hour period. Some THC from each prior use mixes in the blood with THC from the most recent use. However, the amount released from fat cells is too small to make a significant contribution. As a consequence, among both occasional and frequent marijuana smokers, psychoactive effects last for only a few hours. If people smoke marijuana more frequently than shown in figure 16-2 (for example, once every hour), THC levels in the blood and brain would be higher. However, the small amount of previously ingested THC that is steadily released into the bloodstream from fat cells still makes no significant contribution to the level of intoxication.[13]

THC remains in fatty tissue long after people smoke marijuana.[14] However, there are no THC receptors in fat cells and the drug's presence in fatty tissue appears to have no consequences. Despite the often made claim, the brain is not a particularly fatty organ,[15] and THC does not accumulate there.[16] Small amounts of THC accumulate in some other organs, but there is no evidence that it alters cell function or causes structural damage.[17]

THC is eventually biotransformed into inactive metabolites. However, since THC moves so slowly from fatty tissue to sites of biotransformation, it may be days or weeks before the drug and its metabolites are excreted completely. As a consequence, drug testing programs in the workplace and elsewhere identify marijuana users long after the drug was consumed and long after its psychoactive effects have ended.[18]

MYTH

Marijuana use is a major cause of highway accidents. Like alcohol, marijuana impairs psychomotor function and decreases driving ability. If marijuana use increases, an increase in traffic fatalities is inevitable.

> *"Marijuana use diminishes motor control functions, distorts perceptions, and impairs judgement, leading among other things to increased car accidents."[1]*

> *"Recent studies reveal marijuana use is a significant factor in highway fatalities."[2]*

> *"There is a scientific consensus that marijuana—in the 'social' doses commonly used—seriously impairs driving, both while high and possibly for several hours after the subjective intoxication has disappeared."[3]*

> *"Marijuana—like alcohol—seriously impairs driving; in some respects, marijuana is even more impairing than alcohol."[4]*

FACT

There is no compelling evidence that marijuana contributes substantially to traffic accidents and fatalities. At some doses, marijuana affects perceptions and psychomotor performance—changes which could impair driving ability. However, in driving studies, marijuana produces little or no car-handling impairment—consistently less than that produced by low to moderate doses of alcohol and many legal medications. In contrast to alcohol, which tends to increase risky driving practices, marijuana tends to make subjects more cautious. Surveys of fatally injured drivers show that when THC is detected in the blood, alcohol is almost always detected as well. For some individuals, marijuana may play a role in bad driving. The overall rate of highway accidents appears not to be significantly affected by marijuana's widespread use in society.

17

Marijuana and Highway Safety

ALCOHOL'S contribution to highway accidents and fatalities is incontrovertible. Epidemiological surveys have consistently found that one-half or more of drivers in fatal crashes recently consumed alcohol to a level of intoxication, typically defined as a blood-alcohol concentration (BAC) of 0.1 percent.[5] Researchers have shown that alcohol impairs performance in driving simulator studies. They have also demonstrated alcohol-related impairment in studies of actual driving, usually conducted on roads closed to other traffic.

The increase in marijuana use in the 1960s raised concern about marijuana's possible impact on highway safety.[6] Since then, numerous studies have evaluated marijuana's effects on driving, using the same techniques that are used to evaluate the effects of alcohol and legal medications. None of the studies suggest that marijuana contributes substantially to highway accidents or fatalities. Indeed, they suggest the opposite. Researchers who conducted a recent Department of Transportation study said:

Of the many psychoactive drugs, licit and illicit, that are

available and used by people who subsequently drive, marijuana may well be among the least harmful.[7]

In driving simulator studies, researchers have found that marijuana affects some performance measures, particularly those involving visual perception and divided attention,[8] but overall impairment from marijuana is less severe than from alcohol producing BACs well below the 0.1 legal limit.[9] Studies of actual driving have shown that low doses of marijuana cause little or no impairment, and even high doses of marijuana typically cause less impairment than low doses of alcohol.[10] Studies have also found that subjects tend to drive more cautiously after smoking marijuana. They take fewer risks, drive at lower speeds, and maintain a greater distance from other cars.[11]

The most recent marijuana-driving study was conducted at the Institute for Human Pharmacology in the Netherlands. Researchers gave subjects three different doses—one hundred, two hundred, and three hundred micrograms (mcg) of THC per kilogram (kg) of body weight. Then, researchers evaluated subjects' driving performance on the highway. First, subjects drove on a highway closed to traffic, then, on an occupied highway. In both cases, marijuana had an insignificant effect on nearly every measure. Marijuana did make it harder for drivers to maintain a steady lateral position in their lane, particularly at the higher doses. However, even at the 300 mcg/kg dose, marijuana's effect was relatively minor—similar to that observed in drivers using many legal medications. After the 100 mcg/kg dose, subjects were evaluated in a third trial, conducted in high-density urban traffic. Researchers compared marijuana's influence on driving to the influence of low levels of alcohol (.04 percent BAC). Alcohol produced significant reductions in driving ability and marijuana produced none.[12]

Critics of this Dutch study claim that the lack of significant impairment was a result of insufficient dosage.[13] However, there are several reasons to believe that the researchers used appropriate doses. At the lowest dose (100 mcg/kg), subjects reported psychoactive effects, and researchers found expected changes on psychological and physiological measures. In other studies, researchers have found impairment at doses as low as 50 mcg/kg.[14] The largest dose used in the Dutch driving study (300 mcg/kg) is higher than that used in most laboratory studies,[15] and higher than that typically consumed by recreational marijuana smokers.[16] A more reasonable criticism of this and all on-road driving studies is that they seldom require subjects to respond to the kinds of emergencies that can occur in real-life driving situations.

More compelling evidence of marijuana's minimal effect on driving ability comes from epidemiological surveys of drivers involved in fatal highway accidents. Studies in the United States, Canada, and Australia have found THC in the blood of 3 percent to 11 percent of fatally injured drivers. However, in the majority (70 percent to 90 percent) of these cases, alcohol was detected as well.[17] To evaluate marijuana's specific contribution to accidents, some researchers have rated the "culpability" of drivers who test positive only for marijuana. One study found higher culpability for marijuana-positive drivers than drug-free drivers, but it relied on a very small sample, seventeen drivers.[18] Three other studies found not only that marijuana-positive drivers were less culpable than alcohol-positive drivers, but were less culpable than drug-free drivers.[19] That is, fewer drivers in the marijuana-positive group than in the drug-free group were judged to be responsible for the accident. The author of one of these studies suggests "either that cannabis . . . actually increases driving ability or . . . that drivers taking cannabis overcompensate for any loss of driving skills."[20]

It is doubtful that marijuana improves driving ability. In laboratory studies, marijuana impairs subjects' performance on some psychomotor tasks, although typically not as severely as alcohol.[21] What
also makes alcohol more dangerous on the highway is its tendency
to provoke risk-taking behavior. In actual-driving and driving-simu-
lator studies, researchers have consistently found that alcohol makes
subjects less cautious while marijuana makes them more cautious.[22]
In addition, under the influence of marijuana, drivers tend to be
more aware of possible impairment, and seek consciously to compensate for it.[23]

Despite the apparent capacity of many marijuana users to
compensate for impairment of their driving ability, in some individuals, marijuana may increase the risk of an accident. At very
high doses, people may be unable to compensate for marijuana's
psychomotor impairment. Inexperienced marijuana users and inexperienced drivers, in particular, may be unable to drive safely even
after small doses of marijuana. Furthermore, risk-taking individuals may be unwilling to exercise caution, whether they drive under
the influence of marijuana or not. A recent study found that injured motorcycle drivers were more likely than injured automobile
drivers to have used marijuana recently.[24] Another study found that
among people stopped by the police for reckless driving—mostly
young males—one-third were positive for marijuana on a roadside
urine test.[25] These findings may be due to a higher prevalence of
marijuana use among people predisposed to deviant and reckless
behavior.[26] However, it is also likely that marijuana contributes to
bad driving in some individuals.

Currently, there is no reliable measure of marijuana intoxication comparable to the Breathalyzer test for alcohol.[27] However, on

the basis of a failed roadside-sobriety test, the police can require drivers to submit blood samples for analysis. If illegal drugs are detected, the police can make an arrest for "driving under the influence." Under this system, drivers who are impaired by marijuana can be subjected to the same penalties as drivers impaired by alcohol.[28]

Marijuana-related hospital emergencies are increasing, particularly among youth. This is evidence that marijuana is much more harmful than most people previously believed.

> *"Marijuana . . . is not benign, it is not harmless. It's a very dangerous drug that can cause you to fight for your very life in a hospital emergency room."[1]*

> *"Young marijuana users . . . are at greater risk of needing expensive emergency room treatment, which costs us money. . . . In 1993, twice as many teenagers ended up in emergency rooms for marijuana use as for heroin and cocaine combined."[2]*

> *"The fact that . . . annually almost . . . eight thousand persons require emergency hospital care for marijuana use is sufficient evidence of the drug's dangerousness."[3]*

Marijuana does not cause overdose deaths. The number of people in hospital emergency rooms who say they have used marijuana has increased. On this basis, the visit may be recorded as marijuana-related even if marijuana had nothing to do with the medical condition precipitating the hospital visit. Many more teenagers use marijuana than use drugs such as heroin and cocaine. As a result, when teenagers visit hospital emergency rooms, they report marijuana much more frequently than they report heroin or cocaine. In the large majority of cases when marijuana is mentioned, other drugs are mentioned as well. In 1994, fewer than 2 percent of drug-related emergency room visits involved the use of marijuana alone.

18

Marijuana-Related Hospital Emergencies

DATA gathered by the Drug Abuse Warning Network (DAWN) show a recent increase in the number of people "mentioning" marijuana in hospital emergency rooms. When a patient mentions marijuana, it does not mean marijuana *caused* the hospital visit. For every drug-related hospital visit—what DAWN calls a "drug-abuse episode"—hospital staff list up to five drugs that the patient reports having used recently. This includes illicit drugs, prescription drugs, and over-the-counter medications. Emergency room staff also record whether the patient recently consumed alcohol.

The frequency with which any drug is mentioned in hospital emergency rooms depends on its frequency of use, irrespective of its inherent hazards. When a drug increases in popularity, more people mention it when they go to hospital emergency rooms. When a drug decreases in popularity, it gets mentioned less often. Since 1988, the overall number of drug mentions has risen about 40 percent, reaching an all-time high of about one million in 1995.[4] Probably most of this increase is due to the improved reporting procedures that were instituted during this period.[5]

Marijuana is mentioned less often by patients than most other illicit drugs, despite marijuana's being the most frequently used illicit drug in American society. Only LSD and PCP—drugs which few Americans use—are mentioned less often than marijuana. In 1995, for all age groups combined, marijuana represented about 5 percent of all drug mentions, compared to about 15 percent for cocaine and 8 percent for heroin. Together, three over-the-counter medications—aspirin, acetaminophen, and ibuprofen—were mentioned more often than marijuana. These pain medications accounted for 8 percent of total drug mentions while marijuana accounted for 5 percent.

Adolescents in hospital emergency rooms have always mentioned marijuana more often than heroin and cocaine. This is not because marijuana causes more harm than heroin or cocaine. It is because so few adolescents use heroin or cocaine. In a 1995 survey of the general population, 14 percent of youth aged twelve to seventeen said they had used marijuana sometime during the past year. Less than 2 percent said they had used cocaine and less than 1 percent said they had used heroin.[6] That same year, marijuana accounted for 9 percent of the emergency room drug mentions by twelve- to seventeen-year-olds; cocaine accounted for 2 percent and heroin for 0.5 percent. In other words, marijuana is the only one of these three drugs that is mentioned less frequently in hospital emergency rooms than its use in the population.

When marijuana use among youth began increasing in the 1990s, so did the number of young people who mentioned marijuana in hospital emergency rooms. In 1995, youth between the ages of twelve and seventeen mentioned marijuana 8,230 times—more than three times the number of youth mentioning marijuana in 1988. Throughout this period, young people mentioned over-the-counter pain medications much more often than they mentioned marijuana. For example, in 1993, 47 percent of the drug mentions by youth were for over-the-counter pain medications, compared to about 8 percent for marijuana.[7]

Emergency room patients not only mention marijuana less frequently than most other drugs, they rarely mention marijuana alone. In 1994, for all age groups combined, about 80 percent of the time marijuana was mentioned one or more additional drugs were mentioned. Of the forty thousand marijuana mentions, alcohol was mentioned in nineteen thousand and cocaine was mentioned in fourteen thousand. Out of more than five hundred thousand drug-abuse episodes in 1994, slightly more than eight thousand—about 1.6 percent—involved marijuana alone.

Marijuana's wide safety margin is further illustrated by data on drug-related fatalities. In 1993, based on the records of medical examiners, DAWN reported 8,426 drug-related deaths. In 587 of these 8,426 cases (7 percent), the medical examiner found evidence of recent marijuana use by the victim. However, in *all of these cases* other drugs were found as well.[8] Marijuana did not cause a single overdose death. Because marijuana does not profoundly alter cardiovascular and respiratory functions, no dose of marijuana is fatal to humans.

MARIJUANA IS MORE POTENT TODAY THAN IN THE PAST. Adults who used marijuana in the 1960s and 1970s fail to realize that when today's youth use marijuana they are using a much more dangerous drug.

> *"Baby boomers with fond memories of . . . bong hits around the lava lamp may not be particularly alarmed . . . that pot is making a comeback. . . . But the culture of cannabis . . . has grown considerably more dangerous . . . since the flower children left Haight-Ashbury. . . . [Today's marijuana is] twenty times more potent."[1]*

> *"Marijuana is forty times more potent today . . . than 10, 15, 20 years ago."[2]*

> *"To enhance the potency of marijuana [growers use] . . . advanced agronomic practices such as hydroponics, cloning, . . . special fertilizers, plant hormones, steroids, and carbon monoxide."[3]*

> *"Greater potency [means] . . . that small amounts of marijuana now create a significantly higher level of intoxication."[4]*

> *"If people . . . confessing to marijuana use in the late '60s . . . sucked in on one of today's marijuana cigarettes, they'd fall down backwards."[5]*

WHEN TODAY'S YOUTH USE MARIJUANA, THEY ARE USING THE SAME DRUG USED BY YOUTH IN THE 1960S AND 1970S. A small number of low-THC samples seized by the Drug Enforcement Administration in the early 1970s are used to calculate a dramatic increase in potency. However, these samples were not representative of the marijuana generally available to users during this era. Potency data from the early 1980s to the present are more reliable, and they show no increase in the average THC content of marijuana. Even if marijuana potency were to increase, it would not necessarily make the drug more dangerous. Marijuana that varies quite substantially in potency produces similar psychoactive effects.

19

The Potency of Marijuana

WARNINGS about the "new highly potent pot" date back to the mid-1970s.[6] In recent years, the warnings have grown more urgent as marijuana's critics try to convince middle-aged adults, many of whom smoked marijuana in their youth, that today's marijuana is much more dangerous. Estimates of the alleged increase in potency typically range from five- to twenty-five-fold, and occasionally reach as high as sixty-[7] or one-hundred-fold.[8]

For more than twenty years, the Potency Monitoring Project (PMP) at the University of Mississippi has been measuring the percentage of THC (marijuana's chief psychoactive ingredient) in marijuana samples submitted by law enforcement agencies.[9] Since 1980, potency averages have fluctuated between about 2 percent and about 3.5 percent, with no consistent upward or downward trend (see table 19-1). PMP averages in the 1970s were substantially lower, often under 1 percent, with a low of 0.18 percent in 1972. These early PMP averages almost certainly grossly underrepresented the THC content of marijuana available during the 1970s.

Marijuana of less than 0.5 percent potency has essentially no

TABLE 19-1

AVERAGE THC CONTENT OF MARIJUANA
SEIZED BY THE POLICE 1980-1995

	THC Content (%) (Arithmetic Average)	THC Content (%) (Adjusted for Weight)	Number of Seizures
1980	2.06	1.96	153
1981	2.28	2.11	260
1982	3.05	3.34	487
1983	3.23	3.44	1229
1984	3.29	3.96	1119
1985	2.82	2.63	1613
1986	2.30	2.24	1554
1987	2.93	2.23	1699
1988	3.29	3.84	1822
1989	3.06	2.66	1272
1990	3.36	3.82	1263
1991	3.00	3.78	2506
1992	3.10	1.96	3540
1993	3.33	3.33	3354
1994	3.35	0.61	3275

Source: *Quarterly Report, Potency Monitoring Project, Report #60,* University of Mississippi: Research Institute of Pharmaceutical Sciences.

psychoactivity.[10] In laboratory studies, many subjects are unable to distinguish marijuana of less than 1 percent THC from a placebo.[11] People who smoked marijuana during the 1960s and 1970s report having sometimes purchased marijuana that produced no effect.[12] But for marijuana to have become popular, most people must have obtained marijuana with a higher THC content than shown in early reports by PMP.

Independent analyses of marijuana in the 1970s consistently found higher levels of THC than reported by PMP.[13] PharmChem Laboratories analyzed 127 samples of marijuana in 1973—four times the number analyzed by PMP. Average potency in these PharmChem samples was 1.62 percent. Many samples were over 4 percent and the highest sample was 9.5 percent.[14] In 1975, a few of PharmChem's 138 samples had no THC at all, but most were in the range of 2 percent to 5 percent. The highest PharmChem sample in 1975 was 14 percent—about twenty times the 0.71 percent average reported by PMP that year.[15]

The marijuana samples analyzed by independent laboratories in the 1970s were not necessarily representative of the marijuana smoked around the country, but neither were PMP's samples. PMP's samples from the early 1970s were almost entirely from Mexican "kilobricks," always the lowest-potency form of marijuana during this period.[16] Early PMP samples included no high-potency products, such as buds and sinsemilla, despite the fact that these forms of marijuana were available on the retail market.[17] Improper storage of samples, which is known to cause degradation of THC,[18] may also have contributed to PMP's finding of extremely low marijuana potency in the early 1970s.[19]

By the early 1980s, a wider variety of marijuana samples were being sent to PMP. This is because drug enforcement agencies broadened their effort to catch domestic marijuana growers and to intercept smugglers bringing marijuana into the United States from Colombia and the Caribbean.[20] Domestic marijuana and marijuana from Colombia and the Caribbean were available in the United States before law enforcement officials decided to wage offenses against them.[21] Indeed, the police target new drug distribution systems because they have already become important suppliers.[22] The marijuana samples analyzed by PMP in the early 1980s—ranging in potency from 2 to 3 percent—are probably a better reflection of the marijuana available during the 1970s than the samples actually analyzed by PMP during the 1970s.

The number of samples analyzed by PMP increased dramatically during the 1980s, with a yearly average of more than one thousand, compared to less than two hundred per year in the 1970s. Improvements in storage practices and changes in measurement methods may also have increased the amount of THC detected in PMP samples seized after 1980.[23] For all these reasons, the comparison of potency averages across the two decades is inherently misleading. Trends after 1980 are probably more reliable. But at no time do seizures by the police necessarily reflect the marijuana generally available in the country.

Although the average potency of PMP samples has not increased during the past fifteen years, marijuana at the high end of the potency continuum may be somewhat more available today than previously. Some regular marijuana users report having access to high-cost, high-potency products produced from selected seeds under artificial light by small-scale growers. Marijuana samples with very high potency occasionally get sent to the PMP.[24] However, the number of high-potency samples is always too small to have much impact on annual potency averages. What PMP averages reflect—indeed, what they were designed to reflect—is the potency of "commercial grade" marijuana, the marijuana which predominates on the retail market and is used by the majority of consumers.

More potent marijuana is not necessarily more dangerous. There is no possibility of a fatal overdose from smoking marijuana, regardless of THC content. And because THC itself does not cause physiological damage to organs or tissues, high-potency marijuana poses no greater health hazard than marijuana of lower potency. In fact, since the main physiological risk from marijuana is damage to the lungs from smoking (see chapter 15), high-potency marijuana might be slightly less harmful because it permits people to achieve desired psychoactive effects while inhaling less burning plant material.[25] Studies indicate that smokers generally do not adjust their intake in response to marijuana samples that vary only slightly in potency.[26] However, when the variation is more substantial—greater than 100 percent— they tend to smoke less of higher-potency marijuana.[27]

Marijuana that is double or triple in potency does not produce effects that are double or triple in intensity. In laboratory studies, smokers frequently give similar "subjective high" ratings to marijuana samples that vary in potency as much as 100 percent.[28] Even when subjects give higher psychoactive ratings to marijuana of higher potency, the ratings do not escalate in equal proportion to the escalation in THC content. For example, in one study, a 200 percent increase in potency resulted in a 35 percent increase in subjective ratings of the marijuana high.[29] In another study, a 300 percent increase in potency resulted in a 40 percent increase in subjective ratings.[30] These studies suggest that tolerance to THC develops within a single smoking episode—probably as a result of receptor down-regulation, a process that has been demonstrated in animal experiments.[31]

Since illegal drug markets lack quality control, marijuana users always purchase products of unknown potency. From one purchase to the next potency may vary considerably. Nonetheless, for the bulk of marijuana on the retail market, differences in potency may be too small to be of importance. Users may occasionally obtain marijuana of unusually high potency and, as a consequence, experience psychoactive effects more dramatic than usual. However, adverse psychoactive reactions appear to be unrelated to marijuana potency. What marijuana users call bad trips have been reported with marijuana that ranges from quite low (0.7 percent) to quite high (7.5 percent) THC content.[32]

Many experienced marijuana smokers believe that today's marijuana is much more potent than the marijuana they smoked when they were younger. This is not surprising. Older brains are generally less resilient in response to drugs than younger ones. For example, tolerance for alcohol and caffeine diminishes as people get older. As a result, the same dose of either produces more dramatic effects in adults than in youth.[33] Marijuana users probably develop a similar increase in sensitivity—what is sometimes called "reverse tolerance"—to marijuana's effects. In a survey of high school students, there has been essentially no change from 1975 to the present in students' ranking of the intensity or duration of the "high" they get from marijuana.[34] Long-term users believe that marijuana is now more potent because, for them, marijuana has become more powerful.

There is no reason to believe that today's marijuana is stronger or more dangerous than the marijuana smoked during the 1960s and 1970s. A cottage industry has emerged to provide marijuana growers with botanical information and equipment for indoor growing.[35] Nonetheless, no cultivation techniques have been shown to reliably increase marijuana potency. Primarily, they increase yield, making it possible for growers to maximize the amount of marijuana grown in a small space.

MARIJUANA USE CAN BE PREVENTED. Drug education and prevention programs reduced marijuana use during the 1980s. Since then, our commitment has slackened, and marijuana use has been rising. By expanding and intensifying current anti-marijuana messages, we can stop youthful experimentation.

> *"The absence of a concerted effort to discourage marijuana use . . . allowed it to be catapulted back into fashion."[1]*

> *"We are committed to making America a drug-free society. We will do whatever it takes."[2]*

> *"The answer to recent increases in teen drug use is renewed prevention efforts that have at their core a no-use message."[3]*

> *"We have to roll up our sleeves and get busy educating all Americans about the dangers of marijuana use."[4]*

> *"If [we] were doing two to three times what we're doing now through the media . . . we would break the back of the [marijuana] problem in three years. It's predictable."[5]*

> *"We know that a drug-free America is within our grasp. . . . We have learned to reduce demand successfully."[6]*

THERE IS NO EVIDENCE THAT ANTI-DRUG MESSAGES DIMINISH YOUNG PEOPLE'S INTEREST IN DRUGS. Anti-drug campaigns in the schools and the media may even make drugs more attractive. Marijuana use among youth declined throughout the 1980s, and began increasing in the 1990s. This increase occurred despite young people's exposure to the most massive anti-marijuana campaign in American history. In a number of other countries, drug education programs are based on a "harm reduction" model, which seeks to reduce drug-related harm among those young people who do experiment with drugs.

20

Preventing Marijuana Use

TODAY'S adolescents have been bombarded with anti-marijuana messages. They were born in the early 1980s, just as President Ronald Reagan was focusing the drug war on marijuana,[7] and just as Nancy Reagan was introducing her "just say no" slogan to American culture.[8] Today's teenagers have had more drug education than any cohort of young people in American history. About half have received the DARE (Drug Abuse Resistance Education) program, which sends uniformed police officers into the schools to teach anti-drug lessons.[9] Nearly all the rest have received other types of drug education, sometimes as early as kindergarden.[10] Today's teens have seen an average of one Partnership for a Drug-Free America advertisement every day for years.[11] They have seen anti-drug messages on shopping bags, comic books, home videos, restaurant place mats, candy wrappers, bumper stickers, bookmarks, billboards, and the sides of buses.[12] Over and over they have been warned of marijuana's dangers and told that its use is socially unacceptable.

Despite this onslaught of anti-drug messages, the number of teenagers trying marijuana began rising in 1992, and has risen

FIGURE 20-1

TRIED MARIJUANA ONCE OR MORE IN THEIR LIVES
HIGH SCHOOL STUDENTS, GRADES 8, 10, AND 12
1975-1996

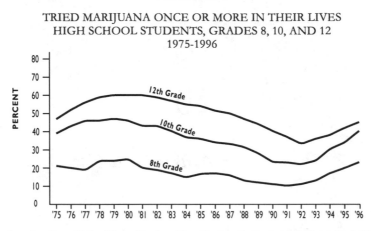

Based on data from *National Survey Results on Drug Use from the Monitoring the Future Study*, National Institute on Drug Abuse. Data for 8th and 10th graders prior to 1991 are retrospective reports fom high school seniors. Prevalence rates for 8th graders prior to 1991 have been adjusted to compensate for seniors' underreporting of 8th-grade use.

every year since (see figure 20-1). Today, as always, rates are higher among older adolescents than younger adolescents. According to a national survey of high school students, in 1996, 45 percent of twelfth graders had tried marijuana, compared to 40 percent of tenth graders and 23 percent of eighth graders.[13]

Fortunately, most youthful marijuana users are experimenters. In 1996, about half of all students who tried marijuana had not used it in the month prior to the survey.[14] Of eighth graders who tried marijuana, nearly half had used it only once or twice.[15] Most young people who try marijuana are normal and well-adjusted. In a recent study, marijuana experimenters were found to have fewer social and psychological problems than their non-marijuana-using peers.[16]

In the last few years, as marijuana use among adolescents has increased, so has the number reporting daily marijuana use (defined as use twenty or more times a month). However, daily marijuana use is still uncommon, and often temporary. About 12 percent of high school seniors reported a period of daily marijuana use at some point in their lives, but nearly two-thirds of this group no longer used marijuana this frequently at the time of the survey. In 1995, less than 1 percent of eighth-grade students reported using marijuana on a daily basis.[17] These young heavy marijuana users often use other drugs heavily, and typically have multiple social and psychological adjustment problems that date back to early childhood.[18]

Government officials have responded to the increase in youthful marijuana use by calling for a redoubling of prevention efforts. Health and Human Services (HHS) Secretary Donna Shalala argues unconvincingly that "the resurgence in marijuana use is happening *despite* the overall success of substance abuse efforts, not as a result of their failure."[19] Shalala's plan for "stopping this new trend in its tracks" is to repeatedly tell American youth that "marijuana is illegal, marijuana is dangerous, marijuana is unhealthy, and marijuana is wrong."[20] National Institute on Drug Abuse (NIDA) director Alan Leshner says, "We must act decisively to remedy these backsliding attitudes."[21] Drug Czar Barry McCaffrey claims that "anti-drug messages have demonstrated the ability to influence attitudes ... [but they] must be repeated with adequate frequency."[22] He predicts that placing $3 million worth of anti-drug advertisements on popular television shows for children "absolutely will turn around drug abuse by youngsters."[23]

Government officials' faith in the power of messages—whatever their origin—to influence the drug-use decisions of young people has no support in the scientific literature. Media campaigns have never been shown to reduce illegal drug use among adults or adolescents.[24] Today's anti-drug ads, compared to those of earlier decades, are technically superb and clever. Some of the Partnership for a Drug-Free America's images—such as the "this is your brain on drugs" fried egg—are remembered by nearly everyone who sees them.[25] Partnership ads have been shown to strengthen anti-drug attitudes among young children and non-drug-using adults. However, they have no apparent effect on the attitudes or drug-taking behavior of teenagers.[26]

Mass campaigns against drugs can even be counterproductive. The primary consequence of public warnings about glue-sniffing in the 1960s seems to have been to introduce glue-sniffing to young people who otherwise might never have heard of it.[27] Today's anti-drug ads—using the same techniques that advertisers use to make consumer products more attractive and desirable—may increase some teens' interest in drugs. The resurgence of marijuana's "glorification" in the popular culture—in movies, music, and hip hop fashion—supports this view.[28] Anti-marijuana campaigns preceded increases in marijuana use during the 1930s and 1960s, and may have contributed to them.[29] Rather than preventing marijuana use, messages that exaggerate marijuana's dangers may actually provoke youthful rebellion.

Similar dilemmas surround school-based anti-drug programs. During the past thirty years, many different approaches to drug education have been tried. Few have been carefully evaluated. When research has been done, it has shown either no effect of drug education on student drug use, or a small effect of short duration.[30]

The most popular form of drug education today is "refusal skills training," which teaches students verbal techniques for resisting pressure by peers to try alcohol, tobacco, and illicit drugs.[31] According to U.S. Department of Education guidelines, refusal skills drug education programs should never reveal that the research on drugs' effects is inconclusive, or that public opinion on the morality of using drugs is divided. The guidelines say that terms such as "casual," "recreational," and "responsible" drug use should not be used because they "tend to foster a belief that some drugs, especially marijuana, are not particularly harmful if used in moderation." Because "it is essential that there be no confusion," the guidelines propose that the zero-tolerance message "be clear, consistent, and positively communicated . . . at every grade level in the K-12 sequence."[32]

Studies show that zero-tolerance refusal skills training programs are no more effective than drug education programs of previous decades. One group of researchers, who designed and evaluated the Midwestern Prevention Project, reported reduced marijuana use up to three years after students received the program.[33] However, most studies have found either no reduction in marijuana use or a slight reduction that disappears quickly after the program has ended.[34] Several recent studies report that DARE—the most popular drug education program in the United States today—has no effect on teenagers' attitudes toward drugs and no effect on their drug-use behavior.[35]

Researchers in California found that a majority of students are dissatisfied with their drug education programs and distrustful of the information presented by their instructors—feelings that increase in intensity as students get older.[36] By the eighth grade, a majority of American youth have obviously rejected the no-use message; about half have used alcohol, nearly as many have smoked tobacco cigarettes, and about 20 percent have tried marijuana or used inhalants.[37] Most schools, as part of a zero-tolerance policy, impose sanctions, including possible expulsion, on detected drug users.[38] Students are, therefore, naturally reluctant to discuss their own drug experiences in drug education classes.[39] Indeed, since the explicit purpose of drug education is to prevent drug experimentation, the topic of drug *use* is practically forbidden. Department of Education guidelines warn teachers to keep all "personal drug experiences" out of the classroom, to avoid "creating conflict and uncertainty in the non-using student."[40] Drug education classes provide no information on the relative risks of different drugs, different doses, different routes of administration, or different patterns of use. In practice, drug education programs in American schools do not provide much education.

In a recent review, the United States General Accounting Office criticized the Department of Education and HHS for "unnecessarily limiting the search for successful drug abuse prevention programs by considering only those with a no-use approach ... despite a lack of evidence demonstrating the superiority of this approach over others."[41] A number of researchers, psychologists, and drug-policy analysts have also criticized current zero-tolerance approaches as ineffective and counterproductive.[42] The alternative approach they offer was endorsed by NIDA in the 1970s[43] and incorporated into some of NIDA's early drug education materials.[44] This alternative approach asserts that moralizing about drugs is ineffective; that exaggerating drugs' dangers is counterproductive; that expecting students to be totally abstinent is unrealistic; and that the appropriate goal of drug education is to reduce drug *abuse* rather than drug *use*. Despite widespread support from drug educators,[45] NIDA abandoned this approach in the early 1980s under pressure from President Ronald Reagan,[46] Secretary of Education William Bennett,[47] and anti-drug organizations.[48] In the years since, zero-tolerance ideas have dominated federally funded drug prevention efforts.

Other countries, such as England, Australia, and the Netherlands, have moved in the direction of "harm reduction" drug education.[49] Proponents of harm reduction do not encourage or condone drug use, but they do assume that most adolescents will eventually experiment with psychoactive substances. In health education classes young people are cautioned about the risks of using drugs. However, most harm reduction programs target teenagers who have already begun to experiment with drugs. For example, in England, an organization called Lifeline[50] produces postcards, posters, and brochures with explicit advice about safer ways to use drugs, and distributes these materials to young people through community organizations, movie theaters, and record stores. Harm reduction workers visit popular dance clubs to urge the users of Ecstasy and other stimulant drugs to consume enough water to avoid dehydration. In some clubs, dancers can submit drug samples to government workers for on-the-spot chemical analysis to detect counterfeiting and contamination.[51] In the Netherlands, government officials deliver brochures to marijuana "coffee shops" to warn consumers—particularly foreign visitors—about possible adverse effects from eating marijuana-laced cookies or brownies.[52]

Harm reduction ideas are not foreign to Americans. For example, campaigns that encourage designated drivers and urge friends not to "let friends drive drunk" represent attempts to lessen the harms of alcohol consumption without necessarily reducing the number of alcohol users.[53] Many parents unconditionally offer to drive their teenagers any time the alternative is accepting a ride from an alcohol-impaired driver. Some parents also offer their children harm reduction advice about marijuana and other drugs.[54] Although nearly all parents hope their teenage children will not use marijuana, many understand that experimentation is common, and does not lead inevitably—or even usually—to regular use.[55]

The British Wootten Report, 1969
The association in legislation of cannabis and heroin . . . is inappropriate and new legislation to deal specifically and separately with cannabis . . . should be introduced as soon as possible. . . . Possession of a small amount of cannabis . . . should not be punished by imprisonment. . . . Sale or supply of cannabis should be punishable . . . with a fine not exceeding £100, or imprisonment for a term not exceeding four months.[1]

The Canadian LeDain Commission Report, 1970
Since cannabis is clearly not a narcotic we recommend that the control of cannabis be removed from the Narcotic Control Act. . . . The Commission is of the opinion that no one should be liable to imprisonment for simple possession.[2]

National Commission on Marihuana and Drug Abuse, 1972
Marihuana's relative potential for harm to the vast majority of individual users and its actual impact on society does not justify a social policy designed to seek out and firmly punish those who use it. . . . Existing social and legal policy is out of proportion to the individual and social harm engendered by the drug.[3]

The Dutch Baan Commission, 1972
The current law does not respect the fact that the risks of the use of cannabis cannot be equaled to the risks of the use of substances that are pharmacologically much more potent. . . . This hurts the credibility of the drug law, and the prevention efforts based on the law are made untrustworthy.[4]

Commission of the Australian Government, 1977
Legal controls [should] not [be] of such a nature as to . . . cause more social damage than use of the drug. . . . Cannabis legislation should be enacted that recognises the significant differences between . . . narcotics and cannabis in their health effects. . . . Possession of marijuana for personal use should no longer be a criminal offence.[5]

National Academy of Sciences Report, 1982
The advantages of a policy of regulation include . . . the savings in economic and social costs of law enforcement . . . , better controls over the quality and safety of the product, and, possibly, increased credibility of warnings about risks.[6]

Australian National Drug Strategy Committee, 1994
Australia experiences more harm . . . from maintaining cannabis prohibition policy than it experiences from the use of the drug. . . . We conclude that cannabis law reform is required in this country.[7]

Report by the Dutch Government, 1995
It has been demonstrated that the more or less free sale of . . . [marijuana] for personal use in the Netherlands has not given rise to levels of use significantly higher than in countries which pursue a highly repressive policy. . . . Dutch policy on drugs over the last twenty years . . . can be considered to have been successful.[8]

Conclusion: Science, Politics
and Policy

IN 1972, after reviewing the scientific evidence, President Nixon's Shafer Commission said it was "of the unanimous opinion that marihuana use is not such a grave problem that individuals who smoke marihuana, and possess it for that purpose, should be subject to criminal prosecution." Between 1969 and 1977, government-appointed commissions in Canada, England, Australia, and the Netherlands issued reports that agreed with the Shafer Commission's conclusions. All found that marijuana's dangers had been greatly exaggerated. All urged lawmakers to drastically reduce penalties for marijuana possession, or eliminate them altogether.

The Shafer Commission

The Shafer Commission was appointed in response to the increase in marijuana use by middle-class youth, which began in the 1960s. By 1970, marijuana had become a mainstream recreational drug. The commission's national survey found that 40 percent of Americans between the ages of eighteen and twenty-five had smoked marijuana. Thirty percent of high school juniors and seniors and

17 percent of freshmen and sophomores had tried marijuana at least once.[9]

The Shafer Commission concluded that, given marijuana's widespread use, law enforcement officials were powerless to stop it. Marijuana use had increased despite harsh criminal penalties against its sale, possession, and use. Arrests for marijuana possession had been increasing steadily and dramatically. In 1965, 18,000 people were arrested for marijuana possession. By 1970, the number had reached 180,000. Most of those arrested were marijuana users who possessed small amounts for personal use. Two-thirds possessed less than one ounce of marijuana and 40 percent possessed less than five grams—the equivalent of one to five joints.[10]

The Shafer Commission argued that arresting and prosecuting youthful marijuana users harmed them irrevocably—disrupting their education, giving them a permanent criminal record, and diminishing their future employment opportunities. Most of the people arrested for marijuana possession in 1970 had never been arrested before. Forty-five percent were employed and 27 percent were full-time students. The commission concluded "that the criminal law is too harsh a tool to apply to personal possession even in the effort to discourage use." A "better method," it said, was "persuasion rather than prosecution."

In other ways as well, the Shafer Commission concluded that marijuana laws in the United States created more harm to users and society than the use of marijuana. Members believed that enforcing the marijuana laws wasted criminal justice resources, and encouraged police tactics that were "on the edge of constitutional limitations." They worried that the "disrespect which the laws and their enforcement engender in the young" would foster "disrespect for all law and the system in general." The commission argued that criminal laws required "an unquestioned consensus . . . about the undesirability of a particular behavior"—near unanimous disapproval of the sort that existed for crimes such as murder, theft, child-beating, and incest. This consensus did not exist for marijuana. The commission conducted a survey of the general population and separate surveys of police officials, prosecutors, and judges. These surveys showed that a substantial minority of Americans supported removing all legal controls over marijuana. A clear majority thought marijuana users should not be arrested and prosecuted.[11] Only 13 percent of judges thought that people possessing marijuana deserved to go to prison.[12]

Based on its assessment of the harms of marijuana and the harms of marijuana policy, the Shafer Commission concluded that the existing marijuana-prohibition system did not serve the best interests of society. It urged Congress and state legislatures to decriminalize marijuana. It said that, for the time being at least, marijuana cultivation and large-scale distribution should remain illegal. However, it recommended that the "possession of marihuana for personal use" and the "casual distribution of small amounts of marihuana" no longer be criminal offenses.

The Marijuana-Law Reform Movement

For a while in the 1970s, it looked as if marijuana decriminalization would be widely implemented in the United States. The Shafer Commission's recommendations were endorsed by many prestigious professional organizations. These included the American Bar Association, the American Medical Association, the National Conference of Commissioners on Uniform State Laws, the National Advisory Commission on Criminal Justice Standards and Goals, the American Public Health Association, the National Council of Churches, the National Education Association,[13] and the New York Academy of Medicine.[14]

Across the country, government officials, lawyers, police chiefs, prosecutors, judges, physicians, newspaper editors, and other public figures repeated the Shafer Commission's arguments in support of marijuana decriminalization.

- President Jimmy Carter said, "Penalties against a drug should not be more dangerous to an individual than use of the drug itself; and where they are they should be changed. Nowhere is this more clear than in the laws against possession of marijuana. . . . Therefore, I support legislation amending federal law to eliminate all federal penalties for the possession of up to one ounce of marijuana."[15]

- Senator Philip Hart, whose teenage son had spent twenty days in jail for possessing less than one joint of marijuana, said, "That is all the evidence I needed to convince me that it—marijuana prosecution policy—was a topsy-turvy operation and made no sense."[16]

- A Mississippi legislator warned parents: "We're putting children in jail and ruining their lives; your children and your neighbors' children are in severe jeopardy."[17]

- In 1975, director of the National Institute on Drug Abuse (NIDA) Robert DuPont argued, "The single most striking characteristic about marijuana is [its] low toxicity. . . . Marijuana use should be discouraged," but "we want to get away from using prison or the threat of prison for the simple possession of marijuana."[18]

- The Commissioner of Public Safety in Alaska stated, "Nobody in law enforcement objects to lessening the penalty for the possession of small amounts by an individual for his own use."[19]

- A sponsor of a decriminalization bill in Minnesota reported, "There are a lot of young people in my district who smoke pot. ... Enforcement of the present law involves a lot of expense."[20]

- U.S. Representative Dan Quayle said, "Congress should definitely consider decriminalizing possession of marijuana. We should concentrate on prosecuting the rapists and burglars who are a menace to society."[21]

- A Colorado district attorney claimed that marijuana criminalization was "the single most destructive force in society—in terms of turning our children against the system."[22]

- A Republican legislator told the Oregon state legislature that "prohibition was not the answer to our alcohol problem in 1919, nor is it the answer to the marihuana problem in 1973."[23]

Even before the Shafer Commission was appointed, Congress and most state legislatures had eliminated mandatory prison terms for marijuana offenses, following the advice of President Kennedy's Advisory Commission on Narcotics and Drug Abuse in 1963[24] and President Johnson's Commission on Law Enforcement and the Administration of Justice in 1967.[25] By 1977, all but eight states had reduced marijuana possession from a felony to a misdemeanor. Ten states had eliminated criminal penalties for possessing up to one ounce of marijuana.[26] By 1978, the marijuana-law reform movement was over. That year, Nebraska, the last state to decriminalize marijuana, made marijuana possession a "civil offense," carrying a maximum fine of $100.[27]

The Anti-Marijuana Movement
In 1974, a small group of scientists and psychiatrists challenged

the Shafer Commission's assessment of marijuana's effects at hearings organized by Senator James Eastland of Mississippi.[28] Many witnesses at the Eastland hearings had themselves conducted animal or cellular studies showing possible biological harm from marijuana. Essentially all thought that using marijuana was immoral. All supported maintaining strict criminal laws over marijuana sale and use. These early opponents of marijuana decriminalization, however, were unable to translate their views into political action.[29]

Throughout the 1970s, marijuana use continued to increase, particularly among adolescents. By 1977, 56 percent of high school seniors, 45 percent of sophomores, and 19 percent of eighth graders had tried marijuana at least once.[30] In response, a grass-roots anti-marijuana movement emerged. It was led by groups of parents who first organized at the local level, primarily for the purpose of preventing their own teenage children from using marijuana. They were angered by NIDA publications which suggested that occasional marijuana use was a relatively harmless activity.[31] Indeed, they blamed this view for marijuana's increasing popularity among American youth.[32]

Within a few years, the parents' groups formed several national associations, including the Parents Resource Institute for Drug Education (PRIDE), the National Federation of Parents for Drug-Free Youth, and Families in Action. These organizations solicited money from civic organizations, businesses, and government agencies, and recruited new members through conferences, workshops, and newspaper advertisements.[33] In communities across the country, and particularly in middle-class suburbs, parents' groups formed, and affiliated with the national associations.[34] Many of the parents who joined these groups had never used marijuana and knew little about its effects. They were certain, however, that they did not want their children to use it. They understood that marijuana's growing acceptance in the culture made it harder for them to produce drug-free children.

The parents' organizations engaged in a variety of political activities aimed at reversing the liberal policies of the 1970s. They lobbied Congress and state legislatures for stricter laws against marijuana, and urged the police to enforce existing laws more vigorously. They pressured school officials to adopt zero-tolerance drug education programs. They pursuaded NIDA to devote more resources to drug prevention, and to eliminate educational materials that were "soft" on marijuana.[35]

Robert DuPont, the first director of NIDA, reports that the concerns of the parents' groups converted him from a marijuana decriminalizer to an anti-marijuana activist.[36] Before leaving NIDA in 1978, DuPont commissioned one of the parents' groups' founders, Marsha Manatt, to write *Parents, Peers, and Pot*, a pamphlet which NIDA distributed widely. This document told the stories of "model children" whose lives had been permanently harmed by marijuana. It claimed that recent scientific studies had found evidence of serious biological harm from marijuana. It said that marijuana damaged the lungs, brain, and heart, caused hormonal abnormalities, infertility, sexual dysfunction, immune impairment and, in adolescent males, was associated with breast enlargement.[37]

In the late 1970s, articles about marijuana's biological, psychological, and social dangers also began appearing in popular magazines such as *Saturday Evening Post, McCalls, Good Housekeeping,* and *Ladies Home Journal.*[38] *Reader's Digest* published several articles about marijuana, including a four-part "Marijuana Alert" series by Peggy Mann, a writer of children's books. These articles were even more alarmist than *Parents, Peers, and Pot.* Mann reported that marijuana has a "dramatically impairing effect on cells," "can damage every human organ," and "can damage man's most precious possessions: the mind, the personality, the spirit." She warned that "pot smokers may be unwittingly damaging their brains, and decreasing their chances of conceiving and producing completely healthy off-spring."[39] Reader's Digest reprinted Mann's series as a pamphlet and distributed over six million copies to schools, churches, youth groups, civic organizations, and businesses.[40]

Around the same time, a number of other individuals and organizations published books and pamphlets describing marijuana's biological toxicity. In 1977, a group of scientists, psychiatrists, and former government drug-abuse officials formed the American Council on Marijuana,[41] an organization dedicated to publicizing the social and health hazards of marijuana.[42] Another anti-drug organization, the Myrin Institute, published and distributed Marijuana Today: A Compilation of Medical Findings for the Layman by biology professor George K. Russell.[43] Long-time anti-marijuana activist and research scientist Gabriel Nahas wrote two alarmist books on marijuana in the 1970s, Marihuana—Deceptive Weed, and Keep Off the Grass.[44] Nahas warned that "time was running out," that "massive doses of positive scientific evidence" were unneccessary. He claimed there was "enough evidence at hand in the laboratory to indicate that marijuana damages cells and slowly erodes vital functions." He urged stricter controls over marijuana and its users, "before its too late for America."[45]

Other anti-marijuana writers drew heavily on Nahas's interpretation of the scientific evidence. Like Nahas, they reviewed only studies suggesting harm from marijuana, failing to note that the findings were often preliminary and had not been confirmed by other researchers. They cited animal and cellular studies, which were of unknown relevance to humans. They ignored entire bodies of research showing no evidence of harm from marijuana. Basically, these books and pamphlets repeated the claims that Gabriel Nahas and others had made at the 1974 Eastland hearings. By the late 1970s, none of the harms that had been reported in animals and cells had been found in human marijuana users. Nonetheless, anti-drug organizations continued to use these studies as proof of marijuana's biological toxicity.

As governor of California in the 1970s, Ronald Reagan opposed marijuana decriminalization.[46] As president, he committed the federal government to waging a war against marijuana[47]—a war that has grown in intensity ever since. NIDA's role increasingly became one of publicizing marijuana's dangers. At a 1981 NIDA conference, "Marijuana and Youth," participants decided that parents and youth should be sent "very tough, clear, unambiguous messages," even in cases where the scientific studies on marijuana had produced ambiguous findings. Former NIDA director Robert DuPont said, "Anytime you talk about evidence that there are a substantial number of marijuana smokers who are not harmed by their use, you are giving permission, if not encouragement, for very heavy use."[48] Donald Ian Macdonald, who would soon become President Reagan's drug adviser, said, "We're in the middle of a major epidemic. . . . Parents have a right to feel terror . . . they need facts about harmful effects."[49] NIDA's 1982 *Marijuana and Health* report to Congress[50] included new warnings about marijuana's biological dangers, despite there having been no new or compelling evidence of biological harm since NIDA's previous *Marijuana and Health* report in 1980.[51]

The Current War on Marijuana

During the past decade, the criminal justice campaign against marijuana has become increasingly punitive.[52] Congress and some state legislatures recently raised penalties for marijuana offenses.[53] Between 1991 and 1995, marijuana arrests doubled. In 1995, state and local law enforcement agencies made more than one-half million marijuana arrests, 86 percent for possession.[54] Tens of thousands of Americans are now in jail or prison for marijuana offenses. Hundreds of thousands more are punished with fines, probation, or forfeiture of their cars, boats, homes, land, or other property. A majority of states revoke the driver's license of anyone arrested for possessing any amount of marijuana, whether or not they were driving at the time of the arrest.[55] Although a number of states have removed criminal penalties for patients who use marijuana as a medicine,[56] federal officials oppose these policies as undermining their dominant message: that marijuana is far too dangerous for anyone to use safely.[57]

In 1989, the Bush administration's National Drug Control Strategy urged families, communities, schools, and employers to join the government in detecting and punishing drug users, so that "the consequences" of using drugs would "outweigh whatever temporary benefits drugs can provide."[58] Today, most schools have strict anti-drug policies, which allow or require administrators to expel students for using marijuana.[59] Most large businesses impose drug tests on job applicants and/or current employees. Applicants who test positive for marijuana are denied employment, regardless of their qualifications; employees who test positive may be fired, regardless of their work performance.[60] Some social welfare agencies impose mandatory drug tests on clients, denying services and benefits to those who test positive.[61] Parents monitor their children closely for signs of possible marijuana use, including searching kids' rooms and administering home drug tests.[62] Police officers who teach drug education courses at school encourage students to report parents, siblings, and friends for smoking marijuana.[63]

Despite all this, marijuana is as readily available as ever. Among adults, marijuana use has remained steady for years, while among adolescents, marijuana use has been rising since the early 1990s.[64] In response to this increase, the federal government, anti-drug organizations, and the media have intensified the campaign against marijuana. The Center on Addiction and Substance Abuse (CASA), which was founded in 1993 by former Health, Education, and Welfare Secretary Joseph Califano, issues reports and press releases about marijuana's harmful effects,[65] which are often cited uncritically by the media. In 1995, NIDA created a new *Marijuana Use Prevention Initiative*, to "show young children, teenagers, and their parents that marijuana use is a serious threat to the health and well-being of our youth."[66] The same year, the Partnership for a Drug-Free America launched a "media blitz" of anti-marijuana advertisements.[67] In 1996, the Department of Health and Human Services (HHS) introduced a *Reality Check* campaign "to increase awareness" that "marijuana is a drug that causes impairment and can lead to many harms, including death."[68] HHS secretary Donna Shalala urges all Americans to send a "clear and consistent message" that "marijuana is illegal, dangerous, unhealthy, and wrong."[69]

Growing Challenge to Marijuana Prohibition

While the United States government has been escalating the war on marijuana, governments in some other Western countries have been moving in the direction of marijuana decriminalization. In the Netherlands, marijuana sale and use has been de facto legal for more than twenty years.[70] In Italy, Spain, Ireland, Switzerland, parts of Germany, and parts of Australia, there are no criminal penalties for marijuana possession and use, and the police generally ignore small-scale dealers if they conduct business in a way that does not disrupt public order.[71] In 1994, the Australian National Task Force on Cannabis urged the government to go even further. It said, "Any social policy should be reviewed when there is reason to believe that the costs of administering it outweigh the harms reduced." It concluded that "Australia experiences more harm . . . from maintaining the cannabis prohibition policy than it experiences from the use of the drug."[72]

Richard J. Bonnie, the principal author of the 1972 Shafer Commission report, has called for a new American commission to evaluate the costs and benefits of current marijuana policy.[73] The Clinton Administration, however, remains steadfastly opposed to even discussing alternatives to strict prohibition.[74] The DEA, CASA, and the California Narcotics Officers' Association recently issued reports in support of current policies, warning Americans that decriminalizing marijuana would lead to escalating rates of marijuana use.[75]

Research indicates that neither harsh nor lenient policies have much influence on marijuana's popularity. Despite having the harshest prohibition system in the Western world, the United States has marijuana-use rates similar to or greater than most other countries. Around the world, marijuana use increased in the 1960s and 1970s, decreased in the 1980s, and has been rising in the 1990s, irrespective of marijuana policy in individual countries.[76] In the United States, in the eleven states that decriminalized marijuana possession in the 1970s, rates of marijuana use remained similar to those in states that retained criminal sanctions.[77]

Public support for marijuana prohibition is waning in the United States. In a recent survey, half of American adults said criminal penalties for marijuana use and possession should be eliminated.[78]

The percentage supporting marijuana's full legalization began rising in 1990, and reached 25 percent by 1995.[79] Forty-eight percent of high school seniors agree that marijuana possession and use should not be criminal offenses, and 30 percent favor legalization.[80] Among college freshmen, support for marijuana legalization doubled from 1990 to 1995, from 17 percent to 34 percent.[81] With regard to marijuana's use as a medicine, two-thirds of Americans say that physicians and patients should make the decision, without fear of criminal prosecution.[82]

Today's parents, like those of previous decades, do not want their children to use marijuana. However, they have not been convinced that marijuana is a very dangerous substance, or that it serves as a "gateway" to other illegal drugs. In fact, they rank marijuana as less risky than most other drugs, including alcohol and tobacco.[83]

More than seventy million Americans—35 percent of those age twenty-six and over—have now used marijuana; one-fifth still smoke marijuana, at least occasionally.[84] Marijuana is the most widely used illicit drug in America. Indeed, it is the only illicit drug that is used widely. Its use occurs in all regions of the country, among people of all social classes, all ethnicities, all occupations, all religions, and all political persuasions. In an important sense, marijuana use is already a "normal" part of the culture. What most makes marijuana deviant is its continued criminalization.

References

Introduction

1 Indian Hemp Drugs Commission, *Report of the Indian Hemp Drugs Commission,* Simla, India: Government Central Printing Office (1894).

2 Canal Zone Committee, *The Panama Canal Zone Military Investigations* (1925).

3 Mayor's Committee on Marihuana, *The Marihuana Problem in the City of New York: Sociological, Medical, Psychological, and Pharmacological Studies,* Lancaster, PA: Jacques Cattel Press (1944).

4 Advisory Committee on Drug Dependence, *Cannabis,* London: Her Majesty's Stationery Office (1969).

5 Canadian Government Commission of Inquiry, *The Non-Medical Use of Drugs,* Ottawa, Canada: Information Canada (1970).

6 National Commission on Marihuana and Drug Abuse, *Marihuana: A Signal of Misunderstanding,* Washington, DC: U.S. Government Printing Office (1972).

7 Werkgroep Verdovende Middelen, *Background and Risks of Drug Use,* The Hague: Staatsuitgeverij (1972).

8 Senate Standing Committee on Social Welfare, *Drug Problems in Australia—An Intoxicated Society?,* Canberra: Australian Commonwealth Government Printing Office (1977).

9 National Research Council, *An Analysis of Marijuana Policy,* Washington, DC: National Academy Press (1982).

10 Ministry of Health, Welfare and Sport, *Drug Policy in the Netherlands: Continuity and Change,* The Netherlands (1995).

11   For a review of the history surrounding marijuana prohibition in the United States, see Bonnie, R.J. and Whitebread, C.H., *The Marihuana Conviction: A History of Marihuana Prohibition in the United States*, Charlottesville: University of Virginia Press (1974); Kaplan, J., *Marijuana: The New Prohibition*, New York: World Publishing Company (1970).

12   For a more recent history of anti-marijuana campaigns in the United States, see Himmelstein, J.L., *The Strange Career of Marihuana: Politics and Ideology of Drug Control in the United States*, Westport, CT: Greenwood Press (1983); Baum, D., *Smoke and Mirrors: The War on Drugs and the Politics of Failure*, Boston: Little, Brown and Company (1996).

1   Marijuana and Science

1   President Bill Clinton, remarks at signing of the Elementary and Secondary Education Act of 1994, Framington, MA (20 October 1994).

2   "Marijuana for the Sick," *New York Times* (30 December 1996), p. A14.

3   Earl Lane, "Reefer Madness Revisited," *Newsday* (3 September 1996), p. B21.

4   California Narcotic Officers' Association, *Marijuana is NOT a Medicine,* Santa Clarita, CA (1996), p. 2.

5   "Taking the Cover Off Pot," *Washington Post* (7 December 1996), p. A24.

6   U.S. Public Law 91-513, Part F, Sec. 601 (1970).

7   National Commission on Marihuana and Drug Abuse, *Marihuana: A Signal of Misunderstanding,* U.S. Government Printing Office (1972), p. 90.

8   National Commission (1972), see note 7, p. 167.

9   *Marijuana Decriminalization,* Hearings Before the Subcommittee to Investigate Juvenile Delinquency of the Committee on the Judiciary, United States Senate (14 May 1975), pp. 2-3.

10   New York Academy of Medicine, Committee on Public Health, "Marihuana and Drug Abuse," *Bulletin of the New York Academy of Medicine* 49: 77-80 (1973).

11   Grinspoon, L., *Marihuana Reconsidered*, Cambridge: Harvard University Press (1971); Kaplan, J., *Marijuana: The New Prohibition*, New York: World Publishing Company (1970); Brecher, E.M., *Licit and Illicit Drugs*, Boston: Little, Brown and Company (1972); Bonnie, R.J. and Whitebread, C.H., *The Marihuana Conviction: A History of Marihuana Prohibition in the United States*, Charlottesville: University of Virginia Press (1974); Kittrie, N.N., "Marijuana—The Right to Truth," *South Carolina Law Review* 23: 361-76 (1971).

12   Commission of Inquiry into the Non-Medical Use of Drugs, *Final Report*, Ottawa: Information Canada (1972); Werkgroep Verdovende Middelen, *Background and Risks of Drug Use*, The Hague: Staatsuitgeverij (1972); Advisory Com-

mittee on Drug Dependence, *Cannabis*, London: H.M. Stationery Office (1968); Senate Standing Committee on Social Welfare, *Drug Problems in Australia—An Intoxicated Society?*, Canberra: Australian Commonwealth Government Printing Office (1977).

13 Nahas, G.G. and Greenwood, A., "The First Report of the National Commission on Marihuana (1972): Signal of Misunderstanding or Exercise in Ambiguity?," *Bulletin of the New York Academy of Medicine* 50: 55-75 (1974); Nahas, G.G., *Marihuana: Deceptive Weed*, New York: Raven Press (1973).

14 Nahas, G.G., *Keep Off the Grass*, New York: Reader's Digest Press (1976).

15 Subcommittee Hearings to Investigate the Administration of the Internal Security Act and Other Internal Security Laws, *Marihuana-Hashish Epidemic and Its Impact on United States Security*, Washington, DC: U.S. Government Printing Office (1974), p. xii.

16 Institute of Medicine, *Marijuana and Health*, Washington, DC: National Academy Press (1982); *Report on Cannabis Use*, Toronto: Addiction Research Foundation (1982).

17 Jones, R., "Clinical Pharmacology of Marijuana," paper presented at National Institutes of Health, Workshop on the Medical Utility of Marijuana, Bethesda, MD (19 February 1997).

18 National Commission (1972), see note 7, p. 8.

19 Ministry of Health, Welfare and Sport, *Drug Policy in the Netherlands: Continuity and Change*, The Netherlands (1995).

20 "Deglamorising Cannabis," *Lancet* 346: 1241 (1995).

2   Marijuana as a Medicine

1 Drug Enforcement Administration, *Drug Legalization: Myths and Misconceptions*, Washington, DC: U.S. Department of Justice (1994), p. 49.

2 Peterson, R.E., *The Marijuana as Medicine Scam*, Lansing, MI: Michigan Office of Drug Control Policy (undated).

3 Richard A. Schwartz and Eric A. Voth, "Marijuana as Medicine: Making a Silk Purse Out of a Sow's Ear," *Journal of Addictive Diseases* 14: 15-21 (1995).

4 Drug Watch International, *By Any Modern Medical Standard, Marijuana is No Medicine*, Omaha (undated).

5 Barry McCaffrey, Director of National Drug Control Policy, Office of National Drug Control Policy Press Release, Washington, DC (15 November 1996).

6 Chang, A.E. et al., "Delta-Nine-Tetrahydrocannabinol as an Antiemetic in Cancer Patients Receiving High-Dose Methotrexate: A Prospective Randomized Evaluation," *Annals of Internal Medicine* 91: 819-24 (1979); Lucas, V.S. and Laszlo, J., "Delta-9-Tetrahydrocannabinol for Refractory Vomiting Induced by Cancer Chemotherapy," *Journal of the American Medical Association* 243: 1241-43

(1980); Orr, L.E. et al., "Antiemetic Effect of Tetrahydrocannabinol Compared with Placebo and Prochlorperazine in Chemotherapy-Associated Nausea and Emesis," *Archives of Internal Medicine* 140: 1431-33 (1980); Ekert, K. et al., "Amelioration of Cancer Chemotherapy Induced Nausea and Vomiting by Delta-9-Tetrahydrocannabinol," *Medical Journal of Australia* 2: 657-59 (1979); Sallan, S.E. et al., "Antiemetic Effect of Delta-9-Tetrahydrocannabinol in Patients Receiving Cancer Chemotherapy," *New England Journal of Medicine* 293: 795-97 (1975); Sallan, S.E. et al., "Antiemetics in Patients Receiving Chemotherapy for Cancer: A Randomized Comparison of Delta-9-Tetrahydrocannabinol and Prochlorperazine," *New England Journal of Medicine* 302: 135-38 (1980); Ungerleider, J.T. et al., "Cannabis and Cancer Chemotherapy: A Comparison of Oral Delta-9-THC and Prochlorperazine," *Cancer* 50: 636-45 (1982); Vinciguerra, V. et al., "Inhalation of Marijuana as an Antiemetic for Cancer Chemotherapy," *New York State Journal of Medicine* 85: 525-27 (1988); Frytak, S. et al., "Delta-9-Tetrahydrocannabinol as an Antiemetic for Patients Receiving Cancer Chemotherapy: A Comparison with Prochlorperazine and a Placebo," *Annals of Internal Medicine* 91: 825-30 (1979); Kluin-Neleman, J.C. et al., "Delta-9-Tetrahydrocannabinol (THC) as an Antiemetic in Patients Treated with Cancerchemotherapy: A Double-Blind Cross-Over Trial Against Placebo," *Veterinary and Human Toxicology* 21: 338-40 (1979).

7   Foltin, R.W. et al., "Behavioral Analysis of Marijuana Effects on Food Intake in Humans," *Pharmacology Biochemistry and Behavior* 25: 577-82 (1986); Foltin, R.W. et al., "Effects of Smoked Marijuana on Food Intake and Body Weight of Humans Living in a Residential Laboratory," *Appetite* 11: 1-14 (1988); Plasse, T.F. et al., "Recent Clinical Experience with Dronabinol," *Pharmacology Biochemistry and Behavior* 40: 695-700 (1991); Regelson, W. et al., "Delta-9-Tetrahydrocannabinol as an Effective Antidepressant and Appetite-Stimulating Agent in Advanced Cancer Patients," pp. 763-76 in Braude, M.C. and Szara, S. (eds), *The Pharmacology of Marihuana*, New York: Raven Press (1976); Gorter, R. et al., "Dronabinol Effects on Weight in Patients with HIV Infection," *AIDS* 6: 127-38 (1992); Greenberg, I. et al., "Effects of Marijuana use on Body Weight and Caloric Intake in Humans," *Psychopharmacology* 49: 79-84 (1976); Ungerleider et al. (1979), see note 6; Ekert et al. (1979), see note 6; Sallan et al. (1980), see note 6.

8   Crawford, W.J. and Merritt, J.C., "Effect of Tetrahydrocannabinol on Arterial and Intraocular Hypertension," *International Journal of Clinical Pharmacology and Biopharmaceutics* 17: 191-96 (1979); Merritt, J.C. et al., "Effects of Marijuana on Intraocular and Blood Pressure in Glaucoma," *Ophthamology* 87: 222-28 (1980); Merritt, J.C. et al., "Oral Delta-9-Tetrahydrocannabinol in Heterogeneous Glaucoma," *Annals of Ophthamology* 12: 947- 50 (1980); Hepler, R.S. and Petrus, R., "Experiences with Administration of Marijuana to Glaucoma Patients," pp. 63-76 in Cohen, S. and Stillman, R. (eds), *The Therapeutic Potential of Marihuana*, New York: Plenum Medical Book Company (1976); Hepler, R.S. et al., "Ocular Effects of Marijuana Smoking," pp. 815-24 in Braude, M.C. and Szara,

S. (eds), *Pharmacology of Marihuana*, New York: Raven Press (1976).

9   Malec, J. et al., "Cannabis Effect on Spasticity in Spinal Cord Injury," *Archives of Physical and Medical Rehabilitation* 63: 116-18 (1982); Dunn, M. and Davis, R., "The Perceived Effects of Marijuana on Spinal Cord Injured Males," *Paraplegia* 12: 175 (1974); Mauer, M. et al., "Delta-9-Tetrahydrocannibinol Shows Antispastic and Analgesic Effects in a Single Case Double-Blind Trial," *European Archives of Psychiatry and Clinical Neuroscience* 240: 1-4 (1990); Hanigan, W.C. et al., "The Effect of Delta-9-THC on Human Spasticity," *Clinical Pharmacology and Therapeutics* 39: 198 (1986).

10 Ungerleider, J.T. et al., "Delta-9-THC in the Treatment of Spasticity Associated with Multiple Sclerosis," *Advances in Alcohol and Substance Abuse* 7: 39-50 (1987); Petro, D.J., "Marijuana as a Therapeutic Agent for Muscle Spasm or Spasticity," *Psychosomatics* 21: 81-85 (1980); Petro, D.J. and Ellenberger, C., "Treatment of Human Spasticity with Delta-9- Tetrahydrocannabinol," *Journal of Clinical Pharmacology* 21: 413-16S (1981); Meinck, H.M. et al., "Effect of Cannabinoids on Spasticity and Ataxia in Multiple Sclerosis," *Journal of Neurology* 236: 120-22 (1989); Consroe, P. et al., "The Perceived Effects of Cannabis Smoking in Patients with Multiple Sclerosis," paper presented at the annual meeting of the International Cannabinoid Research Society (June 1996).

11 Clifford, D.B., "Tetrahydrocannabinol for Tremor in Multiple Sclerosis," *Annals of Neurology* 13: 669-71 (1983).

12 Grinspoon, L. and Bakalar, J.B, *Marihuana: The Forbidden Medicine, Revised and Expanded Edition,* New Haven: Yale University Press (1997); Pertwee, R.G., "Pharmacological, Physiological and Clinical Implications of the Discovery of Cannabinoid Receptors: An Overview," pp. 1-34 in Pertwee, R.G. (ed), *Cannabinoid Receptors*, New York: Academic Press (1995); Consroe, P.F. and Wood, G.C., "Anticonvulsant Nature of Marijuana Smoking," *Journal of the American Medical Association* 243: 306-7 (1975); Noyes, R. and Baram, D.A., "Cannabis Analgesia," *Comprehensive Psychiatry* 15: 531-35 (1974).

13 Cunha, J.M. et al., "Chronic Administration of Cannabidiol to Healthy Volunteers and Epileptic Patients," *Pharmacology* 21: 175-85 (1980); Consroe, P. and Snider, S.R., "Therapeutic Potential of Cannabinoids in Neurological Disorders," pp. 21-50 in Mechoulam, R. (ed), *Cannabinoids as Therapeutic Agents*, Boca Raton: CRC Press (1986).

14 *Uniform Controlled Substances Act of 1970*, 21 U.S., Sec. 800.

15 "MPP Analyzes States' Medicinal Marijuana Laws," *Marijuana Policy Report* 2, 3: 1-6 (1996).

16 Wren, C.S., "Votes on Marijuana Are Stirring Debate," *New York Times* (17 November 1996), p. 16.

17 Cotton, P., "Government Extinguishes Marijuana Access, Advocates Smell Politics," *Journal of the American Medical Association* 267: 2573-74 (1992); Doblin, R., "Reflections on Strategies for Psychedelic Research in Light of the Medical

Marijuana Struggle," *Newsletter of the Multidisciplinary Association for Psychedelic Studies* 3, 2: 6-7 (1992).

18 Randall, R., "How Cancer and AIDS Patients Suffer at the Hands of the DEA," pp. 104-6 in Trebach, A.S. and Zeese, K.B. (eds), *Drug Prohibition and the Conscience of Nations*, Washington, DC: The Drug Policy Foundation (1990); Treaster, J.B., "Healing Herb or Narcotic? Marijuana as Medication," *New York Times* (14 November 1993), p. 37; Meyer, E.L., "Marijuana as Medicine at Heart of Md. Case," *Washington Post* (20 December 1994), p. D1; Goldin, D., "Marijuana Cure: Rx for Arrest," *New York Times* (10 September 1995), p. CY8; "Prohibition of Marijuana Prescribing Will Be Tested in Ohio," *New York Times* (17 September 1995), p. 29.

19 Agurell, S. et al., "Pharmacokinetics and Metabolism of Delta-1-Tetrahydrocannabinol and Other Cannabinoids with Emphasis on Man," *Pharmacological Reviews* 38: 21-43 (1986); Lemberger, L. et al., "Delta-9-Tetrahydrocannabinol: Temporal Correlation of the Psychologic Effects and Blood Levels After Various Routes of Administration," *New England Journal of Medicine* 268: 685-88 (1972); Perez-Reyes, M. et al., "The Clinical Pharmacology and Dynamics of Marijuana Cigarette Smoking," *Journal of Clinical Pharmacology* 21: 201-7S (1981); Wall, M.E. and Perez-Reyes, M., "The Metabolism of Delta-9-Tetrahydrocannabinol and Related Cannabinoids in Man," *Journal of Clinical Pharmacology* 21: 178-89S (1981); Ohlsson, A. et al., "Plasma Delta-9-THC Concentrations and Clinical Effects After Oral and Intravenous Administration and Smoking," *Clinical Pharmacology and Therapeutics* 28: 409-16 (1980); Mason, A.P. and McBay, A.J., "Cannabis: Pharmacology and Interpretation of Effects," *Journal of Forensic Sciences* 30: 615-31 (1985).

20 Mattes, R.D. et al., "Cannabinoids and Appetite Stimulation," *Pharmacology Biochemistry and Behavior* 49: 187-95 (1994); Peat, M.A., "Distribution of Delta-9-Tetrahydrocannabinol and Its Metabolites," *Advances in Analytical Toxicology* 2: 186-217 (1989); Wall, M.E. et al., "Metabolism, Disposition, and Kinetics of Delta-9-Tetrahydrocannabinol in Men and Women," *Clinical Pharmacology and Therapeutics* 34: 352-63 (1983); Agurell et al. (1986), see note 19.

21 Mattes, R.D. et al., "Bypassing the First-Pass Effect for the Therapeutic Use of Cannabinoids," *Pharmacology Biochemistry and Behavior* 44: 745-47 (1993).

22 Mattes et al. (1994), see note 20; Agurell et al. (1986), see note 19; Wall and Perez-Reyes (1981), see note 19.

23 Hollister, L.E. et al., "Do Plasma Concentrations of Delta-9-Tetrahydrocannabinol Reflect the Degree of Intoxication?," *Journal of Clinical Pharmacology* 21: 171-77S (1981); Chait, L.D. and Zacny, J.P., "Reinforcing and Subjective Effects of Oral Delta-9-THC and Smoked Marijuana in Humans," *Psychopharmacology* 107: 255-62 (1992); Ohlsson et al. (1980), see note 19; Peat (1989), see note 20; Lemberger et al. (1972), see note 19.

24 Cone, E.J. et al., "Marijuana-Laced Brownies: Behavioral Effects, Physiological Effects, and Urinalysis in Humans Following Ingestion," *Journal of Analytical*

Toxicology 12: 169-75 (1988); Lemberger et al. (1972), see note 19; Chait and Zacny (1992), see note 23; Ohlsson et al. (1980), see note 19.

25 Perez-Reyes, M., "Pharmacodynamics of Certain Drugs of Abuse," pp. 287-310 in Barnett, G. and Chiang, C.N. (eds), *Pharmacokinetics and Pharmacodynamics of Psychoactive Drugs*, Foster City, CA: Biomedical Publications (1985); Sallan et al. (1975), see note 6; Chait and Zacny (1992), see note 23.

26 Perez-Reyes, M. et al., "Intravenous Injection in Man of Delta-9-Tetrahydro-cannabinol and 11-Hydroxy-Delta-9-Tetrahydrocannabinol," *Science* 177: 633-35 (1972); Perez-Reyes, M. et al., "A Comparison of the Pharmacological Activity of Delta-9-Tetrahydrocannabinol and Its Monohydroxylated Metabolites in Man," *Experentia* 29: 1009-10 (1973); Lemberger, L. et al., "Comparative Pharmacology of Delta-9-Tetrahydrocannabinol and its Metabolite 11-OH-Delta-9-THC," *Journal of Clinical Investigation* 54: 2411-17 (1973); Wall and Perez-Reyes (1981), see note 19; Agurell et al. (1986), see note 19.

27 Mason and McBay (1985), see note 19; Agurell et al. (1986), see note 19; Lemberger et al. (1973), see note 26; Perez-Reyes et al. (1973), see note 26.

28 Mason and McBay (1985), see note 19; Agurell et al. (1986), see note 19; Peat (1989), see note 20; Ohlsson et al. (1980), see note 19.

29 Karniol, G. et al., "Cannabidiol Interferes with the Effects of Delta-9-Tetra-hydrocannabinol in Man," *European Journal of Pharmacology* 28: 172-77 (1974); Zuardi, A.W. et al., "Action of Cannabidiol on the Anxiety and Other Effects Produced by Delta-9-THC in Normal Subjects," *Psychopharmacology* 76: 245-50 (1982).

30 Frytak et al. (1979), see note 6.

31 Schwartz, R.H. and Beveridge, R.A., "Marijuana as an Antiematic Drug: How Useful Today? Opinions From Clinical Oncologists," *Journal of Addictive Diseases* 13: 53-65 (1994).

32 Schwartz, R.H. et al., "Marijuana to Prevent Nausea and Vomiting in Cancer Patients: A Survey of Clinical Oncologists," *Southern Medical Journal* 90: 167-72 (1997).

33 Doblin, R. and Kleiman, M.A.R., "Marijuana as an Anti-Emetic Medicine: A Survey of Oncologists' Attitudes and Experiences," *Journal of Clinical Oncology* 19: 1275-1290 (1991).

34 Schwartz et al. (1997), see note 32.

35 Agurell et al. (1986), see note 19; Ohlsson et al. (1980), see note 19.

36 Elsohly, M.A. et al., "Rectal Bioavailablity of Delta-9-Tetrahydrocannabinol From Various Esters," *Pharmacology Biochemistry and Behavior* 40: 497-502 (1991); Mattes et al. (1993), see note 21.

37 Olsen, J.L. et al., "An Inhalation Aerosol of Delta-9-Tetrahydrocannabinol,"

Journal of Pharmacy and Pharmacology 28: 86 (1976).

38 National Commission on Marihuana and Drug Abuse, *Marihuana: A Signal of Misunderstanding*, Washington, DC: U.S. Government Printing Office (1972); Cohen, S., "Therapeutic Aspects," pp. 194-225 in Petersen, R.C. (ed), *Marihuana Research Findings: 1976*, Rockville, MD: National Institute on Drug Abuse (1977); Cohen, S. and Stillman, R.C. (eds), *The Therapeutic Potential of Marihuana*, New York: Plenum Medical Book Company (1976); National Institute on Drug Abuse, *Marijuana and Health*, Eighth Annual Report to the U.S. Congress from the Secretary of Health and Human Services (1980).

39 "Access to Cannabinoids and Marijuana for Research and Treatment," Appendix III, pp. 175-76 in Mechoulam, R. (ed), *Cannabinoids as Therapeutic Agents*, Boca Raton, FL: CRC Press (1986).

40 Randall, R.C. (ed), *Marijuana, Medicine and the Law*, Washington, DC: Galen Press (1988), pp. 27-50.

41 National Institute on Drug Abuse, *Marihuana and Health*, Sixth Annual Report to the U.S. Congress from the Secretary of Health, Education and Welfare (1976).

42 National Institute on Drug Abuse, *Marihuana and Health*, Seventh Annual Report to the U.S. Congress from the Secretary of Health, Education and Welfare (1977); National Institute on Drug Abuse (1980), see note 37.

43 Drug Policy Office, *Federal Strategy for Prevention of Drug Abuse and Drug Trafficking*, Washington, DC: The White House (1982).

44 National Institute on Drug Abuse, *Marijuana and Health*, Ninth Report to the U.S. Congress from the Secretary of Health and Human Services (1982), p. 5.

45 54 *Federal Register* 53767 (29 December 1989).

46 *In the Matter of Marijuana Rescheduling, Docket 86-22, Opinion, Recommended Ruling, Findings of Fact, Conclusions of Law, and Decision of Administrative Law Judge*, Washington, DC: Drug Enforcement Administration (6 September 1988).

47 *Alliance for Cannabis Therapeutics and NORML v DEA*, 15 F.2d 1131 (D.C. Cir. 1994).

48 57 *Federal Register* 10499 (26 March 1992).

49 Cotton (1992), see note 17; "U.S. Rescinds Approval of Marijuana as Therapy," *New York Times* (11 March 1992), p. A21.

50 Voelker, R., "Medical Marijuana: A Trial of Science and Politics," *Journal of the American Medical Association* 271: 1645 (1994).

51 Drug Enforcement Administration Press Release, "Response to JAMA Article Titled 'Marihuana as Medicine,' " Washington, DC (20 June 1995).

52 Drug Enforcement Administration (1994), see note 1.

53 Doblin, R., "Medical Marijuana Research: NIDA Just Says No to Science," *Newsletter of the Multidisciplinary Association for Psychedelic Studies* 5, 4: 11-13 (1995); Lehrman, S., "U.S. Drug Agencies Resist Medicinal-Pot Plan," *San Francisco*

Examiner (8 January 1995), p. B2; Okie, S., "Plan to Test Drug's Effectiveness in Bureaucratic Limbo," *Washington Post Health* (19 November 1996), p. 7.

54 Barry McCaffrey, Director of National Drug Control Policy, Senate Judiciary Committee Hearings, *Teenage Drug Use* (4 September 1996).

55 Office of National Drug Control Policy, *The Administration's Response to the Passage of California Proposition 215 and Arizona Proposition 200*, Washington, DC (30 December 1996); "Doctors Given Federal Threat on Marijuana: U.S. Acts to Overcome States' Easing of Law," *New York Times* (31 December 1996), p. 1.

56 Lapey, J., *The Medical Marijuana Scam*, Hanover, MA: Concerned Citizens for Drug Prevention, Inc. (1993); Bennett, S.S., *Therapeutic Marijuana: Fact or Fiction*, Portland: Oregon Federation of Parents for Drug Free Youth (1992); Voth, E.A., *The International Drug Strategy Institute Position Paper on the Medicinal Applications of Marijuana*, Drug Watch International, Omaha (no date); Gorman, T.J., *Marijuana is NOT a Medicine*, Santa Clarita, CA: California Narcotics Officers' Association (1996); Center on Addiction and Substance Abuse Press Release, "Majority of Californians Support Marijuana for Terminally Ill But Reject Other Provisions," New York (28 October 1996).

57 Gwynne, P., "Trials of Medical Marijuana's Medical Potential Languish as Government Says Just Say No," *The Scientist* 9, 23: 1-2 (1995).

58 American Public Health Association, *Access to Therapeutic Marijuana/Cannabis*, Resolution 9513 (1995).

59 Federation of American Scientists, *Medical Use of Whole Cannabis* (1994).

60 See *Alliance for Cannabis Therapeutics and NORML v DEA*, 15 F.2d 1131 (D.C. Cir. 1994).

61 "Choice for Surgeon General Favors Medicinal Marijuana Use," *Washington Post* (20 December 1992), p. A16.

62 *Therapeutic Use of Marijuana*, Resolution of the National Association of Attorneys General (25 June 1983).

63 *Resolution Calling for the Reclassification of Marijuana to Schedule II of the Controlled Substances Act*, National Association of Criminal Defense Lawyers (May 1987).

64 Kassirer, J.P., "Federal Foolishness and Marijuana," *New England Journal of Medicine* 336: 366-67 (1997).

65 Grinspoon, L. and Bakalar, J.B., "Marihuana as Medicine: A Plea for Reconsideration," *Journal of the American Medical Association* 273: 1875-76 (1995).

66 "A Medical Opinion on Marijuana," *New York Times* (31 January 1997); "Lift the Ban on Using Marijuana for Medicine," *USA Today* (11 January 1994); "Out-of-Touch Marijuana Ban Ill Serves Patients," *USA Today* (2 January 1997); "Reducing the Drug War to Absurdity," *Chicago Tribune* (11 July 1995); "Giving Suffering Patients a Break," *The Oakland Tribune* (19 January 1994); "Medicinal Marijuana," *The Oakland Tribune* (20 June 1995); "Try Some Mercy," *San Jose Mercury News* (10 January 1994); "Let's OK Pot as Medicine," *The Capital Times*,

Madison, Wisconsin (27 September 1993); "Let Doctors Prescribe Pot," *Albany Times Union* (4 January 1993); "Medical Use of Marijuana: Let Doctors Decide," *The Star Tribune*, Minneapolis (23 March 1992).

67 Beldon & Russonello, "American Voters' Opinions on the Use and Legalization of Marijuana," national random poll conducted for the American Civil Liberties Union, New York (1995); The Field Institute, poll of California voters' support for Proposition 215 (1996); Center on Addiction and Substance Abuse (1996), see note 56; Lake Research, Inc., national random poll conducted for the Lindesmith Center, New York (1997).

68 Hearn, W., "Considering Cannabis," *American Medical News* 38, 37: 11-13 (1995); Wren, C.S., "Doctors Criticize Move Against State Measures," *New York Times* (31 December 1996), p. D18; Goodavage, M., "Calif. to Vote on Legalizing Pot as Medicine," *USA Today* (16 July 1996), p. 10A; Rogers, P., "Pot Charges Against Epileptic Dismissed: Santa Cruz Woman Had Faced Prison Term," *San Jose Mercury News* (27 March 1993), p. B5.

69 Wesner, B., "The Medical Marijuana Issue Among PWAs: Reports of Therapeutic Use and Attitudes Toward Legal Reform," Working Paper, Honolulu: University of Hawaii (1996).

70 Marin, G., "State Pot Order Rejected: S.F. Sheriff Won't Enforce Ban on Club's Sale," *San Francisco Chronicle* (7 August 1996); "Rx to Peddle Pot? Police Say No," *Kentucky Post* (27 February 1996), p. 1; Gorman, P., "Cannabis Provider: Interview with Steven Smith," *High Times*. 5 (April 1994); Peacock, L., "Doctors or Dope Dealers?," *Arkansas Times* (16 December 1993), p. 17; Treaster, J., "Healing Herb or Narcotic? Marijuana as Medicine," *New York Times* (14 November 1993), p. 37; Murphy, K., "Arrest Sounds an Alarm for Medicinal Marijuana Clubs," *Los Angeles Times* (14 June 1995); Goldberg, C., "Marijuana Club Helps Those in Pain," *New York Times* (25 February 1996), p. 16; Fisher, I., "The Marijuana Club," *New York Times* (10 January 1997), p. B1.

71 *Food, Drugs, and Cosmetics Act*, Section 505(d)(7).

72 Pertwee (1995), see note 12.

73 Dansak, D., "In the Matter of Marijuana Rescheduling Petition," affidavit filed in Drug Enforcement Administration Hearing, Docket 86-22 (1987), pp. 149-58 in Randall, R.C. (ed), *Cancer Treatment and Marijuana*, Washington, DC: Galen Press (1990); Vinciguerra et al. (1988), see note 6; Chang et al. (1979), see note 6; Hepler and Petrus (1976), see note 8.

74 Gingrich, N., "Legal Status of Marijuana," *Journal of the American Medical Association* 247: 1563 (1982).

3 Marijuana and Addiction

1 National Institute on Drug Abuse, "Marijuana Treatments Involving Social Support or Relapse Prevention Appear to Reduce Chronic Drug Use," *NIDA Notes* 5, 2 (1990), p. 16.

2   Donna E. Shalala, Secretary of Health and Human Services, "Say 'No' to Legalization of Marijuana," *Wall Street Journal* (18 August 1995), p. A10.

3   Neil Swan, "A Look at Marijuana's Harmful Effects," *NIDA Notes* 9, 2 (1994) p. 16.

4   National Institute on Drug Abuse, *Marijuana: What Parents Need to Know*, Rockville, MD (1995), p.19.

5   Johnston, L.D. et al., *National Survey Results on Drug Use from the Monitoring the Future Study, 1975-1994, Volume II: College Students and Young Adults*, Rockville, MD: U.S. Department of Health and Human Services (1996), p. 43.

6   Substance Abuse and Mental Health Services Administration, *National Household Survey on Drug Abuse: Population Estimates 1994*, Rockville, MD: U.S. Department of Health and Human Services (1995).

7   Grinspoon, L., *Marihuana Reconsidered*, Cambridge, MA: Harvard University Press (1971); Grinspoon, L. and Bakalar, J.B., *Marijuana: The Forbidden Medicine*, New Haven: Yale University Press (1993); Sloman, L., *Reefer Madness: Marijuana in America*, New York: Grove Press (1979); Novak, W., *High Culture: Marijuana in the Lives of Americans*, The Cannabis Institute of America, Inc. (1980).

8   Kandel, D.B. and Davies, M., "Progression to Regular Marijuana Involvement: Phenomenology and Risk Factors for Near Daily Users," pp. 211-54 in Glantz, M. and Pickens, R. (eds), *Vulnerability to Drug Abuse*, Washington, DC: American Psychological Association (1992).

9   Tunving, K. et al., "'A Way Out of the Fog': An Out-Patient Program for Cannabis Abusers," pp. 207-12 in Chesher, G. et al. (eds), *Marijuana: An International Research Report*, Canberra: Australian Government Publishing Service (1988); Hendin, H. et al., *Living High: Daily Marijuana Use Among Adults*, New York: Human Sciences Press (1987); Stephens, R.S. et al., "Adult Marijuana Users Seeking Treatment," *Journal of Consulting and Clinical Psychology* 61: 1100-04 (1993); Novak (1980), see note 7.

10 Jones, R.T., "Marijuana: Health and Treatment Issues," *Psychiatric Clinics of North America* 7: 703-12 (1984); Chalsma, A.L. and Boyum, D., *Marijuana Situation Assessment*, Washington, DC: Office of National Drug Control Policy (1994); U.S. Department of Health and Human Services, *Epidemiological Trends in Drug Abuse, Volume I: Highlights and Executive Summary*, Rockville, MD (1995); Leshner, A.I., "Marijuana, Medicine and the Law," *The Washington Post* (5 October 1994), p. A22.

11 Hubbard, R.L. et al., *Drug Abuse Treatment: A National Study of Effectiveness*, Chapel Hill: University of North Carolina Press (1989); Didcott, P. et al., *A Profile of Addicts in Residential Treatment in New South Wales*, Sidney: New South Wales Department of Health (1988); Stephens et al. (1993), see note 9.

12 Stefanis, C. et al., "Experimental Observations of a 3-Day Hashish Abstinence Period and Reintroduction of Use," *Annals of the New York Academy of Sciences* 282: 113-20 (1976); Mendelson, J.H. et al., "Marijuana Withdrawal Syndrome in a Woman," *American Journal of Psychiatry* 141: 1289-90 (1984); Williams, E.G.

et al., "Studies on Marihuana and Pyrahexl Compound," *Public Health Reports* 61: 1059-83 (1946); Greenberg, I. et al., "Psychiatric and Behavioral Observations of Casual and Heavy Marijuana Users," *Annals of the New York Academy of Sciences* 282: 72-84 (1976); Soueif, M.I., "Hashish Consumption in Egypt, With Special Reference to Psychosocial Aspects," *Bulletin on Narcotics* 19: 1-12 (1967); Bensusan, A.D., "Marihuana Withdrawal Symptoms," *British Journal of Medicine* 3: 112 (1971); Solowij, N. et al., "Biopsychosocial Changes Associated with Cessation of Cannabis Use: A Single Case Study of Acute and Chronic Effects, Withdrawal and Treatment," *Life Sciences* 56: 2127-35 (1995); Miles, C.G. et al., *An Experimental Study of the Effects of Daily Cannabis Smoking on Behavioural Patterns,* Toronto, Canada: Addiction Research Foundation (1974); Mendelson, J.H. et al., "The Effects of Marihuana Use on Human Operant Behavior: Individual Data," pp. 643-53 in Braude, M.C. and Szara, S. (eds), *The Pharmacology of Marihuana,* New York: Raven Press (1976).

13 Jones, R.T. et al., "Clinical Relevance of Cannabis Tolerance and Dependence," *Journal of Clinical Pharmacology* 21: 143-52S (1981).

14 Reported in Gannon, R., "The Truth About Pot," *Popular Science* 192: 76-79 (May 1968).

15 Jones, R.T. et al., "Clinical Studies of Tolerance and Dependence," *Annals of the New York Academy of Sciences* 282: 221-39 (1976).

16 Wiesbeck, G.A. et al., "An Evaluation of the History of a Marijuana Withdrawal Syndrome in a Large Population," *Addiction* 91: 1469-78 (1996).

17 Compton, D.R. et al., "Cannabis Dependence and Tolerance Production," *Advances in Alcohol and Substance Abuse* 9: 129-47 (1990); Jones, R.T., "Cannabis Tolerance and Dependence," pp. 617-90 in Fehr, K.O. and Kalant, H., *Cannabis and Health Hazards,* Toronto: Addiction Research Foundation (1983); Adams, I.B. and Martin, B.R., "Cannabis: Pharmacology and Toxicity in Animals and Humans," *Addiction* 91: 1585-1614 (1996).

18 Aceto, M.D. et al., "Cannabinoid Precipitated Withdrawal by the Selective Cannabinoid Receptor Antagonist, SR 141716A," *European Journal of Pharmacology* 82: R1-2 (1995).

19 Shalala, D., remarks at *National Conference on Marijuana Use: Prevention, Treatment and Research,* sponsored by the National Institute on Drug Abuse, Arlington, VA (July 1995); Swan, N., "Marijuana Antagonist Reveals Evidence of THC Dependence in Rats," *NIDA Notes* 10, 6: 1 (1995); Ferrell, D., "Scientists Unlocking Secrets of Marijuana's Effects," *Los Angeles Times, Washington Edition* (19 December 1996), p. A4.

20 U.S. Department of Health and Human Services, *Drug Abuse and Drug Abuse Research,* Rockville, MD (1991), p. 133.

21 Hilts, P.J., "Is Nicotine Addictive? It Depends on Whose Criteria You Use," *New York Times* (2 August 1994), p. C3.

22 Hall, W. et al., *The Health and Psychological Consequences of Cannabis Use,* Canberra:

Australian Government Publishing Service (1994); Roffman, R.A. and Barnhart, R., "Assessing Need for Marijuana Dependence Treatment Through an Anonymous Telephone Interview," *International Journal of the Addictions* 22: 639-51 (1987).

23 Miller, N.S. and Gold, M.S., "The Diagnosis of Marijuana (*Cannabis*) Dependence," *Journal of Substance Abuse Treatment* 6: 183-92 (1989), p. 184.

24 Gold, M.S., *Marijuana*, New York: Plenum Medical Book Company (1989), p. 96.

25 Gold, M.S., *The Good News About Drugs and Alcohol*, New York: Villard Books (1991); Schwartz, R.H., "Identifying and Helping Patients Who Use Marijuana," *Post Graduate Medicine* 86, 6: 91-95 (1989); Estroff, T.W. and Gold, M.S., "Psychiatric Presentations of Marijuana Abuse," *Psychiatric Annals* 16: 221-24 (1986); Schnoll, S.H. and Daghestani, A.N., "Treatment of Marijuana Abuse," *Psychiatric Annals* 16: 249-54 (1986); Kleber, H.D., "Treatment of Drug Dependence: What Works?" *International Review of Psychiatry* 1: 81-100 (1989); Smith, J.W. et al., "A Marijuana Smoking Cessation Clinical Trial Utilizing THC-Free Marijuana, Aversion Therapy, and Self-Management Counseling," *Journal of Substance Abuse Treatment* 5: 89-98 (1988); Tennant, F.S., "The Clinical Syndrome of Marijuana Dependence," *Psychiatric Annals* 16: 225-34 (1986); Dupont, R.L., *Getting Tough on Gateway Drugs*, Washington, DC: American Psychiatric Press (1984); Gold (1989), see note 23; Miller and Gold (1989), see note 22.

26 Peele, S., *The Diseasing of America*, Lexington, MA: Lexington Books (1989).

27 Normand, J. et al., *Under the Influence: Drugs and the American Workforce*, Washington, DC: National Academy Press (1994); "SmithKline Test Index Shows Continued Drop in Test Positives," *Drug Detection Report* (5 March 1996), p. 1.

28 Zimmer, L. and Jacobs, J.B., "The Business of Drug Testing: Technological Innovation and Social Control," *Contemporary Drug Problems* 19: 1-26 (1992); Jacobs, J.B. and Zimmer, L., "Drug Treatment and Workplace Drug Testing: Politics, Symbolism and Organizational Dilemmas," *Behavioral Sciences and the Law* 9: 345-60 (1991).

4   The Gateway Theory

1 Join Together, *Monthly Action Kit: Increase in Marijuana Use Among Young People*, Boston (1995).

2 Center on Addiction and Substance Abuse, *Cigarettes, Alcohol, and Marijuana: Gateways to Illicit Drugs*, New York (1994), p. 9.

3 Gabriel Nahas, *Keep Off the Grass*, Middlebury, VT: Paul S. Eriksson (1990), p. xxiii.

4 Senator Orrin Hatch, Senate Judiciary Committee Hearings, *Teenage Drug Use* (4 September 1996).

5   Andrew L. Chalsma and David Boyum, *Marijuana Situation Assessment*, Washington, DC: Office of National Drug Control Policy (1994), p. 5.

6   Himmelstein, J.L., *The Strange Career of Marihuana: Politics and Ideology of Drug Control in the United States*, Westport, CT: Greenwood Press (1983); Regush, N.M., *The Drug Addiction Dilemma*, New York: Dial Press (1971).

7   Glaser, D. et al., "Later Heroin Use by Marijuana-Using and Non-Drug-Using Adolescent Offenders in New York City," *International Journal of the Addictions* 4: 145-55 (1969); Goode, E., "Multiple Drug Use Among Marijuana Smokers," *Social Problems* 17: 48-64 (1969).

8   Blum, R.H. et al., *Students and Drugs*, San Francisco: Jossey-Bass (1970); Shick, J.F.E. et al., "Use of Marijuana in the Haight-Ashbury Subculture," *Journal of Psychedelic Drugs* 2: 49-65 (1968); McGlothlin, W.H. and West, L.J., "The Marihuana Problem: An Overview," *American Journal of Psychiatry* 125: 370-78 (1968).

9   Clayton, R.R., "Cocaine Use in the United States," pp. 8-34 in Kozel, N.J. and Adams, E.H. (eds), *Cocaine Use in America: Epidemiologic and Clinical Perspectives*, Rockville, MD: National Institute on Drug Abuse (1985); Yamaguchi, K. and Kandel, D.B., "Patterns of Drug Use from Adolescence to Young Adulthood II," *American Journal of Public Health* 74: 668-72 (1984).

10 Single, E. et al., "Patterns of Multiple Drug Use in High School," *Journal of Health and Social Behavior* 15: 344-57 (1974); Yu, J. and Williford, W.R., "The Age of Onset and Alcohol, Cigarette, and Marijuana Use Patterns: An Analysis of Drug Use Progression of Young Adults in New York State," *International Journal of the Addictions* 27: 1313-23 (1992); Kandel, D.B. et al., "Stages of Progression in Drug Involvement from Adolescence to Adulthood: Further Evidence for the Gateway Theory," *Journal of Studies on Alcohol* 53: 447- 57 (1992); Blum et al. (1970), see note 8.

11 Cohen, P. and Sas, A., "Cannabis Use as a Stepping Stone to Other Drug Use? The Case of Amsterdam," pp.49-82 in Bollinger, L. (ed), *Cannabis Science: From Prohibition to Human Right*, New York: Peter Lang (1997); Blaze-Temple, D. and Lo, S.K., "Stages of Drug Use: A Community Survey of Perth Teenagers," *British Journal of Addiction* 87: 215-25 (1992); Chowdhury, A.N., "Cannabis: A Note from Bengal," *Addiction* 91: 766-67 (1996); Soueif, M.I., "The Use of Cannabis in Egypt: A Behavioral Study," *Bulletin on Narcotics* 23, 4: 17-28 (1971).

12 Substance Abuse and Mental Health Services Administration, *National Household Survey on Drug Abuse: Main Findings 1994*, Rockville, MD: U.S. Department of Health and Human Services (1996), pp. 132-34.

13 Clayton, R.R. and Voss, H.L., *Young Men and Drugs in Manhattan: A Causal Analysis*, Rockville, MD: National Institute on Drug Abuse (1981); Welte, J.W. and Barnes, G.M., "Alcohol: The Gateway to Other Drug Use Among Secondary-School Students," *Journal of Youth and Adolescence* 14: 487-98 (1985); Robins, N.L. and Murphy, G.E., "Drug Use in a Normal Population of Young Negro Men," *American Journal of Public Health* 57: 1580-96 (1967); National Commission on

Marihuana and Drug Abuse, *Marihuana: A Signal of Misunderstanding,* Washington, DC: U.S. Government Printing Office (1972), pp. 340-67; Glaser et al. (1969), see note 7.

14 Substance Abuse and Mental Health Services Administration (1996), see note 12, pp. 27-37; National Institute on Drug Abuse, *National Household Survey on Drug Abuse: Main Findings 1990,* Rockville, MD: U.S. Department of Health and Human Services (1991), pp. 20-30; Johnston, L.D. et al., *National Survey Results on Drug Use from the Monitoring the Future Study, 1975-1994, Volume I: Secondary School Students,* Rockville, MD: U.S. Department of Health and Human Services (1995), pp. 78-82.

15 Substance Abuse and Mental Health Services Administration (1996), see note 12, p. 48.

16 Johnson, V., "A Longitudinal Assessment of Predominant Patterns of Drug Use Among Adolescents and Young Adults," pp. 173-82 in Chesher, G. et al. (eds), *Marijuana: An International Research Report,* Canberra: Australian Government Publishing Service (1988); Mullins, C.J. et al., "Variables Related to Cannabis," *International Journal of the Addictions* 10: 481-502 (1975); Yamaguchi, K. and Kandel, D.P., "Patterns of Drug Use from Adolescence to Young Adulthood III: Predictors of Progression," *American Journal of Public Health* 74: 673-81 (1984); Donovan, J.E. and Jessor, R., "Problem Drinking and the Dimensions of Involvement with Drugs," *American Journal of Public Health* 73: 543-52 (1983); Ellickson, P. et al., "Stepping Through the Drug Use Sequence: Longitudinal Scalogram Analysis of Initiation and Regular Use," *Journal of Abnormal Psychology* 101: 441- 51 (1992); Kandel, D.P. and Yamaguchi, K., "From Beer to Crack: Developmental Patterns of Drug Involvement," *American Journal of Public Health* 83: 851-55 (1993); Inciardi, J.A. and Pottieger, A.E., "Kids, Crack and Crime," *Journal of Drug Issues* 21: 257070 (1991).

17 Golub, A. and Johnson, B.D., "The Shifting Importance of Alcohol and Marijuana as Gateway Substances Among Serious Drug Abusers," *Journal of Studies on Alcohol* 55: 607-14 (1994); Kandel, D.P. and Davies, M., "High School Students Who Use Crack and Other Drugs," *Archives of General Psychiatry* 53: 71-80 (1996); Kandel, D. and Faust, R., "Sequence and Stages in Patterns of Adolescent Drug Use," *Archives of General Psychiatry* 32: 923-32 (1975).

18 Kandel, D.P. et al., "Cocaine Use in Young Adulthood: Patterns of Use and Psychosocial Correlates," pp. 76-110 in Kozel, N.J. and Adams, E.H. (eds), *Cocaine Use in America: Epidemiologic and Clinical Perspectives,* Rockville, MD: National Institute on Drug Abuse (1985).

19 Gove, W.R. et al., "Drug Use and Mental Health Among a Representative National Sample of Young Adults," *Social Forces* 58: 572-90 (1979); Kaplan, H.B. et al., "Pathways to Adolescent Drug Use: Self-Derogation, Peer Influence, Weakening of Social Controls, and Early Substance Use," *Journal of Health and Social Behavior* 25: 270-89 (1982); Donovan, J.E. et al., "Syndrome of Problem Behavior in Adolescence: A Replication," *Journal of Consulting and Clini-*

cal Psychology 56: 762-65 (1988); Scheier, L.M. and Newcombe, M.D., "Psychosocial Predictors of Drug Use Initiation and Escalation: An Expansion of the Multiple Risk Factors Hypothesis Using Longitudinal Data," *Contemporary Drug Problems* 18: 31-73 (1991); Shedler, J. and Block, J., "Adolescent Drug Use and Psychological Health," *American Psychologist* 45: 612-30 (1990); Robins, L.N., "Sturdy Childhood Predictors of Adult Antisocial Behaviour: Replications from Longitudinal Studies," *Psychological Medicine* 8: 611-22 (1978); Farrell, A.D. et al., "Relationship Between Drug Use and Other Problem Behaviors in Urban Adolescents," *Journal of Consulting and Clinical Psychology* 60: 705-12 (1992); Yamaguchi and Kandel (1984), see note 16; Kandel and Davies (1996), see note 17.

20   Johnston, L.D. et al., "Drugs and Delinquency: A Search for Causal Connections," pp. 137-56 in Kandel, D.P. (ed), *Longitudinal Research on Drug Use: Empirical Findings and Methodological Issues*, New York: John Wiley & Sons (1978); Clayton, R.R., "The Delinquency and Drug Use Relationship Among Adolescents: A Critical Review," pp. 82-103 in Lettieri, D.J. and Ludford, J.P., *Drug Abuse and the American Adolescent*, Rockville, MD: National Institute on Drug Abuse (1981); Elliot, D.S. and Ageton, A.R., *Structural Delinquency and Drug Use*, Boulder, CO: Behavioral Research Institute (1976); Donovan, J. and Jessor, R., "Structure of Problem Behavior in Adolescence and Young Adulthood," *Journal of Consulting and Clinical Psychology* 53: 890-904 (1985); Block, J. et al., "Longitudinally Foretelling Drug Usage in Adolescence: Early Childhood Personality and Environmental Precursors," *Child Development* 59: 336-55 (1988); Robins, L.N. and McEvoy, L., "Conduct Problems as Predictors of Substance Abuse," pp. 182-204 in Robins, L.N. and Rutter, M. (eds), *Straight and Devious Pathways From Childhood to Adulthood*, Cambridge: Cambridge University Press (1990).

21   Center on Addiction and Substance Abuse (1994), see note 2.

22   Tanda, G. et al., "Cannabinoid and Heroin Activation of Mesolimbic Dopamine Transmission by a Common μ, Opioid Receptor Mechanism," *Science* 276: 2048-50 (1997).

23   Blakeslee, S., "Brain Studies Tie Marijuana to Other Drugs," *New York Times* (27 June 1997), p. A16.

24   Casteneda, E. et al., "THC Does Not Affect Striatal Dopamine Release: Microdialysis in Freely Moving Rats," *Pharmacology Biochemstry and Behavior* 40: 587-91 (1991); Herkenham, M., "Localization of Cannabinoid Receptors in Brain and Periphery," pp. 145-66 in Pertwee, R. (ed), *Cannabinoid Receptors*, New York: Academic Press (1995)..

5   *Marijuana Law and Punishment*

1   Robert E. Peterson, *The Success of Tough Drug Enforcement*, Vestal, NY: Performance Accountability Evaluations (1996), p. iv.

2 Robert E. Pierre, "Marijuana's Violent Side," *Washington Post* (9 September 1996), p. 1.

3 Patrick McGowan, Minnesota sheriff, quoted in Suro, R., "Political Rhetoric Overlooks Change in Drug-Use Patterns," *Washington Post* (24 September 1996), p. 1.

4 William Bennett, Director of National Drug Control Policy, quoted in "Too Easy on Drugs, Bennett Tells," *The Sacramento Bee* (19 June 1990), p. 1.

5 Senator Mitch McConnell, Senate Judiciary Committee Hearings, *Teenage Drug Use* (4 September 1996).

6 National Commission on Marihuana and Drug Abuse, *Marihuana: A Signal of Misunderstanding*, Washington, DC: U.S. Government Printing Office (1972), p. 152.

7 National Research Council, *An Analysis of Marijuana Policy*, Washington, DC: National Academy Press (1982).

8 Office of National Drug Control Policy, *National Drug Control Strategy*, Washington, DC: The White House (1996); Office of National Drug Control Policy, *National Drug Control Strategy: Budget Summary*, Washington, DC: The White House (1995).

9 U.S. Sentencing Commission, *Annual Report*, Washington, DC: United States Sentencing Commission (1994), p. 119.

10 Uniform Crime Report data, provided by State of Georgia, Bureau of Investigation (August 1996).

11 Wisconsin Office of Justice Assistance, *Drug Problems in Wisconsin*, Madison: Statistical Analysis Center (1997).

12 Uniform Crime Report data, provided by New York State Division of Criminal Justice Services (22 August 1996); Krauss, C., "Crackdown Is Intensified in Quality-of-Life Crimes," *New York Times* (6 March 1996), p. B3.

13 Substance Abuse and Mental Health Services Administration, *National Household Survey on Drug Abuse: Population Estimates 1994*, Rockville, MD: U.S. Department of Health and Human Services (1995).

14 U.S. Sentencing Commission, *Annual Report*, Washington, DC: U.S. Sentencing Commission (1995), p. 103.

15 Illinois Department of Corrections, personal communication (1 October 1996).

16 California Department of Justice, *Crime and Delinquency in California, 1994*, Sacramento (1995).

17 New York State Division of Criminal Justice Services, *Characteristics of 1995 Adult Arrestees for Marijuana*, New York (July 1996).

18 National Criminal Justice Association, *A Guide to State Controlled Substances Acts*, Washington, DC (1991); Bureau of Justice Statistics, *Drugs, Crime and the Justice*

System, Washington, DC: U.S. Department of Justice (1992), pp. 178-81; Thomas, C., *Citizens' Guide to Marijuana Laws*, Washington, DC: National Organization for the Reform of Marijuana Laws (1994).

19 Federal Bureau of Prisons, personal communication to the Marijuana Policy Project, Washington, DC (8 November 1995); U.S. Sentencing Commission (1995), see note 14, p. 110.

20 Thomas, C., *Marijuana Arrests and Incarceration in the United States: Preliminary Report*, Washington, DC: Marijuana Policy Project (1995).

21 Michigan Department of Corrections, *1995 Statistical Report*, Lansing (1996).

22 New York State Division of Criminal Justice Services, *Sentences for Marijuana Convictions in 1995*, New York (July 1996).

23 Criminal Justice Policy Council, *Arrests and Dispositions, Texas Narcotics Control Program, Calendar Year 1989*, Austin (1991).

24 State of Georgia, Department of Corrections, personal communication (23 August 1996).

25 Department of Corrections, *Characteristics of Population in California State Prisons, By Institution*, Sacramento (1996).

26 Butterfield, F., "Tough Law on Sentences is Criticized," *New York Times* (8 March 1996), p. A8.

27 Thomas (1994), see note 18.

28 *Anti-Drug Abuse Act of 1988*, 42 U.S.C., section 5301; Bureau of Justice Statistics (1992), see note 18, p. 184.

29 Marijuana Policy Project, *Smoke a Joint, Lose Your License: July 1995 Status Report*, Washington, DC (1995).

30 Erickson, P.G., *Cannabis Criminals*, Toronto: Addiction Research Foundation (1980); Schain, R., "Doing Major Time for a Minor Crime," *New York Times* (10 March 1996), p. 23.

31 Treaster, J., "Miami Beach's New Drug Weapon Will Fire Off Letters to the Employer," *New York Times* (23 February 1991), p. 9.

32 Gerstein, D.R. and Harwood, H.J., *Treating Drug Problems, Volume I*, Washington, DC: National Academy Press (1990); Erwin, B.S., "Old and New Tools for the Modern Probation Officer," *Crime and Delinquency* 36: 61-74 (1990); Navarro, M., "Experimental Courts are Using New Strategies to Blunt the Lure of Drugs," *New York Times* (17 October 1996), p. A25.

33 *Anti-Drug Abuse Act of 1988*, 42 U.S.C., section 1437; Webster, B. and Connors, E.F., *The Police, Drugs, and Public Housing*, Washington, DC: U.S. Department of Justice (1992).

34 Bureau of Justice Statistics (1992), see note 18, p. 187.

35 Hyde, H., *Forfeiting Our Property Rights*, Washington, DC: Cato Institute (1995); Duke, S.B. and Gross, A.C., *America's Longest War*, New York: G.P. Putnam's Sons (1993); Reed, T.G., "American Forfeiture Law: Property Owners Meet

the Prosecutor," *Policy Analysis* 179: 1-32 (1992).

36 O'Hair, J.D., "Campaign Push-Off," pp. 38-42 in *Beyond Convictions: Prosecutors As Community Leaders in the War on Drugs*, Alexandria, VA: American Prosecutors Research Institute (1993).

37 Reed (1992), see note 35; Gross and Duke (1993), see note 35.

38 Hyde (1995), see note 35, pp. 12-13.

39 Office of National Drug Control Policy (1996), see note 8, p. 50.

40 Hyde (1995), see note 35, p. 327.

41 American Management Association, *1994 Survey on Workplace Drug Testing and Drug Abuse Policies*, New York (1994).

42 Morgan, J.P., "The 'Scientific' Justification for Urine Drug Testing," *Kansas Law Review* 36: 683-97 (1988); Normand, J. et al., *Under the Influence: Drugs and the American Workforce*, Washington, DC: National Academy Press (1994).

43 Office of National Drug Control Policy, *National Drug Control Strategy*, Washington, DC: The White House (1989); U.S. Department of Education, *What Works: Schools Without Drugs*, Washington, DC (1992); Shinonara, R., "Bird Seed Snack Brings 10-Day School Suspension," *Anchorage Daily News* (25 October 1996), p. 1.

44 Booth, W., "Florida County Sets Drug Tests for Welfare Clients," *Washington Post* (17 September 1996), p. A3.

45 Dao, J., "Stricter Rules Imposed at New York State Homeless Shelters," *New York Times* (9 November 1995), p. B1.

46 Johnston, L.D. et al., *National Survey Results on Drug Use from the Monitoring the Future Study, 1975-1994, Volume I: Secondary School Students*, Rockville, MD: U.S. Department of Health and Human Services (1995), p. 247.

47 Johnston, L.D. et al., (1995), see note 46.

48 Substance Abuse and Mental Health Services Administration, *National Household Survey on Drug Abuse: Main Findings 1994*, Rockville, MD: U.S. Department of Health and Human Services (1996).

6   Dutch Marijuana Policy

1   A.M. Rosenthal, "While the Children Sleep," *New York Times* (22 September 1995), p. A31.

2   Joseph A. Califano, "Legalization: The Reality," *The Prevention Pipeline* 8,5 (1995), p. 12.

3   Lee Brown, Director of Office of National Drug Control Policy, quoted in "Top Cop in the War on Drugs," *San Francisco Examiner and Chronicle* (12 March 1995), p. 4.

4   Robert Peterson, *The Success of Tough Drug Enforcement*, Vestal, NY: Performance

Accountability Evaluations (1996), p. 12.

5   Stevenson, R., *Winning the War on Drugs: To Legalize or Not?*, London: Institute of Economic Affairs (1994); Zimmer, L., "The Ascendancy and Decline of Worldwide Cannabis Prohibition," pp. 15-30 in Bollinger, L. (ed), *Cannabis Science: From Prohibition to Human Right*, New York: Peter Lang (1997).

6   Silvis, J., "Enforcing Drug Laws in the Netherlands," pp. 41-58 in Leuw, E. and Marshall, I.H. (eds), *Between Prohibition and Legalization: The Dutch Experiment in Drug Policy*, Amsterdam: Kugler Publications (1994).

7   Jansen, A.C.M., "The Development of a 'Legal' Consumers' Market for Cannabis—The 'Coffee Shop' Phenomenon," pp. 169-82 in Leuw, E. and Marshall, I.H. (eds), *Between Prohibition and Legalization: The Dutch Experiment in Drug Policy*, New York: Kugler Publications (1994); Netherlands Institute on Alcohol and Drugs, "Cannabis Policy Fact Sheet," *Netherlands Alcohol and Drug Report* 1 (1995); Silvis (1994), see note 6.

8   Leuw, E., "Initial Construction and Development of the Official Dutch Drug Policy," pp. 23-40 in Leuw, E. and Marshall, I.H. (eds), *Between Prohibition and Legalization: The Dutch Experiment in Drug Policy*, Amsterdam: Kugler Publications (1994); Kaplan, C.D. et al., "Is Dutch Drug Policy an Example to the World?" pp. 311-35 in Leuw, E. and Marshall, I.H. (eds), *Between Prohibition and Legalization: The Dutch Experiment in Drug Policy*, Amsterdam: Kugler Publications (1994); Engelsman, E.L., "Dutch Policy on the Management of Drug-Related Problems," *British Journal of Addiction* 84: 211-18 (1989).

9   Marshall, I.H. and Marshall, C.E., "Drug Prevention in the Netherlands—A Low Key Approach," pp. 205-32 in Leuw, E. and Marshall, I.H. (eds), *Between Prohibition and Legalization: The Dutch Experiment in Drug Policy*, Amsterdam: Kugler Publications (1994).

10 Netherlands Institute for Alcohol and Drugs (1995), see note 7.

11 Fromberg, E., "The Case of the Netherlands: Contradictions and Values," pp. 113-24 in *Questioning Prohibition: 1994 International Report on Drugs*, Brussels: International Antiprohibitionist League (1994); Leuw (1994), see note 8.

12 Sandwijk, J.P. et al., *Licit and Illicit Drug Use in Amsterdam II*, Amsterdam: University of Amsterdam (1995).

13 Substance Abuse and Mental Health Services Administration, *Preliminary Estimates from the 1995 National Household Survey on Drug Abuse*, Advance Report Number 18, Washington, DC: U.S. Department of Health and Human Services (1996), p. 92.

14 Adlaf, E. et al., *The Ontario Student Drug Use Survey: 1975-1995*, Toronto: Addiction Research Foundation (1995); Donnelly, N. and Hall, W., *Patterns of Cannabis Use in Australia*, Canberra: Australian Government Publishing Service (1994); Harrison, L.D., "More Cannabis in Europe? Perspectives from the USA," paper presented at the Seventh Annual Conference on Drug Use and Drug Policy, European Research Group on Drug Issues and Drug Policy, Amsterdam (September 1996); Quensel, S. et al., "Zur Cannabis-Situation in der

Bundesrepublik Deutschland," pp. 17-77 in Cohen, P.D.A. and Sas, A. (eds), *Cannabisbeleid in Duitsland, Frankrijk en de Verenigde Staten,* The Netherlands: University of Amsterdam (1996).

15 De Zwart, W.M. et al., *Key Data: Smoking, Drinking, Drug Use and Gambling Among Pupils Aged 10 Years and Older,* Utrecht: Netherlands Institute on Alcohol and Drugs (1994).

16 Sandwijk et al. (1995), see note 12.

17 Van Solinge, T.B., "Cannabis in Frankrijk," pp. 79-128 in Cohen, P.D.A. and Sas, A. (eds), *Cannabisbeleid in Duitsland, Frankrijk en de Verenigde Staten,* The Netherlands: University of Amsterdam (1996); Quensel et al. (1996), see note 14.

18 Sandwijke et al. (1995), see note 12.

19 Substance Abuse and Mental Health Services Administration, *National Household Survey on Drug Abuse: Population Estimates 1994,* Rockville, MD: U.S. Department of Health and Human Services (1995), p. 92.

20 Cohen, P. and Sas, A., "Cannabis Use, a Stepping Stone to Other Drug Use? The Case of Amsterdam," pp.49-82 in Bollinger, L. (ed), *Cannabis Science: From Prohibition to Human Right,* New York: Peter Lang (1997).

21 Sifaneck, S.J. and Kaplan, C.D., "Keeping Off, Stepping On and Stepping Off: The Steppingstone Theory Reevaluated in the Context of the Dutch Cannabis Experience," *Contemporary Drug Problems* 22: 483-512 (1995); van Vliet, H.J., "Separation of Drug Markets and the Normalization of Drug Problems in the Netherlands: An Example for Other Nations?," *Journal of Drug Issues* 20: 463-71 (1990).

22 Ministry of Health, Welfare and Sport, *Drug Policy in the Netherlands: Continuity and Change,* The Netherlands (1995); "Netherlands' Neighbors Worry Which Way the Drug Wind Blows," *International Herald Tribune* (20 October 1994).

23 Gunning, K.F., "Crime Rate and Drug Use in Holland," Rotterdam: Dutch National Committee on Drug Prevention (1993); Jorritsma, R.E., "The Drug Toleration Policy for Cannabis Products in the Netherlands," *Prevention Pipeline* 8, 5: p. 13 (1995).

24 Ministry of Health, Welfare and Sport (1995), see note 22.

25 Bertrand, M., "New Players and New Strategies," pp. 5-11 in *Questioning Prohibition: 1994 International Report on Drugs,* Brussels: International Antiprohibitionist League (1994); Europe Against Drugs, "Four Steps in the Development of a Narcotic Epidemic," *EURAD News* 2 (1990); Branegan, J., "Dutch Dilemma: Drugs'R'Us?" *Time Magazine,* European Edition, April 29: 28-30 (1996); Solomon, G.B.H., *Congressional Record,* p. E813 (6 April 1995).

26 Blom, T. and van Mastrigt, H., "The Future of the Dutch Model in the Context of the War on Drugs," pp. 255-82 in Leuw, E. and Marshall, I.H. (eds), *Between Prohibition and Legalization: The Dutch Experiment in Drug Policy,* Amsterdam: Kugler Publications (1994).

27 *Reuter News Service*, The Hague (2 March 1996).

28 Ministry of Justice and Ministry of Welfare, Health and Cultural Affairs, *The Drug Policy in the Netherlands*, The Netherlands (1994); Zaal, L., "Police Policy in Amsterdam," pp. 90-94 in O'Hare, P.A. et al. (eds), *The Reduction of Drug-Related Harm*, New York: Routledge (1992); Ministry of Health, Welfare and Sport (1995), see note 22.

29 Leuw (1994), see note 8.

30 Ministry of Health, Welfare and Sport (1995), see note 22.

7 Marijuana and the Brain

1 Connie Moulton and Otto Moulton, "Synopsis of Marijuana," *Drug Awareness Information Newsletter*, Danvers, CT: Committees of Correspondence (undated).

2 Peggy Mann, *Marijuana Alert*, New York: McGraw-Hill Book Company (1985), p. 185.

3 Office for Substance Abuse Prevention, *Drug-Free Communities: Turning Awareness into Action*, Rockville, MD: U.S. Department of Health and Human Services (1989), p. 26.

4 Robert Heath, *Marijuana and the Brain*, Rockville, MD: American Council for Drug Education (1981), p. 10.

5 Kolansky, H. and Moore, W.T., "Effects of Marijuana on Adolescents and Young Adults," *Journal of the American Medical Association* 216: 486-92 (1971); Tennant, F.S. and Groesbeck, C.J., " Psychiatric Effects of Hashish," *Archives of General Psychiatry* 27: 133-36 (1972); Powelson, D.H., "Marijuana: More Dangerous Than You Know," *Reader's Digest* 105: 95-99 (December 1974).

6 Nattrass, F.J., "Cerebral Atrophy in Young Cannabis Smokers," *Lancet* 2: 374 (1971); Kolansky, H. and Moore, W.T., "Toxic Effects of Chronic Marijuana Use," *Journal of the American Medical Association* 222: 35-41 (1972); Powelson, D.H., Subcommittee Hearings to Investigate the Administration of the Internal Security Act and Other Internal Security Laws, Senate Judiciary Committee, *Marihuana-Hashish Epidemic and Its Impact on United States Security*, Washington, DC: U.S. Government Printing Office (1974); Russell, W.R., "Cerebral Atrophy in Young Marijuana Smokers," *Lancet* 2: 1314 (1971); Schwarz, C.J., "Cerebral Atrophy in Young Cannabis Smokers," *Lancet* 1: 374 (1972).

7 Campbell, A.M.G. et al., "Cerebral Atrophy in Young Cannabis Smokers," *Lancet* 2: 1219-26 (1971).

8 National Institute of Mental Health, *Marijuana and Health*, Second Annual Report to Congress from the Secretary of Health, Education and Welfare (1972); Bull, J., "Cerebral Atrophy in Young Cannabis Smokers," *Lancet* 2: 1420 (1971); Susser, M., "Cerebral Atrophy in Young Cannabis Smokers," *Lancet* 1: 41-42 (1972); Brewer, C., "Cerebral Atrophy in Young Cannabis Smokers," *Lancet* 1:

143 (1972); Grinspoon, L., "Marijuana and Brain Damage: A Criticism of the Study by A.M.G. Campbell et al.," *Contemporary Drug Problems* 1: 811-14 (1972).

9   Kuehnle, J. et al., "Computed Tomographic Examination of Heavy Marihuana Smokers," *Journal of the American Medical Association* 237: 1231-21 (1977); Hannerz, J. and Hindmarsh, T., "Neurological and Neuroradiological Examination of Chronic Cannabis Smokers," *Annals of Neurology* 13: 207-10 (1983).

10 Co, B.T. et al., "Absence of Cerebral Atrophy in Chronic Cannabis Users: Evaluation by Computerized Transaxial Tomography," *Journal of the American Medical Association* 237: 1229-30 (1977).

11 Struve, F.A. and Straumanis, J.J., "Electroencephalographic and Evoked Potential Methods in Human Marijuana Research: Historical Review and Future Trends," *Drug Development Research* 20: 369-88 (1990).

12 Struve, F. et al., "Topographic Quantitative EEG Findings in Subjects with 15+ Years of Cumulative Daily THC Exposure," p. 451 in Harris, L. (ed), *Problems of Drug Dependence 1991*, Rockville, MD: National Institute on Drug Abuse (1992); Struve, F.A. et al., "Persistent Topographic Quantitative EEG Sequelae of Chronic Marijuana Use: A Replication Study and Initial Discriminant Function Analysis," *Clinical Electroencephalography* 25: 63-73 (1994).

13 Solowij. N. et al., "Effects of Long-Term Cannabis Use on Selective Attention: An Event-Related Potential Study," *Pharmacology Biochemistry and Behavior* 40: 683-88 (1991); Solowij, N. et al., "Differential Impairments of Selective Attention Due to Frequency and Duration of Cannabis Use," *Biological Psychiatry* 37: 731-39 (1995); Straumanis, J. et al., "Cognitive Evoked Potentials in Chronic Marijuana Users, pp. 21-24 in Racagni, G. et al. (eds), *Biological Psychiatry*, Vol. 2, New York: Elsevier Science Publishers (1991).

14 Patrick, G. et al., "Auditory and Visual P300 Event Related Potentials Are Not Altered in Medically and Psychiatrically Normal Chronic Marijuana Users," *Life Sciences* 56: 2135-40 (1995).

15 Scallet, A.C., "Neurotoxicology of Cannabis and THC: A Review of Chronic Exposure Studies in Animals," *Pharmacology Biochemistry and Behavior* 40: 671-82 (1991).

16 Heath, R.G., "Marijuana: Effects on Deep and Surface Electroencephalograms of Rhesus Monkeys," *Neuropharmacology* 12: 1-14 (1973).

17 Heath, R.G., Subcommittee Hearings to Investigate the Administration of the Internal Security Act and Other Internal Security Laws, Senate Judiciary Committee, *Marihuana-Hashish Epidemic and Its Impact on United States Security*, Washington, DC: U.S. Government Printing Office (1974).

18 Heath, R.G., "Marihuana and Delta-9-THC: Acute and Chronic Effects on Brain Function of Monkeys," pp. 345-56 in Braude, M.C. and Szara, S. (eds), *Pharmacology of Marihuana*, New York: Raven Press (1976).

19 Harper, J.W. et al., "Effects of Cannabis Sativa on Ultrastructure of the Synapse in Monkey Brain," *Journal of Neuroscience Research* 3: 87-93 (1977); Meyers,

W.A. and Heath, R.G., "Cannabis Sativa: Ultrastructural Changes in Organelles of Neurons in Brain Septal Region of Monkeys," *Journal of Neuroscience Research* 4: 9-17 (1979).

20 Heath, R.G. et al., "Cannabis Sativa: Effects on Brain Function and Ultrastructure in Rhesus Monkeys," *Biological Psychiatry* 15: 657-90 (1980).

21 Subcommittee Hearings to Investigate the Administration of the Internal Security Act and Other Internal Security Laws, Senate Judiciary Committee, *Marihuana-Hashish Epidemic and Its Impact on United States Security*, Washington, DC: U.S. Government Printing Office (1974); Maugh, T.H., "Marihuana (II): Does it Damage the Brain," *Science* 185: 775-76 (1974); Kolansky, H. and Moore, W.T., "Marihuana: Can it Hurt You?," *Journal of the American Medical Association* 232: 923-24 (1975).

22 Ali, S.F. et al., "Chronic Marijuana Smoke Exposure in the Rhesus Monkey IV: Neurochemical Effects and Comparison to Acute and Chronic Exposure to Delta-9-Tetrahydrocannabinol (THC) in Rats," *Pharmacology Biochemistry and Behavior* 40: 677-82 (1991).

23 Westlake, T.M. et al., "Chronic Exposure to Delta-9-Tetrahydrocannabinol Fails to Irreversibly Alter Brain Cannabinoid Receptors," *Brain Research* 544: 145-49 (1991).

24 Slikker, W. et al., "Behavioral, Neurochemical, and Neurohistological Effects of Chronic Marijuana Smoke Exposure in the Nonhuman Primate," pp. 219-74 in Murphy, L. and Bartke, A. (eds), *Marijuana/Cannabinoids: Neurobiology and Neurophysiology*, Boca Raton: CRC Press (1992).

25 Mathias, R., "Studies Show Cognitive Impairments Linger in Heavy Marijuana Users," *NIDA Notes* 11, 3 (1996), p. 9,

26 U.S. Department of Justice, Drug Enforcement Administration, *Drug Legalization: Myths and Misconceptions*, Washington, DC (1994); National Institute on Drug Abuse, *Marijuana: What Parents Need to Know*, Rockville, MD: U.S. Department of Health and Human Services (1995); Mann, P., *The Sad Story of Mary Wanna*, New York: Woodmere Press (1988); U.S. Department of Health and Human Services, Office for Substance Abuse Prevention, *Drug-Free Communities: Turning Awareness Into Action*, Rockville, MD (1989); Spence, W.R., *Marijuana and Its Effects and Hazards*, Waco, TX: Health Edco (undated); Fitzpatrick, P., *Chemical Health Program Newsletter*, St. Paul, MN: St. Paul Public Schools (April 1992); Moulton and Moulton (undated), see note 1.

8   Motivation and Performance

1   Donna Shalala, Secretary of Health and Human Services, "Say 'No' to Legalization of Marijuana," *Wall Street Journal* (18 August 1995), p. A10.

2   National Institute on Drug Abuse, *The Facts About Marijuana*, Rockville, MD:

U.S. Department of Health and Human Services (undated).

3   Ernie D. Preate, *Blowing Away the Marijuana Smoke Screen*, Scranton: Pennsylvania Office of Attorney General (undated).

4   Sidney Cohen, *Marijuana: National Impact on Education*, Rockville, MD: American Council for Drug Education (1982), p. 24.

5   Himmelstein, J.L., *The Strange Career of Marihuana: Politics and Ideology of Drug Control in America*, Westport, CT: Greenwood Press (1983).

6   Indian Hemp Drugs Commission, *Report of the Indian Hemp Drugs Commission*, Simla, India: Government Central Printing Office(1894); Benabud, A., "Psychopathological Aspects of the Cannabis Situation in Morocco, *Bulletin on Narcotics* 9: 1-16 (1957); Chopra, I.C. and Chopra, R.N., "The Use of Cannabis Drugs in India," *Bulletin on Narcotics* 9: 17-29 (1957); Nahas, G.G., "Hashish and Drug Abuse in Egypt During the 19th and 20th Centuries," *Bulletin of New York Academy of Medicine* 61: 428-44 (1985).

7   McGlothlin, H.W. and West, L.J., "The Marihuana Problem: An Overview," *American Journal of Psychiatry* 125: 1126-34 (1968); Smith, D.E., "The Acute and Chronic Toxicity of Marijuana," *Journal of Psychedelic Drugs* 2: 37-48 (1968); Kolansky, H. and Moore, W.T., "Effects of Marihuana on Adolescents and Young Adults," *Journal of the American Medical Association* 216: 486-92 (1971); Kolansky, H. and Moore, W.T., "Toxic Effects of Chronic Marihuana Use," *Journal of the American Medical Association* 222: 35-41 (1972).

8   Walters, P.A., "Drug Use and Life-Style Among 500 College Undergraduates," *Archives of General Psychiatry* 26: 92-96 (1972); Pope, H.G. et al., "Drug Use and Life-Style Among College Undergraduates: Nine Years Later," *Archives of General Psychiatry* 38: 588-91 (1981); Pope, H.G. et al., "Drug Use and Life Style Among College Undergraduates in 1989: A Comparison With 1969 and 1978," *American Journal of Psychiatry* 147: 998-1001 (1990).

9   Hogan, R. et al., "Personality Correlates of Undergraduate Marijuana Use," *Journal of Consulting and Clinical Psychology* 35: 58-63 (1970); Brill, N.Q. et al., "Personality Factors in Marihuana Use: A Preliminary Report," *Archives of General Psychiatry* 24: 163-65 (1971); Miranne, A.C., "Marijuana Use and Achievement Orientations of College Students," *Journal of Health and Social Behavior* 20: 194-99 (1979); Hochman, J.S. and Brill, N.Q., "Chronic Marihuana Use and Psychosocial Adaptation," *American Journal of Psychiatry* 130: 132-40 (1973).

10   Mellinger, G.D. et al., "Drug Use, Academic Performance, and Career Indecision: Longitudinal Data in Search of a Model," pp. 157-77 in Kandel, D.B. (ed), *Longitudinal Research on Drug Use: Empirical Findings and Methodological Issues*, Washington, DC: American Psychological Association (1978); Hochman and Brill (1973), see note 9; Walters (1972), see note 8.

11   Brill, N.O. and Christie, R.L., "Marihuana Use and Psychosocial Adaptation," *Archives of General Psychiatry* 31: 713-19 (1974); Johnson, B.D., *Marihuana Users and Drug Subcultures*, New York: John Wiley & Sons (1973); Hochman and Brill

(1973), see note 9.

12   Kupfer, D.J. et al, "A Comment on the Amotivational Syndrome in Marihuana Smokers," *American Journal of Psychiatry* 130: 1319-22 (1973); Anker, J.L. et al., "Drug Usage and Related Patterns of Behavior in University Students: I. General Survey and Marihuana Use," *Journal of American College Health Association* 19: 178-86 (1971); Brill and Christie (1974), see note 11; Hochman and Brill (1973), see note 9; Walters et al. (1972), see note 8; Miranne (1979), see note 9; Pope et al. (1981), see note 8; Pope et al. (1990), see note 8.

13   Goode, E., "Drug Use and Grades in College," *Nature* 234: 225-27 (1971); Gergen, M.K. et al., "Correlates of Marijuana Use Among College Students," *Journal of Applied Social Psychology* 2: 1-16 (1972); Blum, R., *Students and Drugs,* San Francisco: Jossey-Bass (1969); Mellinger et al. (1978), see note 10.

14   Jessor, R. et al., "Psychosocial Correlates of Marijuana Use and Problem Drinking in a National Sample of Adolescents," *American Journal of Public Health* 70: 604-13 (1980); Brook, J.S. et al., "Stability of Personality During Adolescence and its Relationship to Stage of Drug Use," *Genetic, Social, and General Psychology* 111: 317-30 (1985); Block, J. et al., "Longitudinally Foretelling Drug Usage in Adolescence: Early Childhood Personality and Environmental Precursors," *Child Development* 59: 336-55 (1988); Kandel, D.B. and Davies, M., "High School Students Who Use Crack and Other Drugs," *General Archives of Psychiatry* 53: 71-80 (1996); Kandel, D.B. and Logan, J.A., "Patterns of Drug Use from Adolescence to Young Adulthood: I. Periods of Risk for Initiation, Continued Use and Discontinuation," *American Journal of Public Health* 74: 660-66 (1984); Hawkins, J.D. et al., "Risk and Protective Factors for Alcohol and Other Drug Problems in Adolescence and Early Adulthood: Implications for Substance Abuse Prevention," *Psychological Bulletin* 112: 64-105 (1992).

15   Shedler, J. and Block, J., "Adolescent Drug Use and Psychosocial Health," *American Psychologist* 45: 612-30 (1990); Block et al. (1988), see note 14.

16   Farrell, A.D. et al., "Relationship Between Drug Use and Other Problem Behaviors in Urban Adolescents," *Journal of Consulting and Clinical Psychology* 60: 705-12 (1992); Kleinman, P.H. et al., "Daily Marijuana Use and Problem Behaviors Among Adolescents," *International Journal of the Addictions* 23: 87-107 (1988); Dembo, R. et al., "A Longitudinal Study of the Relationships Among Alcohol Use, Marijuana/Hashish Use, Cocaine Use, and Emotional/Psychological Functioning Problems in a Cohort of High-Risk Youth," *International Journal of the Addictions* 25: 1341-82 (1990); Tubman, J.G. et al., "Qualitative Changes in Relationships Between Substance Use and Adjustment During Adolescence," *Journal of Substance Abuse* 3: 405-14 (1991); Donovan, J.E. and Jessor, R., "Structure of Problem Behavior in Adolescence and Young Adulthood," *Journal of Consulting and Clinical Psychology* 53: 890-904 (1985); Scheier, L.M. and Newcombe, M.D., "Psychosocial Predictors of Drug Use Initiation and Escalation: An Expansion of the Multiple Risk Factors Hypothesis Using Longitudinal Data," *Contemporary Drug Problems* 18: 31-73 (1991).

17   Johnson, V., "A Longitudinal Assessment of Predominant Patterns of Drug

Use Among Adolescents and Young Adults," pp. 173-82 in Chesher, G. et al. (eds), *Marijuana: An International Research Report*, Canberra: Australian Government Publishing Service (1988); Yamaguchi, K. and Kandel, D.P., "Patterns of Drug Use from Adolescence to Young Adulthood III: Predictors of Progression," *American Journal of Public Health* 74: 673-81 (1984); Donovan, J.E. and Jessor, R., "Problem Drinking and the Dimensions of Involvement with Drugs," *American Journal of Public Health* 73: 543-52 (1983); Kandel, D.P. and Yamaguchi, K., "From Beer to Crack: Developmental Patterns of Drug Involvement," *American Journal of Public Health* 83: 851-55 (1993); Kandel, D.P. and Davies, M., "High School Students Who Use Crack and Other Drugs," *Archives of General Psychiatry* 53: 71-80 (1996).

18 Hall, W., et al., *The Health and Psychological Consequences of Cannabis Use*, Canberra: Australian Government Publishing Service (1994).

19 Hendin, H. et al., *Adolescent Marijuana Users and Their Families*, Rockville, MD: National Institute on Drug Abuse (1981).

20 Musty, R.E. and Kaback, L., "Relationships Between Motivation and Depression in Chronic Marijuana Users," *Life Sciences* 56: 2151-58 (1995).

21 Comitas, L., "Cannabis and Work in Jamaica: A Refutation of the Amotivational Syndrome," *Annals of the New York Academy of Science* 282: 24-32 (1976); Bowman, M. and Pihl, R.O., "Cannabis: Psychological Effects of Chronic Heavy Use: A Controlled Study of Intellectual Functioning in Chronic Users of High Potency Cannabis," *Pharmacologia* 29: 150-79 (1973).

22 Carter, W.E. and Doughty, P.L., "Social and Cultural Aspects of Cannabis Use in Costa Rica," *Annals of the New York Academy of Science* 282: 2-16 (1976).

23 Boulougouris, C.J. et al., "Social Traits of Heavy Hashish Users and Matched Controls," *Annals of the New York Academy of Science* 282: 17-23 (1976).

24 Bowman and Pihl (1973), see note 21.

25 Kandel, D.B. and Davies, M., "Labor Force Experiences of a National Sample of Young Adult Men," *Youth and Society* 21: 411-45 (1990); Register, C.A. and Williams, D.R., "Labor Market Effects of Marijuana and Cocaine Use Among Young Men," *Industrial and Labor Relations Review* 45: 435-51 (1992); Kaestner, R., "The Effect of Drug Use on the Wages of Young Adults," *Journal of Labor Economics* 9: 381-412 (1991); Kaestner, R., "New Estimates of the Effect of Marijuana and Cocaine Use on Wages," *Industrial and Labor Relations Review* 47: 454-70 (1994); Gill, A.M. and Michaels, R.J., "Does Drug Use Lower Wages?," *Industrial and Labor Relations Review* 45: 419-34 (1992); Sickels, R. and Taubman, P., "Who Uses Illegal Drugs?," *American Economic Review* 81: 248-51 (1991); Kandel, D. et al., "The Impact of Drug Use on Earnings: A Life-Span Perspective," *Social Forces* 74: 243-70 (1995).

26 Kandel and Davies (1990), see note 25.

27 Kaestner, R., "The Effect of Illicit Drug Use on the Labor Supply of Young Adults," *The Journal of Human Resources* 29: 126-55 (1994).

28 Cohen, S., "The 94-Day Cannabis Study," *Annals of the New York Academy of Sciences* 282: 211-20 (1976); Lessin, P.J. and Thomas, S.A., "Assessment of the Chronic Effects of Marihuana on Motivation and Achievement: A Preliminary Report," pp. 681-97 in Braude, M.C. and Szara, S., *Pharmacology of Marihuana, Volume 2,* New York: Raven Press (1976).

29 Mendelson, J.H. et al., "The Effects of Marihuana Use on Human Operant Behavior: Individual Data," pp. 643-53 in Braude, M.C. and Szara, S. (eds), *The Pharmacology of Marihuana, Volume 2,* New York: Raven Press (1976); Mendelson, J.H. et al., "Operant Acquisition of Marihuana in Man," *Journal of Pharmacology and Experimental Therapeutics* 198: 42-53 (1976).

30 Miles, C.G. et al., *An Experimental Study of the Effects of Daily Cannabis Smoking on Behavioural Patterns,* Toronto, Canada: Addiction Research Foundation (1974); Campbell, I., "The Amotivational Syndrome and Cannabis Use with Emphasis on the Canadian Scene," *Annals of the New York Academy of Sciences* 282: 33-36 (1976).

31 Foltin, R.W. et al., "Motivational Effects of Smoked Marijuana: Behavioral Contingencies and Low-Probability Activities," *Journal of the Experimental Analysis of Behavior* 53: 5-19 (1990).

32 Kandel et al. (1995), see note 25.

33 Foltin et al. (1990), see note 31, p. 18.

9 Memory and Cognition

1 Joseph A. Califano, *The 1996 CASA National Survey of Parents and Teenagers,* New York: Center on Addiction and Substance Abuse (1996), p. 3.

2 National Institute on Drug Abuse, *The Facts About Marijuana,* Rockville, MD: U.S. Department of Health and Human Services (undated).

3 Gabriel G. Nahas, American Bar Association Hearings, *Drug Legalization—Yes or No,* Chicago (6 August 1995).

4 Robert G. Heath, *Marijuana and the Brain,* Rockville, MD: American Council for Drug Education (1981). p. 5.

5 National Institute on Drug Abuse, "Facts About Marijuana and Marijuana Abuse," *NIDA Notes* 11, 2 (1996) p. 5.

6 Ferraro, D.P., "Acute Effects of Marijuana on Human Memory and Cognition," pp. 98-119 in Petersen R.C. (ed), *Marijuana Research Findings: 1980,* Rockville, MD: National Institute on Drug Abuse (1980); Jaffe, J.H., "Drug Addiction and Drug Abuse," pp. 522-73 in Goodman, L. and Gilman, A.E. (eds), *The Pharmacological Basis of Therapeutics,* New York: Pergamon Press (1990).

7 Darley, C.F., "Influence of Marihuana on Storage and Retrieval Processes in Memory," *Memory and Cognition* 1: 196-200 (1973); Darley, C.F. et al., "Marijuana Effects on Long-Term Memory Assessment and Retrieval," *Psychopharm-*

acology 52: 239-41 (1977); Abel, E.L., "Retrieval of Information After Use of Marihuana," pp. 121-24 in Abel, E.L. (ed), *The Scientific Study of Marihuana*, Chicago: Nelson-Hall Publishers (1976a); Abel, E.L., "Marihuana and Memory: Acquisition or Retrieval?" pp. 125-32 in Abel, E.L. (ed), *The Scientific Study of Marihuana*, Chicago: Nelson-Hall Publishers (1976b); Wetzel, C.D. et al., "Remote Memory During Marijuana Intoxication," *Psychopharmacology* 76: 278-81 (1982); Dornbush, R.L., "Marijuana and Memory Effects of Smoking on Storage," *Annals of the New York Academy of Sciences* 234: 94-100 (1974).

8   Miller, L.L. et al., "Marijuana: Effects on Pulse Rate, Subjective Estimates of Intoxication and Multiple Measures of Memory," *Life Sciences* 25: 1325-30 (1979); Dornbush (1974), see note 7; Darley et al. (1977), see note 7.

9   Miller, L. et al., "Effects of Marihuana on Recall of Narrative Material and Stroop Colour-Word Performance," pp. 117-20 in Abel, E.L. (ed), *The Scientific Study of Marihuana*, Chicago: Nelson-Hall Publishers (1976); Miller, L. et al., "Effects of Marijuana on Recall of Narrative Material and Stroop Colour-Word Performance," *Nature* 19: 172-73 (1972); Miller, L. et al., "Marijuana: An Analysis of Storage and Retrieval Deficits in Memory With the Technique of Restricted Reminding," *Pharmacology Biochemistry and Behavior* 8: 327-32 (1978); Dornbush, R.L., "Marijuana, Memory, and Perception," *American Journal of Psychiatry* 128: 194-97 (1971); Dittrich, A. et al., "Effects of (-)Delta-9-trans-Tetrahydrocannabinol (THC) on Memory, Attention, and Subjective State: A Double-Blind Study," *Psychopharmacologia* 33: 369-76 (1973); Block, R.I. et al., "Acute Effects of Marijuana on Cognition: Relationships to Chronic Effects and Smoking Techniques," *Pharmacology Biochemistry and Behavior* 43: 907-17 (1992); Hooker, W.D., and Jones, R.T., "Increased Susceptibility to Memory Intrusions and the Stroop Interference Effect During Acute Marijuana Intoxication," *Psychopharmacology* 91: 20-24 (1987); Abel (1976a), see note 7; Miller et al. (1979), see note 8; Darley et al. (1973), see note 7.

10   Dornbush, R.L. and Kokkevi, A., "Acute Effects of Cannabis on Cognitive, Perceptual, and Motor Performance in Chronic Hashish Users," *Annals of the New York Academy of Sciences* 282: 213-22 (1976); Peters, B.A., "Sensory, Perceptual, Motor and Cognitive Functioning and Subjective Reports Following Oral Administration of Delta-9-Tetrahydrocannabinol," *Psychopharmacology* 47: 141-48 (1976); Tinklenberg, J.R. et al., "Time Production and Memory Functions," *Archives of General Psychiatry* 27: 812-15 (1972).

11   Clark, L.D. et al., "Experimental Studies of Marihuana," *American Journal of Psychiatry* 125: 379-84 (1968); Borg, G. and Gershon, S., "Dose Effects of Smoked Marihuana on Human Cognitive and Motor Functions," *Psychopharmacologia* 42: 211-18 (1975); Kiplinger, G.F. et al., "Dose-Response Analysis of the Effects of Tetrahydrocannabinol in Man," *Clinical Pharmacology and Therapeutics* 12: 650-57 (1971); Manno, J.F. et al., "Comparative Effects of Smoking Marihuana or Placebo on Human Motor and Mental Performance," *Clinical Pharmacology and Therapeutics* 11: 208-15 (1970); Klonoff, H. et al., "Neu-

ropsychological Effects of Marijuana," *Canadian Medical Association Journal* 108: 150-57 (1973); Rafaelsen, L. et al., "Effects of Cannabis and Alcohol on Psychological Tests," *Nature* 172: 117-18 (1973); Weckowicz, T.E. et al., "Effect of Marijuana on Divergent and Convergent Production Cognitive Tests," *Journal of Abnormal Psychology* 84: 386-98 (1975).

12 Bromberg, W., "Marihuana Intoxication: A Clinical Study of Cannabis Sativa Intoxication," *American Journal of Psychiatry* 91: 303-30 (1934); Tart, T.C., "Marijuana Intoxication: Common Experiences," *Nature* 226: 701-04 (1970); Adamec, C. et al., "An Analysis of the Subjective Marijuana Experience," *International Journal of the Addictions* 11: 295-307 (1976).

13 McGlothlin, W.H. et al., "Marijuana Use Among Adults," *Psychiatry* 33: 433-43 (1970); Fisher, G. and Steckler, A., "Psychological Effects, Personality and Behavioral Changes Attributed to Marihuana," *International Journal of the Addictions* 9: 101-26 (1974); Grinspoon, L., *Marihuana Reconsidered*, Cambridge: Harvard University Press (1971); Pihl, R.O. et al., "Dimensions of the Subjective Marijuana Experience," *International Journal of the Addictions* 14: 63-71 (1979); Hochman, J.S. and Brill, N.Q., "Chronic Marijuana Use and Psychosocial Adaptation," *American Journal of Psychiatry* 130: 132-40 (1973).

14 Carlin, A.S. et al., "Social Facilitation of Marijuana Intoxication: Impact of Social Set and Pharmacological Activity," *Journal of Abnormal Psychology* 80: 132-40 (1972); Zinberg, N.E., *Drug, Set, and Setting*, New Haven: Yale University Press (1984).

15 Soueif, M.I., "The Use of Cannabis in Egypt: A Behavioural Study," *Bulletin on Narcotics* 23, 4: 17-28 (1971); Soueif, M.I., "Chronic Cannabis Users: Further Analysis of Objective Test Results," *Bulletin on Narcotics* 27, 4: 1-26 (1975).

16 Fletcher, J.M. and Satz, P., "A Methodological Commentary on the Egyptian Study of Chronic Hashish Use," *Bulletin on Narcotics* 29, 2: 1-43 (1977); Carlin, A.S., "Neuropsychological Consequences of Drug Abuse," pp. 478-97 in Grant, I. and Adams, K.M. (eds), *Neuropsychological Assessment of Neuropsychiatric Disorders*, New York: Oxford University Press (1986).

17 Harrison, L., and Gfroerer, J., "The Intersection of Drug Use and Criminal Behavior," *Crime and Delinquency* 38: 422-43 (1992); Leukefeld, C.G. and Clayton, R., "Drug Abuse and Delinquency: A Study of Youths in Treatment," pp. 213-28 in Bescher, G. and Friedman, A. (eds), *Youth Drug Abuse: Problems, Issues and Treatment*, Lexington, MA: DC Heath (1979); Dembo, R. et al., "Examination of the Relationships Among Drug Use, Emotional/Psychological Problems, and Crime Among Youths Entering a Juvenile Detention Center," *International Journal of Addictions* 25: 301-40 (1990); Farrell, A.D. et al., "Relationship Between Drug Use and Other Problem Behaviors in Urban Adolescents," *Journal of Consulting and Clinical Psychology* 60: 705-12 (1992); Fagan, J. et al., "Delinquency and Substance Use Among Inner-City Students," *Journal of Drug Issues* 20: 351-402 (1990); Johnson, V., "A Longitudinal Assessment of Predominant Patterns of Drug Use Among Adolescents and Young Adults," pp. 173-82 in

Chesher, G. et al. (eds), *Marijuana: An International Research Report*, Canberra: Australian Government Publishing Service (1988); Yamaguchi, K. and Kandel, D.P., "Patterns of Drug Use from Adolescence to Young Adulthood III: Predictors of Progression," *American Journal of Public Health* 74: 673-81 (1984); Kandel, D.P. and Yamaguchi, K., "From Beer to Crack: Developmental Patterns of Drug Involvement," *American Journal of Public Health* 83: 851-55 (1993); Kandel, D.P. and Davies, M., "High School Students Who Use Crack and Other Drugs," *Archives of General Psychiatry* 53: 71-80 (1996).

18 Rubin, V. and Comitas, L., *Ganja in Jamaica: A Medical and Anthropological Study of Chronic Marijuana Use*, The Hague: Mouton (1975); Kokkevi, A. and Dornbush, R., "Psychological Test Characteristics of Long-Term Hashish Users," pp. 43-47 in Stefanis, C. et al. (eds), *Hashish: Studies of Long-Term Users*, New York: Raven Press (1977); Satz, P. et al., "Neuropsychologic, Intellectual, and Personality Correlates of Chronic Marijuana Use in Native Costa Ricans," *Annals of the New York Academy of Medicine* 282: 266-306 (1976).

19 Bowman, M. and Pihl, R.O., "Cannabis: Psychological Effects of Chronic Heavy Use: A Controlled Study of Intellectual Functioning in Chronic Users of High Potency Cannabis," *Pharmacologia* 29: 159-70 (1973).

20 Page, J.B. et al., "Psychosociocultural Perspectives on Chronic Cannabis Use: The Costa Rican Follow-up," *Journal of Psychoactive Drugs* 20: 57-65 (1988).

21 Fletcher, J.M. et al., "Cognitive Correlates of Long-Term Cannabis Use in Costa Rican Men," *Archives of General Psychiatry* 53: 1051-57 (1996).

22 Page et al. (1988), p. 61.

23 Wig, N.N. and Varma, V.K., "Patterns of Long-Term Heavy Cannabis Use in North India and Its Effects on Cognitive Functions: A Preliminary Report," *Drug and Alcohol Dependence* 2: 211-19 (1977); Mendhiratta, S.S. et al., "Some Psychological Correlates of Long-Term Heavy Cannabis Use," *British Journal of Psychiatry* 132: 482-86 (1978); Mendhiratta, S.S. et al., "Cannabis and Cognitive Functions: A Reevaluation Study," *British Journal of Addiction* 83: 749-53 (1988).

24 Ray, R. et al., "Chronic Cannabis Use and Cognitive Functions," *Indian Journal of Medical Research* 69: 996-1000 (1979); Venkoba Rao, A. et al., "Cannabis (Ganja) and Cognition," *Indian Journal of Psychiatry* 17: 233-37 (1975); Varma, V.K. et al., "Cannabis and Cognitive Functions: A Prospective Study," *Drug and Alcohol Dependence* 21: 147-52 (1988).

25 Entin, E.E. and Goldzung, P.J., "Residual Effects of Marihuana Usage on Learning and Memory," *Psychological Record* 23: 169-78 (1973); Gianutsos, R. and Litwak, A.R., "Chronic Marijuana Smokers Show Reduced Coding into Long-Term Storage," *Bulletin of the Psychonomic Society* 7: 277-79 (1976).

26 Rossi, A.M. et al., "Effects of Marihuana on Reaction Time and Short-Memory in Human Volunteers," *Pharmacology Biochemistry and Behavior* 6: 73-77 (1977); Carlin, A.S. and Trupin, E.W., "The Effect of Long-Term Chronic Marijuana Use on Neuropsychological Function," *International Journal of the Addictions* 12:

617-24 (1977); Weckowicz, T.E. et al., "Field Dependence, Cognitive Functions, Personality Traits, and Social Values in Heavy Cannabis Users and Non-user Controls," *Psychological Record* 41: 291-302 (1977).

27   Rossi et al. (1977), see note 26; Entin and Goldzung (1973), see note 25.

28   Schaeffer, J. et al., "Cognition and Long-Term Use of Ganja (Cannabis)," *Science* 213: 465-66 (1981).

29   Weckowicz, T.E. and Janssen, D.V., "Cognitive Functions, Personality Traits, and Social Values in Heavy Marijuana Smokers and Nonsmoker Controls," *Journal of Abnormal Psychology* 81: 264-69 (1973); Weckowicz et al. (1977), see note 26; Carlin and Trupin (1977), see note 26.

30   Block, R.I. and Ghoneim, M.M., "Effects of Chronic Marijuana Use on Human Cognition," *Psychopharmacology* 110: 219-28 (1993).

31   Block, R.I. et al., "Long-Term Marijuana Use and Subsequent Effects on Learning and Cognitive Functions Related to School Achievement: Preliminary Study," pp. 96-111 in Spencer, J.W. and Boren, J.J. (eds), *Residual Effects of Abused Drugs on Behavior*, Rockville, MD: National Institute on Drug Abuse (1990).

32   Pope, H.G. and Yurgelun-Todd, D., "The Residual Cognitive Effects of Heavy Marijuana Use," *Journal of the American Medical Association* 275: 521-27 (1996).

33   Schwartz, R.H. et al.,"Short-Term Memory Impairment in Cannabis-Dependent Adolescents," *American Journal of Diseases of Children* 143: 1214-18 (1989), p. 1215.

34   Schwartz et al. (1989), see note 33, p. 1214.

35   Nahas, G. and Latour, C., "The Human Toxicity of Marijuana," *The Medical Journal of Australia* 156: 495-97 (1992); Hall, W. et al., *The Health and Psychological Consequences of Cannabis Use*, Canberra: Australian Government Publishing Service (1994); Adams, I.B. and Martin, B.R., "Cannabis: Pharmacology and Toxicity in Animals and Humans," *Addiction* 91: 1585-1614 (1996).

36   Schwartz et al. (1989), see note 33, p. 1218.

37   In the part of the paper describing the data analysis (p. 1217), the community sample (Group B) is mislabeled Group C. Figure 2 (p. 1218) presents a graphic illustration of scores on the Wechsler Test, with the community sample and the program sample labeled properly. Schwartz et al. (1988), see note 33.

38   Deadwyler, S.A. et al., "The Effects of Delta-9-THC on Mechanisms of Learning and Memory," pp. 79-83 in Erinoff, L. (ed), *Neurobiology of Drug Abuse: Learning and Memory*, Rockville, MD: National Institute on Drug Abuse (1990); Lichtman, A.H. et al., "Systemic or Intrahippocampal Cannabinoid Administration Impairs Spatial Memory in Rats," *Psychopharmacology* 119: 282-90 (1995).

10   Pyschology and Insanity

1   Janet D. Lapey, *Marijuana Update 1996*, Drug Watch International, Omaha (1996).

2   Thomas J. Gorman, *Marijuana is NOT a Medicine*, Santa Clarita, CA: California Narcotic Officers' Association (1996), p. 33.

3   Center for Substance Abuse Prevention, *Reality Check: Questions and Answers*, Rockville, MD: U.S. Department of Health and Human Services (1996).

4   Gabriel G. Nahas and Colette Latour, "The Human Toxicity of Marijuana," *Medical Journal of Australia* 156 (1994), p. 497.

5   Fossier, A.E., "The Marihuana Menace," *New Orleans Medical and Surgical Journal* 84: 247-52 (1931); Merrill, F.T., *Marihuana: The New Dangerous Drug*, Washington, DC: Foreign Policy Association (1938); Rowell, E.A. and Rowell, R., *On the Trail of Marihuana, the Weed of Madness*, Mountain View, CA: Pacific Press Publishing Association (1939).

6   Chopra, G.S., "Man and Marihuana," *International Journal of the Addictions* 4: 215-47 (1969); Brill, H. and Nahas, G.G., "*Cannabis* Intoxication and Mental Illness," pp. 263-305 in Nahas, G.G. (ed), *Marihuana in Science and Medicine*, New York: Raven Press (1984).

7   Grinspoon, L., *Marihuana Reconsidered*, Cambridge, MA: Harvard University Press (1971); Kaplan, J., *Marijuana: The New Prohibition*, New York: World Publishing Company (1970); National Commission on Marihuana and Drug Abuse, *Marihuana: A Signal of Misunderstanding*, Washington, DC: U.S. Government Printing Office (1972).

8   Allebeck, P. et al., "Cannabis and Schizophrenia: A Longitudinal Study of Cases Treated in Stockholm County," *Acta Psychiatrica Scandinavica* 88: 21-24 (1993).

9   Hall, W. et al., *The Health and Psychological Consequences of Cannabis Use*, Canberra: Australian Government Publishing Service (1994); Thornicroft, G., "Cannabis and Psychosis: Is There Epidemiological Evidence for Association?" *British Journal of Psychiatry* 157: 25-33 (1990); Hollister, L.E., "Health Aspects of Cannabis," *Pharmacological Reviews* 38: 1-20 (1986).

10   Negrete, J.C. et al., "Cannabis Affects the Severity of Psychiatric Symptoms: Results of a Clinical Survey," *Psychological Medicine* 16: 515-20 (1986).

11   Mueser, K.T. et al., "Prevalence of Substance Abuse in Schizophrenia: Demographic and Clinical Correlates," *Schizophrenia Bulletin* 16: 31-56 (1990); Warner, R. et al., "Substance Use Among the Mentally Ill: Prevalence, Reasons for Use, and Effects on Illness," *American Journal of Orthopsychiatry* 64: 30-39 (1994).

12   Andreasson, S. et al., "Cannabis and Schizophrenia: A Longitudinal Study of Swedish Conscripts," *Lancet* 2: 1483-86 (1987).

13   Andreasson, S. et al., "Schizophrenia in Users and Nonusers of Cannabis: A Longitudinal study in Stockholm County," *Acta Psychiatrica Scandinavica* 79: 505-10 (1989).

14   Johnson, B.A. et al., "Cannabis and Schizophrenia," *Lancet* 1: 592-93 (1988); Negrete, J.C., "Cannabis and Schizophrenia," *British Journal of Addiction* 84: 349-51 (1989).

15 Der, G. et al., "Is Schizophrenia Disappearing," *Lancet* 1: 513-16 (1990).

16 McGlothlin, W.H. and West, L.J., "The Marihuana Problem: An Overview," *American Journal of Psychiatry* 125: 370-78 (1968); Kolansky, H. and Moore, W.T., "Clinical Effects of Marihuana on the Young," *International Journal of Psychiatry* 10: 55-67 (1972); Rodgers, T.C., "Discussion," *American Journal of Psychiatry* 130: 139-40 (1973).

17 Jessor, R. et al., "Psychosocial Correlates of Marijuana Use and Problem Drinking in a National Sample of Adolescents," *American Journal of Public Health* 70: 604-13 (1980); Pandina, R.J. et al., "The Impact of Prolonged Marijuana Use on Personal and Social Competence in Adolescence," pp. 183-200 in Chesher, G. et al. (eds), *Marijuana: An International Research Report*, Canberra: Australian Government Publishing Service (1988); Shedler, J. and Block, J., "Adolescent Drug Use and Psychological Health: A Longitudinal Inquiry," *American Psychologist* 45: 612-30 (1990); Dembo, R. et al., "A Longitudinal Study of the Relationship Among Alcohol Use, Marijuana/Hashish Use, Cocaine Use, and Emotional/Psychological Functioning Problems in a Cohort of High-Risk Youths," *International Journal of the Addictions* 25: 1341-82 (1990).

18 MacDonald, D.I., " The Relationship of Moderate Marijuana Use and Adolescent Behavior," pp. 45-51 in *Marijuana and Youth: Clinical Observations on Motivation and Learning*, Rockville, MD: National Institute on Drug Abuse (1982); Voth, H.M., "The Effects of Marijuana on the Young," pp. 51-55 in *Marijuana and Youth: Clinical Observations on Motivation and Learning*, Rockville, MD: National Institute on Drug Abuse (1982); Gold, M.S., *Marijuana*, New York: Plenum Medical Book Company (1989); DuPont, R.L., *Getting Tough on Gateway Drugs: A Guide for the Family*, Washington, DC: American Psychiatric Press (1984); Millman, R.B. and Sbriglio, R., "Patterns of Use and Psychopathology in Chronic Marijuana Users," *Pediatric Clinics of North America* 9: 533-45 (1986).

19 Farrell, A.D. et al., "Relationship Between Drug Use and Other Problem Behaviors in Urban Adolescents," *Journal of Consulting and Clinical Psychology* 60: 705-12 (1992); Donovan, J.E. and Jessor, R., "Structure of Problem Behavior in Adolescence and Young Adulthood," *Journal of Consulting and Clinical Psychology* 53: 890-904 (1985); Hendin, H. et al., *Adolescent Marijuana Abusers and Their Families*, Rockville, MD: National Institute on Drug Abuse (1981); Kellam, S. et al., "The Prevention of Teenage Substance Use: Longitudinal Research and Strategy," pp. 171-200 in Petersen, A. and Perry, C. (eds), *Promoting Adolescent Health: A Dialogue on Research and Practice*, New York: Academic Press (1982); Block, J. et al., "Longitudinally Foretelling Drug Usage in Adolescence: Early Childhood Personality and Environmental Precursors," *Child Development* 59: 336-55 (1988); Johnston, L.D. et al., "Drugs and Delinquency: A Search for Causal Connections," pp. 137-56 in Kandel, D.B. (ed), *Longitudinal Research on Drug Use: Empirical Findings and Methodological Issues*, New York: John Wiley & Sons (1978); Tubman, J.G. et al., "Qualitative Changes in Relationships Between Substance Use and Adjustment During Adolescence," *Journal of Sub-*

stance Abuse 3: 405-14 (1991); Shedler and Block (1990), see note 15; Pandina et al. (1988), see note 15; Dembo et al. (1990), see note 15.

20 Hendin, H. et al., *Adolescent Marijuana Abusers and Their Families*, Rockville, MD: National Institute on Drug Abuse (1981).

21 Jessor, R., "Marihuana: A Review of Recent Psychosocial Research," pp. 337-55 in DuPont, R.L. et al. (eds), *Handbook on Drug Abuse*, Rockville, MD: National Institute on Drug Abuse (1979); Eisenman, R. et al., "Undergraduate Marijuana Use as Related to Internal Sensation, Novelty Seeking and Openness to Experience," *Journal of Clinical Psychology* 36: 1013-19 (1980); Satinder, K.P. and Black, A., "Cannabis Use and Sensation Seeking Behavior," *Journal of Psychology* 116: 101-05 (1984); Kandel, D.B., "Marijuana Users in Young Adulthood," *Archives of General Psychiatry* 41: 200-09 (1984); Mayer, J.E. and Ligman, J.D., "Personality Characteristics of Adolescent Marijuana Users," *Adolescence* 24: 965-76 (1989); Fisher, G. and Steckler, A., "Psychological Effects, Personality and Behavioral Changes Attributed to Marihuana," *International Journal of the Addictions* 9: 101- 26 (1974); Brook, J.S., "Family Socialization and Adolescent Personality and Their Association with Adolescent Use of Marijuana," *Journal of Genetic Psychology* 133: 261-71 (1978).

22 Kay, E.J. et al., "A Longitudinal Study of the Personality Correlates of Marijuana Use," *Journal of Consulting and Clinical Psychology* 46: 470-77 (1978); Pederson, W., "Mental Health, Sensation Seeking and Drug Use Patterns: A Longitudinal Study," *British Journal of Addiction* 86: 195-204 (1991); Smith, G.M. and Fogg, C.P., "Psychological Predictors of Early Use, Late Use, and Nonuse of Marijuana Among Teenage Students," pp. 101-13 in Kandel, D.P. (ed), *Longitudinal Research on Drug Use: Empirical Findings and Methodological Issues*, New York: John Wiley & Sons (1978).

23 Hogan, R. et al., "Personality Correlates of Undergraduate Marijuana Use," *Journal of Consulting and Clinical Psychology* 35: 58-63 (1970); McAree, C.P. et al., "Personality Factors and Patterns of Drug Usage in College Students," *American Journal of Psychiatry* 129: 890-93 (1972); Richek, H.G. et al., "Personality/Mental Health Correlates of Drug Use by High School Students," *Journal of Nervous and Mental Disease* 160: 435-42 (1975); Goldstein, J.W. and Sappington, J.T., "Personality Characteristics of Students Who Became Heavy Drug Users: An MMPI Study of an *Avant-Guard*," *American Journal of Drug and Alcohol Abuse* 4: 401-12 (1977); Hochman, J.S. and Brill, N.Q., "Chronic Marihuana Use and Psychosocial Adaptation," *American Journal of Psychiatry* 130: 132-40 (1973).

24 Shedler and Block (1990), see note 17.

25 Weil, A., "Adverse Reactions to Marijuana: Classification and Suggested Treatment," *New England Journal of Medicine* 282: 997-1000 (1970); Smith, D.E., "Acute and Chronic Toxicity of Marijuana," *Journal of Psychedelic Drugs* 2: 37-47 (1968); Meyer, M.E., "Psychiatric Consequences of Marihuana Use: The State of the Evidence," pp. 133-52 in Tinklenberg, J.R. (ed), *Marihuana and Health Hazards: Methodologic Issues in Current Research*, New York: Academic Press (1975); Abruzzi,

W., "Drug-Induced Psychosis," *International Journal of the Addictions* 12: 183-93 (1977).

26 Mason, A.P. and McBay, A.J., "Cannabis: Pharmacology and Interpretation of Effects," *Journal of Forensic Sciences* 30: 615-31 (1985); Wall, M.E. and Perez-Reyes, M., "The Metabolism of Delta-9-Tetrahydrocannabinol and Related Cannabinoids in Man," *Journal of Clinical Pharmacology* 21: 178-89S (1981).

27 Perez-Reyes, M. et al., "Intravenous Injection in Man of Delta-9-Tetrahydrocannabinol and 11-Hydroxy-Delta-9-Tetrahydrocannabinol," *Science* 177: 633-35 (1972); Perez-Reyes, M. et al., "A Comparison of the Pharmacological Activity of Delta-9-Tetrahydrocannabinol and Its Monohydroxylated Metabolites in Man," *Experientia* 29: 1009-10 (1973); Lemberger, L. et al., "Comparative Pharmacology of Delta-9-Tetrahydrocannabinol and its Metabolite 11-OH-Delta-9-THC," *Journal of Clinical Investigation* 54: 2411-17 (1973); Agurell, S. et al., "Pharmacokinetics and Metabolism of Delta-9-Tetrahydrocannabinol and Other Cannabinoids with Emphasis on Man," *Pharmacological Reviews* 38: 21-43 (1986).

28 Jones, R. et al., "Clinical Studies of Cannabis Tolerance and Dependence," *Annals of the New York Academy of Sciences* 282: 221-39 (1976).

29 Ritzlin, R.S. et al., "Delta-9-Tetrahydrocannabinol Levels in Street Samples of Marijuana and Hashish: Correlation to User Reactions," *Clinical Toxicology* 15: 45-53 (1979).

30 Ungerleider, J.T. and Andrysiak, T., "Bias and the Cannabis Researcher," *Journal of Clinical Pharmacology* 21: 153-58S (1981).

31 Mathers, D.C. and Ghodse, A.H., "Cannabis and Psychotic Illness," *British Journal of Psychiatry* 161: 648-53 (1992); Thomas, H., "Psychiatric Symptoms in Cannabis Users," *British Journal of Psychiatry* 163: 141-49 (1993).

32 Grossman, W., "Adverse Reactions Associated with Cannabis Products in India," *Annals of Internal Medicine* 70: 529-33 (1969); Chopra, G.S. and Smith, J.W., "Psychotic Reactions Following Cannabis Use in East Indians," *Archives of General Psychiatry* 30: 24-27 (1974); Chaudry, H.R. et al., "Cannabis Psychosis Following Bhang Ingestion," *British Journal of Addiction* 86: 1075-81 (1991).

33 Hollister (1986), see note 9.

34 Keeler, M.H. et al., "Spontaneous Recurrence of Marihuana Effect," *American Journal of Psychiatry* 125:384-86 (1968); Annis, H.M. and Smart, R.G., "Adverse Reactions and Recurrences from Marijuana Use," *British Journal of Addiction* 68: 315-19 (1973); Edwards, G., "Cannabis and the Psychiatric Position," pp. 320-40 in Graham, J.D.P., *Cannabis and Health*, New York: Academic Press (1976); Stanton, M.D. et al., "Drug Flashbacks. II. Some Additional Findings," *International Journal of the Addictions* 11: 53-69 (1976); Brown, A. and Stickgold, A., "Marijuana Flashback Phenomena," *Journal of Psychedelic Drugs* 8: 275-83 (1976).

35 Weil, A., *The Natural Mind*, Boston: Houghton Mifflin Company (1972).

11   Marijuana, Deviance and Crime

1   Donna Shalala, Secretary of Health and Human Services, "Say 'No' to Legalization of Marijuana," *Wall Street Journal* (18 August 1995), p. A10.

2   Lee Brown, Director of National Drug Control Policy, remarks at *National Conference on Marijuana Use: Prevention, Treatment, and Research*, sponsored by the National Institute on Drug Abuse, Arlington, VA (July 1995).

3   Richard H. Schwartz, "Marijuana: A Crude Drug with a Spectrum of Unappreciated Toxicity," *Pediatrics* 73 (1984), p. 457.

4   Bonnie, R.J. and Whitebread, C.H., *The Marihuana Conviction: A History of Marihuana Prohibition in the United States*, Charlottesville: University of Virginia Press (1974); Kaplan, J., *Marijuana: The New Prohibition*, New York: The World Publishing Company (1970).

5   Anslinger, H.J. and Cooper, C., "Assassin of Youth," *American Magazine* 124 (July 1937).

6   National Commission on Marihuana and Drug Abuse, *Marihuana: A Signal of Misunderstanding*, Washington, DC: U.S. Government Printing Office (1972), p. 77.

7   *Drug Use Forecasting: 1993 Annual Report on Juvenile Arrestees/Detainees*, Washington, DC: U.S. Department of Justice (1994); Harrison, L. and Gfroerer, J., "The Intersection of Drug Use and Criminal Behavior," *Crime and Delinquency* 38: 422-43 (1992); Leukefeld, C.G. and Clayton, R., "Drug Abuse and Delinquency: A Study of Youths in Treatment," pp. 213-28 in Bescher, G. and Friedman, A. (eds), *Youth Drug Abuse: Problems, Issues and Treatment*, Lexington, MA: DC Heath (1979); O'Donnell, J.A. et al., *Young Men and Drugs: A Nationwide Survey*, Rockville, MD: National Institute on Drug Abuse (1976); Dembo, R. et al., "Examination of the Relationships Among Drug Use, Emotional/Psychological Problems, and Crime Among Youths Entering a Juvenile Detention Center," *International Journal of Addictions* 25: 301-40 (1990); Anthony, J.C., "Young Adult Marijuana Use in Relation to Antecedent Misbehavior," pp. 238-44 in Harris, L.S. (ed), *Problems of Drug Dependence, 1984*, Rockville, MD: National Institute on Drug Abuse (1985); Jessor, R. and Jessor, S.L., *Problem Behavior and Psychosocial Development: A Longitudinal Study of Youth*, New York: Academic Press (1977); Farrell, A.D. et al., "Relationship Between Drug Use and Other Problem Behaviors in Urban Adolescents," *Journal of Consulting and Clinical Psychology* 60: 705-12 (1992).

8   Fagan, J. et al., "Delinquency and Substance Use Among Inner-City Students," *Journal of Drug Issues* 20: 351-402 (1990); Ausubel, D.B., *Drug Addiction: Physiological, Psychological and Sociological Aspects*, New York: Random House (1958); Johnson (1973), see note 7.

9   Simonds, J.F. and Kashani, J., "Specific Drug Use and Violence in Delinquent Boys," *American Journal of Drug and Alcohol Abuse* 7: 305-22 (1980); Johnston, L.D. et al., "Drugs and Delinquency: A Search for Causal Connections," pp. 137-56 in Kandel,

D.B. (ed), *Longitudinal Research on Drug Use: Empirical Findings and Methodological Issues*, New York: John Wiley & Sons (1978); Goode, E., "Marijuana and Crime," pp. 447-53 in National Commission on Marihuana and Drug Abuse, *Marihuana: A Signal of Misunderstanding, Appendix I*, Washington, DC: U.S. Government Printing Office (1972).

10   Clayton, R.R., "The Delinquency and Drug Use Relationship Among Adolescents," pp. 82-103 in Lettieri, D.J. and Ludford, J.P. (eds), *Drug Abuse and the American Adolescent*, Rockville, MD: National Institute on Drug Abuse (1981); Jessor, R. "Marihuana: A Review of Recent Psychosocial Research," pp. 337-56 in DuPont, R.L. et al (eds), *Handbook on Drug Abuse*, Rockville, MD: National Institute on Drug Abuse (1979).

11   Tinklenberg, J.R. et al., "Drugs and Criminal Assaults by Adolescents: A Replication Study," *Journal of Psychoactive Drugs* 13: 277-87 (1981); Goode (1972), see note 9.

12   Hendin, H. et al., *Adolescent Marijuana Users and Their Families*, Rockville, MD: National Institute on Drug Abuse (1981).

13   Watts, W.D. and Wright, L.S., "The Drug Use-Violent Delinquency Link Among Adolescent Mexican-Americans," pp. 112-35 in DeLaRosa, M. et al. (eds), *Drugs and Violence: Causes, Correlates, and Consequences*, Rockville, MD: National Institute on Drug Abuse (1990); Abram, K.M. and Teplin, L.A., "Drug Disorder, Mental Illness, and Violence," pp. 222-38 in *Drugs and Violence: Causes, Correlates, and Consequences*, Rockville, MD: National Institute on Drug Abuse (1990); Simonds, J.F. and Kashani, J. "Specific Drug Use and Violence in Delinquent Boys," *American Journal of Drug and Alcohol Abuse* 7: 305-22 (1980); Johnston et al. (1978), see note 9.

14   Spunt, B. et al., "The Role of Marijuana in Homicide," *International Journal of the Addictions* 29: 195-213 (1994).

15   Cherek, D.R. et al., "Acute Effects of Marijuana Smoking on Aggressive, Escape and Point-Maintained Responding of Male Drug Users," *Psychopharmacology* 111: 163-68 (1993).

16   Cherek, D.R. and Dougherty, D.M., "Provocation Frequency and its Role in Determining the Effects of Smoked Marijuana on Human Aggressive Responding," *Behavioural Pharmacology* 6: 405-12 (1995); Cherek, D.R. and Steinberg, J.L., "Effects of Drugs on Human Aggressive Behavior," pp. 239-90 in Burrows, G.D. and Werry, J.S. (eds), *Advances in Human Psychopharmacology, Volume IV*, Greenwich, CT (1987); Hollister, L.E. et al., "Comparison of Tetrahydrocannabinol and Synhexyl in Man," *Clinical Pharmacology and Therapeutics* 9: 783-88 (1968); Jones, R.T. and Benowitz, N., "The 30-Day Trip: Clinical Studies of Cannabis Tolerance and Dependence," pp. 627-42 in Braude, M.C. and Szara. S. (eds), *Pharmacology of Marihuana*, New York: Raven Press (1976); Mendelson, J.H. and Meyer, R.E., "Behavioral and Biological Concomitants of Chronic Marihuana Smoking by Heavy and Chronic Users," pp. 68-246 in *Marihuana: Signal of Misunderstanding, Appendix I*, Washington, DC: U.S. Govern-

ment Printing Office (1972).

17   Myerscough, R. and Taylor, S.P., "The Effects of Marijuana on Human Physical Aggression," *Journal of Personality and Social Psychology* 49: 1541-46 (1985).

18   Ginsberg, H.J. et al., "Delta-9-Tetrahydrocannabinol Affects Consummatory But Not Appetite Sequence of Interspecific Aggression in the Mongolian Gerbil," *Bulletin of the Psychonomic Society* 10: 361-63 (1977); Sieber, B. et al., "Behavioural Effects of Hashish Extract in Mice in Comparison with Other Psychoactive Drugs," *General Pharmacology* 13: 315-20 (1982); Ferraro, D.P., "Preclinical Effects: Unlearned Behavior," pp. 86-102 in Petersen, R.C. (ed), *Marihuana Research Findings 1976*, Rockville, MD: National Institute on Drug Abuse (1977).

19   Carlini, E.A. et al., "Factors Influencing the Aggressive Behavior Induced by Marihuana in Starved Rats," *British Journal of Pharmacology* 44: 794-804 (1972); Miczek, K.A. et al., "Does THC Induce Aggression? Suppression Reactions by Chronic and Acute Delta-9-Tetrahydrocannabinol Treatment in Laboratory Rats," pp. 499-514 in Braude, M.C. and Szara, S. (eds), *The Pharmacology of Marihuana*, New York: Raven Press (1976).

12   Marijuana, Sex Hormones and Reproduction

1   Parents Resource Institute for Drug Education, *Marijuana and Cocaine*, Atlanta, GA: PRIDE (1990).

2   Center for Substance Abuse Prevention, *Female Adolescents and Marijuana Use; Fact Sheet for Adults*, Rockville, MD: U.S. Department of Health and Human Services (1995).

3   Center for Substance Abuse Prevention, *Marijuana: Tips for Teens*, Rockville, MD: U.S. Department of Health and Human Services (1995).

4   Neil Swan, "A Look at Marijuana's Harmful Effects," *NIDA Notes* 9, 2 (1994), p. 16.

5   President Bill Clinton, speech at Framingham High School, Framingham, Massachusetts (20 October 1994).

6   Harmon, J. and Aliapoulios, M.A., "Gynecomastia in Marijuana Users," *New England Journal of Medicine* 287: 936 (1972).

7   Cates, W. and Pope, J.N., "Gynecomastia and Cannabis Smoking: A Nonassociation Among U.S. Soldiers," *American Journal of Surgery* 134: 613-15 (1977).

8   Kolodny, R.C. et al., "Plasma Testosterone and Semen Analysis in Male Homosexuals," *New England Journal of Medicine* 285: 1170-74 (1971).

9   Kolodny, R.C. et al., "Depression of Plasma Testosterone Levels After Chronic Intensive Marijuana Use," *New England Journal of Medicine* 290: 872-74 (1974).

10   Kolodny, R.C. et al., "Depression of Plasma Testosterone with Acute Mari-

huana Administration," pp. 217-25 in Braude, M.C. and Szara, S. (eds), *Pharmacology of Marihuana*, New York: Raven Press (1976).

11   Mendelson, J.H. et al., "Plasma Testosterone Levels Before, During, and After Chronic Marijuana Smoking," *New England Journal of Medicine* 291: 1051-55 (1974); Schaefer, C.F. et al., "Normal Plasma Testosterone Concentrations After Marijuana Smoking," *New England Journal of Medicine* 292: 867-68 (1975); Mendelson, J.H. et al., "Effects of Chronic Marijuana Use on Integrated Plasma Testosterone and Luteinizing Hormone Levels," *Journal of Pharmacology and Experimental Therapeutics* 207: 611-17 (1978); Hembree, W.C. et al., "Marihuana's Effects on Human Gonadal Function," pp. 521-32 in Nahas, G.G. (ed), *Marihuana: Chemistry, Biochemistry, and Cellular Effects*, New York: Springer-Verlag (1976); Cone, E.J. et al., "Acute Effects of Marijuana on Hormones, Subjective Effects and Performance in Male Human Subjects," *Pharmacology Biochemistry and Behavior* 24: 1749-54 (1986).

12   Cushman, P., "Plasma Testosterone Levels in Healthy Male Marijuana Smokers," *American Journal of Drug and Alcohol Abuse* 2: 269-75 (1975); Block, R.I. et al., "Effects of Chronic Marijuana Use on Testosterone, Luteinizing Hormone, Follicle Stimulating Hormone, Prolactin and Cortisol in Men and Women," *Drug and Alcohol Dependence* 28: 121-28 (1991); Coggins, W.J. et al., "Health Status of Chronic Heavy Cannabis Users," *Annals of the New York Academy of Sciences* 282: 148-61 (1976);

13   Kolodny et al. (1974), see note 9.

14   Chausom, A.M. and Safer, B., "Marijuana and Sex," *New England Journal of Medicine* 291: 308 (1974).

15   Hembree, W.C. et al., "Changes in Human Spermatozoa Associated with High Dose Marihuana Smoking," pp. 429-39 in Nahas, G.G. and Paton, W.D.M. (eds), *Marihuana: Biological Effects*, Oxford: Pergamon Press (1979).

16   Bauman, J., "Marijuana and the Female Reproductive System," pp. 85-88 in *Health Consequences of Marijuana Use*, Washington, DC: U.S. Government Printing Office (1980).

17   Mendelson, J.H. et al., "Acute Effects of Marijuana Smoking on Prolactin Levels in Human Females," *Journal of Pharmacology and Experimental Therapeutics* 232: 220-22 (1985).

18   Block et al. (1991), see note 12.

19   Harclerode, J., "Endocrine Effects of Marijuana in the Male: Preclinical Studies," pp. 46-64 in Braude, M.C. and Ludford, J.L. (eds), *Marijuana Effects on the Endocrine and Reproductive Systems*, Rockville, MD: National Institute on Drug Abuse (1984); Bloch, E., "Effects of Marijuana and Cannabinoids on Reproduction, Endocrine Function, Development and Chromosomes," pp. 355-432 in Fehr, K.O. and Kalant, H. (eds), *Cannabis and Health Hazards*, Toronto: Addiction Research Foundation

(1983); Mendelson, J.H. and Mello, N.K., "Effects of Marijuana on Neuroendocrine Hormones in Human Males and Females," pp. 97-114 in Braude, M.C. and Ludford, J.P. (eds), *Marijuana Effects on the Endocrine and Reproductive Systems*, Rockville, MD: National Institute on Drug Abuse (1984); Smith, C.G. and Asch, R.H., "Acute, Short-Term, and Chronic Effects of Marijuana on the Female Primate Reproductive Function," pp. 82-96 in Braude, M.C. and Ludford, J.P. (eds), *Marijuana Effects on the Endocrine and Reproductive Systems*, Rockville, MD: Department of Health and Human Services (1984); Wenger, T. et al., "Effects of Delta-9-Tetrahydrocannabinol on Pregnancy, Puberty, and the Neuroendocrine System," pp. 539-560 in Murphy, L. and Bartke, A. (eds), *Marijuana/Cannabinoids: Neurobiology and Neurophysiology*, Boca Raton: CRC Press (1992).

20 Smith, C.G. et al., "Tolerance Develops to the Disruptive Effects of Delta-9-Tetrahydrocannabinol on the Primate Menstrual Cycle," *Science* 219: 1453-55 (1983).

21 Yang, Z.M. et al., "Activation of Brain-Type Cannabinoid Receptors Interferes with Preimplantation Mouse Embryo Development," *Biology of Reproduction* 55: 756-61 (1996).

22 Leshner, A., quoted in U.S. Department of Health and Human Services Press Release, "Early Pregnancy Halted by Chemicals in Marijuana," Rockville, MD (11 October 1996).

23 Mueller, B.A. et al., "Recreational Drug Use and the Risk of Primary Infertility," *Epidemiology* 1: 195-200 (1990).

24 Wilcox, A.J. et al., "Risk Factors for Early Pregnancy Loss," *Epidemiology* 1: 382-85 (1990).

25 Abel, E.L., "Marijuana and Sex: A Critical Survey," *Drug and Alcohol Dependence* 8: 1- 22 (1981); Ehrenkranz, J.R.L. and Hembree, W.C., "Effects of Marijuana on Male Reproductive Function," *Psychiatric Annals* 16: 243-49 (1986).

26 Copeland, K.C. et al., "Marijuana Smoking and Pubertal Arrest," *Journal of Pediatrics* 96: 1079-80 (1980).

27 Wenger, et al. (1992), see note 19; Smith and Asch (1984), see note 19; Harclerode (1984), see note 19.

28 Bauman (1980), see note 16.

29 Block et al. (1991), see note 12.

30 Block et al. (1991), see note 12; Kolodny et al. (1974), see note 9; Abel (1981), see note 23.

31 Kolodny et al. (1976), see note 10; Cone et al. (1986), see note 11.

13 Marijuana Use During Pregnancy

1 Peggy Mann, *The Sad Story of Mary Wanna*, NY: Woodmere Press (1988), p. 30.

2 Peter Fried, quoted in "Marijuana: Its Use and Effects," *Prevention Pipeline* 8, 5 (1995), p. 4.

3   American Council for Drug Education, *Drugs and Pregnancy*, Rockville, MD (1994).

4   Neil Swan, "A Look at Marijuana's Harmful Effects," *NIDA Notes* 9, 2: 14-15 (1994).

5   Parents Resource Institute for Drug Education, "Marijuana—Effects on the Female," Atlanta, GA: PRIDE (1996).

6   Hecht, F. et al., "Lysergic-Acid-Diethylamide and Cannabis as Possible Teratogens in Man," *Lancet* 2: 1087 (1968); Carakushansky, G. et al., "Lysergide and Cannabis as Possible Teratogens in Man," *Lancet* 1: 150-51 (1969).

7   Maugh, T.H., "Marihuana: The Grass May No Longer Be Greener," *Science* 185: 683-85 (1974).

8   Matsuyama, S. and Jarvik, L., "Effects of Marihuana on the Genetic and Immune Systems," pp. 179-93 in Petersen, R.C. (ed), *Marihuana Research Findings, 1976*, Rockville, MD: National Institute on Drug Abuse (1977); Morishima, K., "Effects of Cannabis and Natural Cannabinoids on Chromosomes and Ova," pp. 25-45 in Braude, M.C. and Ludford, J.L. (eds), *Marijuana Effects on the Endocrine and Reproductive Systems*, Rockville, MD: National Institute on Drug Abuse (1984).

9   Parents Resource Institute for Drug Education, *Marijuana: Effects on the Male*, Atlanta, GA: PRIDE (1996); Spence, W.R., *Marijuana: Its Effects and Hazards*, Waco, TX: Health Edco (undated); Mann (1988), see note 1.

10 Herclerode, J., "The Effect of Marijuana on Reproduction and Development," pp. 137-66 in Petersen, R.C. (ed), *Marijuana Research Findings: 1980*, Rockville, MD: National Institute on Drug Abuse (1980); Abel, E.L., "Effects of Prenatal Exposure to Cannabinoids," pp. 20-35 in Pinkert, T.M. (ed), *Current Research on the Consequences of Maternal Drug Abuse*, Rockville, MD: National Institute on Drug Abuse (1985); Hutchings, D. and Dow-Edwards, D., "Animal Models of Opiate, Cocaine, and Cannabis Use," *Clinics in Perinatology* 18: 1-22 (1991); Behnke, M. and Eyler, F.D., "The Consequences of Prenatal Substance Use for the Developing Fetus, Newborn, and Young Child," *International Journal of the Addictions* 28: 1341-91 (1993); Wenger, T. et al., "Effects of Delta-9-Tetrahydrocannabinol on Pregnancy, Puberty, and the Neuroendocrine System," pp. 539-60 in Murphy, L. and Bartke, A. (eds), *Marijuana/Cannabinoids: Neurobiology and Neurophysiology*, Boca Raton, FL: CRC Press (1992).

11 Rudolph, A.M., "Animal Models for Study of Fetal Drug Exposure," pp. 5-16 in Chiang, C.N. and Lee, C.C. (eds), *Prenatal Drug Exposure: Kinetics and Dynamics*, Rockville, MD: National Institute on Drug Abuse (1985).

12 Fried, P.A., "Postnatal Consequences of Maternal Marijuana Use," pp. 61-72 in Pinkert, T.M. (ed), *Current Research on the Consequences of Maternal Drug Abuse*, Rockville, MD: National Institute on Drug Abuse (1985); Golub, M.S. et al., "Peer and Maternal Social Interaction Patterns in Offspring of Rhesus Monkeys Treated Chronically with Delta-9-Tetrahydrocannabinol," pp. 657-67 in Agurell, S., *The Cannabinoids: Chemical, Pharmacological, and Therapeutic Aspects*, Orlando: Aca-

demic Press (1984); Herclerode (1980), see note 10.

13 Grilly, D.M. et al., "Observations on the Reproductive Activity of Chimpanzees Following Long-Term Exposure to Marijuana," *Pharmacology* 11: 304-07 (1974).

14 Linn, S. et al., "The Association of Marijuana Use with Outcome of Pregnancy," *American Journal of Public Health* 73:1161-64 (1983).

15 Shiono, P.H. et al., "The Impact of Cocaine and Marijuana Use on Low Birth Weight and Preterm Birth: A Multicenter Study," *American Journal of Obstetrics and Gynecology* 172: 19-27 (1995); Knight, E.M. et al., "Relationships of Serum Illicit Drug Concentrations During Pregnancy to Maternal Nutritional Status," *Journal of Nutrition* 124: 973-80S (1994); Tennes, K. and Blackard, C., "Maternal Alcohol Consumption, Birthweight, and Minor Physical Abnormalities," *American Journal of Obstetrics and Gynecology* 138: 774-80 (1980); Hayes, J. et al., "Newborn Outcomes with Maternal Marijuana Use in Jamaican Women," *Pediatric Nursing* 14: 107-10 (1988); Fried, P.A. and O'Connell, C.M., "A Comparison of the Effects of Prenatal Exposure to Tobacco, Alcohol, Cannabis and Caffeine on Birth Size and Subsequent Growth," *Neurotoxicology and Teratology* 9: 79-85 (1987); O'Connell, C.M. and Fried, P.A., "An Investigation of Prenatal Cannabis Exposure and Minor Physical Anomalies in a Low Risk Population," *Neurobehavioral Toxicology and Teratology* 6: 345-50 (1984); Richardson, G.A. et al., "The Effect of Prenatal Alcohol, Marijuana and Tobacco Exposure on Neonatal Behavior," *Infant Behavioral Development* 12: 199-209 (1989); Astley, S., "Analysis of Facial Shape in Children Gestationally Exposed to Marijuana, Alcohol, and/or Cocaine," *Pediatrics* 89: 67-77 (1992); Witter, F.R. and Niebyl, J.R., "Marijuana Use in Pregnancy and Pregnancy Outcome," *American Journal of Perinatology* 7: 36-38 (1990).

16 Dreher, M.C. et al., "Prenatal Exposure and Neonatal Outcomes in Jamaica: An Ethnographic Study," *Pediatrics* 93: 254-60 (1994); Tennes, K. et al., "Marijuana: Prenatal and Postnatal Exposure in the Human," pp. 48-60 in Pinkert, T.M. (ed), *Current Research on the Consequences of Maternal Drug Abuse*, Rockville, MD: National Institute on Drug Abuse (1985).

17 Hatch, E.E. and Braken, M.B., "Effect of Marijuana Use in Pregnancy on Fetal Growth," *American Journal of Epidemiology* 124: 986-93 (1986); Kline, J. et al., "Cigarettes, Alcohol and Marijuana: Varying Associations with Birthweight," *International Journal of Epidemiology* 16: 44-51 (1987); Zuckerman, B. et al., "Effects of Maternal Marijuana and Cocaine Use on Fetal Growth," *New England Journal of Medicine* 320: 762-68 (1989); Fried, P.A. et al., "Marijuana Use During Pregnancy and Decreased Length of Gestation," *American Journal of Obstetrics and Gynecology* 150: 23-26 (1984); Hingson, R. et al., "Effects of Maternal Drinking and Marijuana Use on Fetal Growth and Development," *Pediatrics* 70: 539-46 (1982); Fried, P.A. and Makin, J.E., "Neonatal Behavioral Correlates of Prenatal Exposure to Marijuana, Cigarettes and Alcohol in a Low Risk Population," *Neurotoxicology and Teratology* 9: 1-7 (1987); Cornelius, M.D. et al., "Prenatal Tobacco and Marijuana Use Among Adolescents: Effects on Offspring Ges-

tational Age, Growth, and Morphology," *Pediatrics* 95: 738-43 (1995); Day, N. et al., "Prenatal Marijuana Use and Neonatal Outcome," *Neurotoxicology and Teratology* 13: 329-34 (1991).

18   Day, N.L. and Richardson, G.A., "Prenatal Marijuana Use: Epidemiology, Methodologic Issues, and Infant Outcome," *Clinics in Perinatology* 18: 77-91 (1991); Richardson, G.A. et al., "The Impact of Marijuana and Cocaine Use on the Infant and Child," *Clinical Obstetrics and Gynecology* 36: 302-18 (1993); Cornelius et al. (1995), see note 17; Coles, C.D. et al., "Effects of Cocaine, Alcohol, and Other Drug Use in Pregnancy on Neonatal Growth and Neurobehavioral Status," *Neurotoxicology and Teratology* 14: 22-33 (1992).

19   Day et al. (1991), see note 17.

20   Hatch and Bracken (1986), see note 17.

21   Fried et al. (1984), see note 16.

22   Tennes et al. (1985), see note 16.

23   Day, N.L. et al., "Effect of Prenatal Marijuana Exposure on the Cognitive Development of Offspring at Age Three," *Neurotoxicology and Teratology* 16: 169-75 (1994).

24   Streissguth, A.P. et al., "IQ at Age 4 in Relation to Maternal Alcohol Use and Smoking During Pregnancy," *Developmental Psychology* 25: 3-11 (1989).

25   Day et al. (1994), see note 23.

26   Center on Addiction and Substance Abuse, *Legalization: Panacea or Pandora's Box*, New York (1995); Drug Watch Oregon, *Marijuana Research Review* 2, 4 (1995).

27   Robison, L.L. et al., "Maternal Drug Use and Risk of Non-Lymphoblastic Leukemia Among Offspring," *Cancer* 63: 1904-11 (1989).

28   Grufferman, S. et al., "Parents' Use of Cocaine and Marijuana and Increased Risk of Rhabdomyosarcoma in Their Children," *Cancer Causes and Control* 4: 217-24 (1993).

29   Day, N.L. et al., "The Epidemiology of Alcohol, Marijuana and Cocaine Use Among Women of Childbearing Age and Pregnant Women," *Clinical Obstetrics and Gynecology* 36: 232-45 (1993).

30   Grufferman, S. et al., "Environmental Factors in the Etiology of Rhabdomyosarcoma in Childhood," *Journal of the National Cancer Institute* 68: 107-13 (1982).

31   National Toxicology Program, *Toxicology and Carcinogenesis: Studies of 1-Trans-Delta-9-Tetrahydrocannabinol in F344/N Rats and B6c3F1 Mice*, Rockville, MD: U.S. Department of Health and Human Services (1996).

32   Fried, P.A. and Watkinson, B., "12- and 24-Month Neurobehavioral Follow-Up of Children Prenatally Exposed to Marijuana, Cigarettes and Alcohol," *Neurotoxicology and Teratology* 10: 305-13 (1988).

33   Fried, P.A. and Watkinson, B., "36- and 48-Month Neurobehavioral Follow-Up of Children Prenatally Exposed to Marijuana, Cigarettes, and Alcohol,"

Developmental and Behavioral Pediatrics 11: 49-58 (1990).

34 Fried and Watkinson (1990), see note 33.

35 Fried, P.A. et al., "60- and 72-Month Follow-Up of Children Prenatally Exposed to Marijuana, Cigarettes, and Alcohol: Cognitive and Language Assessment," *Journal of Developmental and Behavioral Pediatrics* 13: 383-91 (1992).

36 Fried, P.A. et al., "A Follow-Up Study of Attentional Behavior in 6-Year-Old Children Exposed Prenatally to Marijuana, Cigarettes, and Alcohol," *Neurotoxicology and Teratology* 14: 299-311 (1992).

37 O'Connell, C.M. and Fried, P.A., "Prenatal Exposure to Cannabis: A Preliminary Report of Postnatal Consequences in School-Age Children," *Neurotoxicology and Teratology* 13: 631-39 (1991).

38 Fried, P.A., "Prenatal Exposure to Marijuana and Tobacco During Infancy, Early and Middle Childhood: Effects and Attempts at a Synthesis," *Archives of Toxicology* 17:240-241 (1995).

39 Fried, P.A., "The Ottawa Prenatal Prospective Study (OPPS): Methodological Issues and Findings—It's Easy to Throw the Baby Out With the Bath Water," *Life Sciences* 56: 2159-68 (1995).

40 *National Conference on Marijuana Use: Prevention, Treatment, and Research,* sponsored by the National Institute on Drug Abuse, Arlington, VA (July 1995).

41 Center for Substance Abuse Prevention, "Marijuana: Its Uses and Effects," *Prevention Pipeline* 8, 5: 3-5 (1995).

42 Fried, P.A., "Prenatal Exposure to Tobacco and Marijuana: Effects During Pregnancy, Infancy, and Early Childhood," *Clinical Obstetrics and Gynecology* 36: 319-37 (1993).

43 Fried (1993), see note 42.

44 Fried, P.A., "Cigarettes and Marijuana: Are There Measurable Long-Term Neurobehavioral Teratogenic Effects?" *Neurotoxicology* 10: 577-84 (1989); Day, N. et al., "The Effects of Prenatal Tobacco and Marijuana Use on Offspring Growth From Birth Through 3 Years of Age," *Neurotoxicology and Teratology* 14: 407-14 (1992); Barr, H.M. et al., "Infant Size at 8 Months of Age: Relationship to Maternal Use of Alcohol, Nicotine, and Caffeine During Pregnancy," *Pediatrics* 74: 336-41 (1984); Fried and Watkinson (1990), see note 31; Streissguth et al. (1989), see note 24; Cornelius et al. (1990), see note 17; Kline et al. (1987), see note 17; Fried (1995), see note 38.

14 Marijuana and the Immune System

1 Parents Resource Institute for Drug Education, *Marijuana and Cocaine*, Atlanta: PRIDE (1990).

2 Ernest D. Preate, *Blowing Away the Marijuana Smokescreen*, Scranton: Pennsylvania Office of Attorney General (no date), p. 2.

3   W.R. Spence, *Marijuana: Its Effects and Hazards*, Waco: Health Edco (no date).

4   Eric A. Voth, *The International Drug Strategy Institute Position Paper on the Medical Applications of Marijuana*, Omaha: Drug Watch International (undated).

5   Drug Watch International, *By Any Modern Medical Standard, Marijuana is No Medicine*, Omaha (undated).

6   Nahas, G.G., *Marihuana—Deceptive Weed*, New York: Raven Press (1973).

7   Nahas, G.G., *Keep Off the Grass*, New York: Reader's Digest Press (1976).

8   Nahas, G.G. et al., "Inhibition of Cellular Mediated Immunity in Marihuana Smokers," *Science* 183: 419-20 (1974).

9   Nahas (1976), see note 7.

10   Lau, R.J. et al., "Phytohemagglutinin-Induced Lymphocyte Transformation in Humans Receiving Delta-9-Tetrahydrocannabinol," *Science* 192: 805-07 (1976); White, S.C. et al., "Mitogen-Induced Blastogenetic Responses to Lymphocytes from Marihuana Smokers," *Science* 188: 71-72 (1975); Dax, E.M. et al., "The Effects of 9-ENE-Tetrahydrocannabinol on Hormone Release and Immune Function," *Journal of Steroid Biochemistry* 34: 263-70 (1989); Kaklamani, E. et al., "Hashish Smoking and T-Lymphocytes," *Archives of Toxicology* 40: 97-101 (1978).

11   Nahas, G.G., *Keep Off the Grass*, 5th edition, Middlebury, VT: Paul S. Eriksson (1990).

12   Hollister, L.E., "Marijuana and Immunity," *Journal of Psychoactive Drugs* 24: 159-64 (1992).

13   Holsapple, M.P. et al., "Molecular Mechanisms of Toxicant-Induced Immuno-suppression: Role of Second Messengers," *Annual Review of Pharmacology and Toxicology* 36: 131-59 (1996); Spector, S. et al., "Delta-9-Tetrahydrocannabinol Augments Murine Retroviral Induced Immunosuppression and Infection," *International Journal of Immunopharmacology* 13: 411-17 (1991); Klein, T.W. et al., "The Effect of Delta-9-Tetrahydrocannabinol and 11-Hydroxy-Delta-9-Tet-rahydrocannabinol on T-Lymphocyte and B-Lymphocyte Mitogen Responses," *Journal of Immunopharmacology* 7: 451-66 (1985); Nahas, G.G. et al., "Natural Cannabinoids: Apparent Depression of Nucleic Acids and Protein Synthesis in Cultured Human Lymphocytes," pp. 177-203 in Braude, M.C. and Szara, S. (eds), *Pharmacology of Marihuana*, New York: Raven Press (1976); Watzl, B. et al., "Influence of Marijuana Components (THC and CBD) on Human Mono-nuclear Cell Cytokine Secretion *In Vitro*," pp. 63-70 in Friedman, H. et al. (eds), *Drugs of Abuse, Immunity, and Immunodeficiency*, New York: Plenum Press (1991).

14   Banchereau, J. et al., "Inhibitory Effects of Delta-9-Tetrahydrocannabinol and Other Psychotropic Drugs on Cultured Lymphocytes," pp. 129-44 in Nahas, G.G. and Paton, W.D.M. (eds), *Marihuana: Biological Effects*, New York: Pergamon Press (1979); Nahas et al. (1976), see note 13.

15   Munson, A.E. and Fehr, K.O., "Immunological Effects of Cannabis," pp. 257-353 in Fehr, K.O. and Kalant, H. (eds), *Cannabis and Health Hazards*, Toronto:

Addiction Research Foundation (1983).

16   Cabral, G.A. et al., "Effect of Delta-9-Tetrahydrocannabinol on Herpes Simplex Virus Type 2 Vaginal Infection in the Guinea Pig," *Proceedings of the Society for Experimental Biology and Medicine* 182: 181-86 (1986).

17   Mishkin, E.M. and Cabral, G.A., "Delta-9-Tetrahydrocannabinol Decreases Host Resistance to Herpes Simplex Virus Type 2 Vaginal Infection in the BGC3F1 Mouse," *Journal of General Virology* 66: 2539-49 (1985).

18   Silverstein, M.J. and Lensin, P., "2, 4-Dinitrochlorobenzene Skin Testing in Chronic Marihuana Users," pp. 199-203 in Braude, M.C. and Szara, S. (eds), *Pharmacology of Marihuana*, New York: Raven Press (1976).

19   Munson and Fehr (1983), see note 15, p. 338.

20   "Marinol," pp. 2129-31 in *Physician's Desk Reference*, Forty-Ninth Edition, Montvale, NJ: Medical Economics (1995).

21   Food and Drug Administration, "Unimed's Marinol (Dronabinol) Gains Indication for Anorexia in AIDS Patients," *Food, Drug, and Cosmetic Reporter*: 14 (4 January 1993).

22   Huber, G.L. et al., "Marijuana: Tetrahydrocannabinol and Pulmonary Antibacterial Defenses," *Chest* 77: 403-10 (1980).

23   Cabral, G.A. et al., "Chronic Marijuana Smoke Alters Alveolar Macrophage Morphology and Protein Expression," *Pharmacology Biochemistry and Behavior* 40: 643-50 (1991).

24   Barbers, R.G. et al., "Enhanced Alveolar Monocytic Phagocyte (Macrophage) Proliferation in Tobacco and Marijuana Smokers," *American Review of Respiratory Disease* 143: 1092-95 (1991); Barbers, R.G. et al., "Differential Examination of Bronchoalveolar Lavage Cells in Tobacco and Marijuana Smokers," *American Review of Respiratory Disease* 135: 1271-75 (1987).

25   Wallace, J.M. et al., "Lymphocytic Subpopulation Profiles in Bronchoalveolar Lavage Fluid and Peripheral Blood from Tobacco and Marijuana Smokers," *Chest* 105: 847-52 (1994); Sherman, M.P. et al., "Marijuana Smoking, Pulmonary Function, and Lung Macrophage Oxidant Release," *Pharmacology Biochemistry and Behavior* 40: 663-69 (1991); Sherman, M.P. et al., "Effects of Smoking Marijuana, Tobacco or Cocaine Alone or in Combination on DNA Damage in Human Alveolar Macrophages," *Life Sciences* 56: 2201-07 (1995).

26   Nieman, R.B. et al., "The Effect of Cigarette Smoking on the Development of AIDS in HIV-1-Seropositive Individuals," *AIDS 7: 705-10 (1993)*; Bushkin, S.E. et al., "Heavy Smoking Increases the Risk of Pneumocystis Carinii Pneumonia (PCP)," paper presented at the International Conference on AIDS, Amsterdam (1992).

27   Caiaffa, W.T. et al., "Drug Smoking, *Pneumocystis Carinii* Pneumonia, and Immunosuppression Increase Risk of Bacterial Pneumonia in Human Immunodeficiency Virus-Seropositive Injection Drug Users," *American Journal*

of Respiratory and Critical Care Medicine 150: 1493-98 (1994).

28 Coates, R.A. et al., "Cofactors of Progression to Acquired Immunodeficiency Syndrome in a Cohort of Male Sexual Contacts of Men with Immunodeficiency Virus Disease," *American Journal of Epidemiology* 132: 717-22 (1990); Kaslow, R.A. et al., "No Evidence for a Role of Alcohol or Other Psychoactive Drugs in Accelerating Immunodeficiency in HIV-1-Positive Individuals," *Journal of the American Medical Association* 261: 3424-29 (1989).

29 McCaffery, B., remarks on C-SPAN (December 21, 1996); Drug Enforcement Administration, *Drug Legalization: Myths and Misconceptions*, Washington, DC (1994); Gorman, T.J., *Marijuana is NOT a Medicine*, Santa Clarita, CA: California Narcotics Officers' Association (1996); Drug Watch International, *By Any Modern Medical Standard, Marijuana is No Medicine*, Omaha (undated); Drug Watch Oregon, *Marijuana Research Review* (February 1994); Peterson, R.E., *The Marijuana as Medicine Scam*, Lansing, MI: Michigan Office of Drug Control Policy (undated).

30 Chusid, M.J. et al., "Pulmonary Aspergillosis, Inhalation of Contaminated Marijuana Smoke, Chronic Granulomatous Disease," *Annals of Internal Medicine* 82: 682-83 (1975).

31 Sutton, S. et al., "Possible Risk of Invasive Pulmonary Aspergillosis with Marijuana Use During Chemotherapy for Small Cell Lung Cancer," *Drug Intelligence and Clinical Pharmacology* 20: 289-90 (1986); Denning, D.W. et al., "Pulmonary Aspergillosis in the Acquired Immunodeficiency Syndrome," *New England Journal of Medicine* 324: 654-62 (1991).

15 Marijuana Smoking and the Lungs

1 Center on Addiction and Substance Abuse, *Legalization: Panacea or Pandora's Box*, New York (1995), p. 36.

2 Carlton E. Turner, *The Marijuana Controversy*, Rockville, MD: American Council for Drug Education (1981).

3 Gabriel G. Nahas and Nicholas A. Pace, "Marijuana as Chemotherapy Aid Poses Hazards," letter to the editor, *New York Times* (4 December 1993), p. 20.

4 Darryl S. Inaba and William E. Cohen, *Uppers, Downers, All-Arounders: Physical and Mental Effects of Psychoactive Drugs*, 2nd Edition, Ashland, OR: CNS Productions, Inc. (1995), p. 174.

5 Tomatis, L. (ed), *Cancer: Causes, Occurrence and Control*, Lyon: International Agency on Cancer (1990); Department of Health and Human Services, *The Health Consequences of Smoking: Chronic Obstructive Lung Disease*, Washington, DC: U.S. Government Printing Office (1984).

6 Huber, G.L. et al., "Marijuana and Tobacco Smoke: Gas-Phase Cytoxins," *Pharmacology Biochemistry and Behavior* 40: 629-36 (1991).

7 Wu, T. et al., "Pulmonary Hazards of Smoking Marijuana as Compared with

Tobacco," *New England Journal of Medicine* 318: 347-51 (1988).

8 Tashkin, D.P. et al., "Effects of Habitual Use of Marijuana and/or Cocaine on the Lung," pp. 63-87 in Chiang, N. and Hawkins, R.L. (eds), *Research Findings on Smoking of Abused Substances*, Rockville, MD: National Institute on Drug Abuse (1990); Sherrill, D.L. et al., "Respiratory Effects of Non-Tobacco Cigarettes: A Longitudinal Study in the General Population," *International Journal of Epidemiology* 20: 132-37 (1991).

9 Polen, M.R., "Health Care Use by Frequent Marijuana Smokers Who Do Not Smoke Tobacco," *Western Journal of Medicine* 158: 596-601 (1993).

10 Tashkin, D. quoted in Gagnon, L., "Marijuana Less Harmful to Lungs than Cigarettes," *Medical Post* (Quebec) (6 September 1994).

11 Tashkin, D.P., "Heavy Habitual Marijuana Smoking Does Not Cause an Accelerated Decline in FEV1 With Age," *American Journal of Respiratory and Critical Care Medicine* 155: 141-48 (1997).

12 Didcott, P. et al., *Long-Term Cannabis Users on the New South Wales North Coast*, Canberra: Australian Government Publishing Service (1997).

13 Glatt, H. et al., "Delta-1-Tetrahydrocannabinol and 1 Alpha, 2 Alpha-Epoxyhexahydrocannabinol: Mutagenicity Investigation in the Ames Test," *Mutation Research* 66: 329-35 (1979); Zimmerman, S. and Zimmerman, A.M., "Genetic Effects of Marijuana," *International Journal of the Addictions* 25: 19-33 (1990-91).

14 Leuchtenberger, C., "Effects of Marijuana (Cannabis) Smoke on Cellular Biochemistry of *In Vitro* Test Systems," pp. 177-224 in Fehr, K.O. and Kalant, K. (eds), *Cannabis and Health Hazards*, Toronto: Addiction Research Foundation (1983).

15 Novotny, M. et al., "Possible Basis for the Higher Mutagenicity of Marijuana Smoke as Compared to Tobacco Smoke," *Experientia* 32: 280-82 (1975); Hoffman, D. et al, "On the Carcinogenicity of Marijuana Smoke," *Recent Advances in Phytochemistry* 9: 63-81 (1975).

16 Harvey, R.G., *Polycyclic Aromatic Hydrocarbons: Chemistry and Carcinogenicity*, Cambridge: Oxford University Press (1991).

17 Huber, G.L. et al., "The Effects of Marijuana on the Respiratory and Cardiovascular Systems," pp. 3-18 in Chesher, G. et al. (eds), *Marijuana: an International Research Report*, Canberra: Australian Government Publishing Service (1988).

18 Fligiel, S.E.G. et al., "Bronchial Pathology in Chronic Marijuana Smokers: A Light Electron Microscope Study," *Journal of Psychoactive Drugs* 20: 33-42 (1988).

19 Fligiel, S.E.G. et al., "Pulmonary Pathology in Marijuana Smokers," pp. 43-47 in Chesher, G. et al. (eds), *Marijuana: An International Research Report*, Canberra: Autralian Government Publishing Service (1988).

20 Sridhar, K. et al., "Possible Role of Marijuana Smoking as a Carcinogen in the Development of Lung Cancer at a Young Age," *Journal of Psychoactive Drugs* 26:

285-88 (1994).

21 Substance Abuse and Mental Health Services Administration, *National House-hold Survey on Drug Abuse: Main Findings 1994*, Rockville, MD: U.S. Department of Health and Human Services (1996), pp. 46, 49.

22 Doblin, R., "The MAPS/California NORML Marijuana Waterpipe/Vaporizer Study," *Newsletter of the Multidisciplinary Association for Psychedelic Studies* 5, 1: 19-22 (1994).

23 Agurell, S. and Leander, K., "Stability, Transfer and Aborption of Cannabinoid Constituents of Cannabis (Hashish) Smoking," *Acta Pharmaceutica Suecica* 8: 391-402 (1971); Zacny, J.P. and Chait, L.D., "Breathhold Duration and Response to Marijuana Smoke," *Pharmacology Biochemistry and Behavior* 33: 481-84 (1989); Zorilosa, J. et al., "Marijuana Smoking: Effects of Varying Puff Volumes and Breathholding Duration," *Journal of Pharmacology and Experimental Therapeutics* 272: 560-69 (1995).

16 Marijuana's Persistence in the Body

1 Committees of Correspondence, *Drug Abuse Newsletter* 16 (March 1984).

2 Peggy Mann, *Marijuana Alert*, New York: McGraw-Hill Book Company (1985), p. 184.

3 Gabriel Nahas, "When Friends or Patients Ask About Marihuana," *Journal of the American Medical Association* 233 (1979), p. 79.

4 Robert DuPont, *Getting Tough on Gateway Drugs*, Washington, DC: American Psychiatric Press, Inc. (1984), p. 68.

5 Martin, B.R., "Cellular Effects of Cannabinoids," *Pharmacological Reviews* 38: 45-74 (1986).

6 Agurell, S. et al., "Pharmacokinetics and Metabolism of Delta-1-Tetrahydrocannabinol and Other Cannabinoids with Emphasis on Man," *Pharmacological Reviews* 38: 21-43 (1986); Cone, E.J. et al., "Acute Effects of Smoking Marijuana on Hormones, Subjective Effects and Performance in Male Human Subjects, *Pharmacology Biochemistry and Behavior* 24: 1749-54 (1986).

7 Barnett, G. et al., "Behavioral Pharmacokinetics of Marijuana," *Psychopharmacology* 85: 51-56 (1985); Cone, E.J. and Huestis, M.A., "Relating Blood Concentrations of Tetrahydrocannabinol and Metabolites to Pharmacologic Effects and Time of Marijuana Usage," *Therapeutic Drug Monitoring* 15: 527-32 (1993); Morgan, J.P., "Marijuana Metabolism in the Context of Urine Testing for Cannabinoid Metabolite," *Journal of Psychoactive Drugs* 20: 107-15 (1988).

8 Swatek, R., "Marijuana Use: Persistence and Urinary Elimination," *Journal of Substance Abuse Treatment* 1: 265-70 (1984).

9 Garrett, E.R., "Pharmacokinetics and Disposition of Delta-9-Tetrahydrocannabinol and its Metabolites," *Advances in Bioscience* 22-23: 105-21 (1978).

10 Hollister, L.E., "Health Aspects of Cannabis," *Pharmacological Reviews* 38:1-20 (1986).

11 Moscowitz, H. et al., "Duration of Skills Performance Impairment Under Marijuana," *American Association for Automotive Medicine Proceedings* 181: 87-96 (1979); Chait, L.D. et al., "'Hangover' Effects The Morning After Marijuana Smoking," *Drug and Alcohol Dependence* 15: 229-38 (1985); Yesavage, J.A. et al., "Carry-Over Effects of Marijuana Intoxication on Aircraft Pilot Performance: A Preliminary Report," *American Journal of Psychiatry* 142: 1325-29 (1985); Leirer, V.O. et al., "Marijuana Carry-Over Effects on Aircraft Pilot Performance," *Aviation, Space, and Environmental Medicine* 62: 221-27 (1991).

12 Chait, L.D., "Subjective and Behavioral Effects of Marijuana the Morning After," *Psychopharmacology* 100: 328-33 (1990); Cocchetto, D.M. et al., "Relationship Between Plasma Delta-9-Tetrahydrocannabinol Concentration and Pharmacologic Effects in Man," *Psychopharmacology* 75: 158-64 (1981); Hollister, L.E. et al., "Do Plasma Concentrations of Delta-9-Tetrahydrocannabinol Reflect the Degree of Intoxication?," *Journal of Clinical Pharmacology* 21: 171-77S (1981); Lindgren, J.C. et al., "Clinical Effects and Plasma Levels of Delta-9-Tetrahydrocannabinol (Delta-9-THC) in Heavy and Light Users of Cannabis," *Psychopharmacology* 74: 802-12 (1981); Perez-Reyes, M. et al., "The Clinical Pharmacology and Dynamics of Marijuana Cigarette Smoking," *Journal of Clinical Pharmacology* 21: 201-07S (1981); Perez-Reyes, M. et al., "Comparison of Effects of Marijuana Cigarettes of Three Different Potencies," *Clinical Pharmacology and Therapeutics* 31: 617-24 (1982); Ohlsson, A. et al., "Plasma Delta-9-Tetrahydrocannabinol Concentrations and Clinical Effects After Oral and Intravenous Administration and Smoking," *Clinical Pharmacology and Therapeutics* 28: 409-16 (1980); Leirer, V.O. et al., "Marijuana, Aging, and Task Difficult Effects on Pilot Performance," *Aviation, Space, and Environmental Medicine* 60: 1145-52 (1989); Janowsky, D.S. et al., "Marijuana Effects on Simulated Flying Ability," *American Journal of Psychiatry* 133: 384-88 (1976); Cone et al. (1986), see note 6.

13 Hollister (1986), see note 10.

14 Kreuz, D.S. and Axelrod, J., "Delta-9-Tetrahydrocannabinol: Localization in Body Fat," *Science* 179: 391-92 (1973); Johansson, E. et al, "Analysis of Delta-1-Tetrahydrocannabinol (Delta-1-THC) in Human Plasma and Fat After Smoking," pp. 291-96 in Chesher, E. et al. (eds), *Marijuana: An International Report*, Canberra: Australian Government Publishing Service (1988).

15 Siegel, G.J. et al., *Basic Neurochemistry*, New York: Raven Press (1989).

16 Ryrfeldt, A., "Whole Body Autoradiography of Delta-1-Tetrahydrocannabinol and Delta-6-Tetrahydrocannabinol in Mouse," *Acta Pharmaceutica Suecica* 10: 13-28 (1973); Nahas, G. et al., "The Kinetics of Cannabinoid Distribution and Storage with Special Reference to the Brain and Testes," *Journal of Clinical Pharmacology* 21: 208-14S (1981); Bronson, M. et al., "Distribution and Disposition of Delta-9-Tetrahydrocannabinol (THC) in Different Tissues of the Rat," pp. 309-17 in Agurell, S. et al. (eds), *The Cannabinoids: Chemical, Pharmacologic, and*

Therapeutic Aspects, Orlando: Academic Press (1984); Kreuz and Axelrod (1973), see note 14.

17 Hollister (1986), see note 10.

18 Morgan, J.P., "Urine Testing for Cannabinoid Metabolite; Technical and Practical Problems," pp. 333-44 in Chesher, G. et al. (eds), *Marijuana: An International Report*, Canberra: Australian Government Publishing Service (1988).

17 *Marijuana and Highway Safety*

1 Center on Addiction and Substance Abuse, *Legalization: Panacea or Pandora's Box*, New York (1995), p. 36.

2 Neil Swan, "A Look at Marijuana's Harmful Effects," *NIDA Notes* 9, 2 (1994), p. 14.

3 Herbert Moskowitz and Robert Petersen, *Marijuana and Driving: A Review*, Rockville, MD: American Council for Drug Education (1982), p. 7.

4 Peggy Mann, *Marijuana Alert*, New York: McGraw-Hill (1985), p. 265.

5 Jacobs, J.B., *Drunk Driving: An American Dilemma*, Chicago: University of Chicago Press (1989).

6 National Commission on Marihuana and Drug Abuse, *Marihuana: A Signal of Misunderstanding*, Washington, DC: U.S. Government Printing Office (1972).

7 Robbe, H. and O'Hanlon, J., *Marijuana and Actual Driving Performance*, Washington, DC: Department of Transportation (1993), p. 107.

8 Moskowitz, H., "Marijuana and Driving," *Accident Analysis and Prevention* 17: 323-45 (1985).

9 Stein, A.C. et al., *A Simulator Study of the Combined Effects of Alcohol and Marijuana on Driving Behavior; Phase II*, Washington, DC: U.S. Department of Transportation (1983); Hansteen, R.W. et al., "Effects of Cannabis and Alcohol on Automobile Driving and Psychomotor Tracking," *Annals of New York Academy of Sciences* 282: 240-56 (1976); Moskowitz, H. et al., "Marihuana: Effects on Simulated Driving Performance," *Accident Analysis and Prevention* 8: 45-50 (1976); Crancer, A. et al., "Comparison of the Effects of Marihuana and Alcohol on Simulated Driving Performance," *Science* 164: 851-54 (1969).

10 Klonoff, H., "Marijuana and Driving in Real-Life Situations," *Science* 186: 317-24 (1974); Sutton, L.R., "The Effects of Alcohol, Marijuana and Their Combination on Driving Ability," *Journal of Studies on Alcohol* 44: 438-45 (1983); Peck, R.C. et al., "The Effects of Marijuana and Alcohol on Actual Driving Performance," *Alcohol, Drugs and Driving* 2: 135- 54 (1986); Hansteen et al. (1976), see note 9.

11 Smiley, A., "Marijuana: On-Road and Driving Simulator Studies," *Alcohol, Drugs and Driving* 2: 121-34 (1986); Chesher, G.B., "Cannabis and Road Safety: An Outline of the Research Studies to Examine the Effects of Cannabis on Driv-

ing Skills and On Actual Driving Performance," pp. 67-96 in *Inquiry into the Effects of Drugs (Other than Alcohol) on Road Safety in Victoria*, Report of the Parliament of Victoria, Melbourne: Government Printer (1995); Dott, A.B., *Effect of Marihuana on Risk Acceptance in a Simulated Passing Task*, Rockville, MD: U.S. Department of Health, Education, and Welfare (1972); Moskowitz (1985), see note 8.

12 Robbe and O'Hanlon (1993), see note 7.

13 Mathias, R., "Marijuana Impairs Driving-Related Skills and Workplace Performance," *NIDA Notes* 11, 1: 6 (1996).

14 Moskowitz, H. and McGlothlin, W., "Effects of Marihuana on Auditory Signal Detection," *Psychopharmacology* 40: 137-40 (1974); Moskowitz et al. (1976), see note 9.

15 Barnett, G. et al., "Behavioral Pharmacokinetics of Marijuana," *Psychopharmacology* 85: 51-56 (1985); Smiley (1986), see note 11.

16 Martin, B.R., "Cellular Effects of Cannabinoids," *Pharmacological Reviews* 38: 45-74 (1986).

17 McBay, A.J. and Owens, S.M., "Marijuana and Driving," pp. 257-63 in Harris, L.S. (ed), *Problems of Drug Dependence 1980*, Washington, DC: U.S. Government Printing Office (1981); Terhune, K.W. et al., *The Incidence and Role of Drugs in Fatally Injured Drivers*, Washington, DC: Department of Transportation (1992); Cimbura, G. et al., "Incidence and Toxicological Aspects of Drugs Detected in 484 Fatally Injured Drivers and Pedestrians in Canada," *Journal of Forensic Sciences* 27: 855-67 (1982); Mason, A.P. and McBay, A.J., "Ethanol, Marijuana, and Other Drug Use in 600 Drivers Killed in Single-Vehicular Crashes in North Carolina," *Journal of Forensic Sciences* 29: 987-1026 (1984); Crouch, D.J. et al., "The Prevalence of Drugs and Alcohol in Fatally Injured Truck Drivers," *Journal of Forensic Sciences* 38: 1342-53 (1993); Drummer, O.H., "A Review of the Contribution of Drugs in Drivers to Road Accidents," pp. 1-28 in *Inquiry into the Effects of Drugs (Other than Alcohol) on Road Safety in Victoria*, Report of the Parliament of Victoria, Melbourne: Government Printer (1995); Cimbura, G. et al., "Incidence and Toxicological Aspects of Cannabis and Ethanol in 1394 Fatally Injured Drivers and Pedestrians in Ontario (1982-1984)," *Journal of Forensic Sciences* 35: 1035-41 (1990).

18 Terhune, K., *The Role of Alcohol, Marijuana and Other Drugs in the Accidents of Injured Drivers*, Washington, DC: Department of Transportation (1982).

19 Williams, A. et al., "Drugs in Fatally Injured Young Male Drivers," *Public Health Reports* 100: 19-25 (1985); Terhune et al. (1992), see note 17; Drummer (1995), see note 17.

20 Drummer (1995), see note 17, p 13.

21 Chait, L.D. and Pierri, J., "Effects of Smoked Marijuana on Human Performance: A Critical Review," pp. 387-424 in Murphy, L. and Bartke, A. (eds),

Marijuana/Cannabinoids: Neurobiology and Neurophysiology, Boca Raton: CRC Press (1992).

22 Ellingstad, V.S. et al., *Alcohol, Marihuana, and Risk Taking,* Washington, DC: National Highway Traffic Safety Administration (1973); Stein et al. (1983), see note 9; Dott (1972), see note 11.

23 Cappell, H.D. and Pliner, P.L., "Volitional Control of Marijuana Intoxication: A Study of the Ability to 'Come Down' on Command," *Journal of Abnormal Psychology* 82: 428-34 (1973); Smiley (1986), see note 11.

24 Mayhew, D.R. et al., "Alcohol and Cannabis Among Fatally Injured Motorcyclists," pp. 267-70 in Noordzj, P.C. et al. (eds), *Alcohol, Drugs and Traffic Safety,* Amsterdam: Excerpta Medica (1987); Soderstrom, C.A. et al., "Marijuana and Alcohol Use Among 1,023 Trauma Patients," *Archives of Surgery* 123: 733-37 (1988); Soderstrom, C.A. et al., "Marijuana and Other Drug Use Among Automobile and Motorcycle Drivers Treated at a Trauma Center," *Accident Analysis and Prevention* 27: 131-35 (1995).

25 Brookoff, D. et al., "Testing Reckless Drivers for Cocaine and Marijuana," *New England Journal of Medicine* 331: 518-22 (1994).

26 Johnson, V. and White, H.R., "An Investigation of Factors Related to Intoxicated Driving Behaviors Among Youth," *Journal of Studies on Alcohol* 50: 320-30 (1989).

27 Reeve, V.C. et al., "Hemolyzed Blood and Serum Levels of Delta-9-THC: Effects on the Performance of Roadside Sobriety Tests," *Journal of Forensic Sciences* 28: 963-71 (1983); Cocchetto, D.M., "Relationship Between Plasma Delta-9-Tetrahydrocannabinol Concentration and Pharmacologic Effects in Man," *Psychopharmacology* 75: 158-64 (1981); Chesher (1995), see note 11.

28 Page, T.E., "The Drug Recognition Expert Response," pp. 121-47 in *Inquiry in the Effects of Drugs (Other than Alcohol) on Road Safety in Victoria,* Report of the Parliament of Victoria, Melbourne: Government Printer (1995); Brookoff et al. (1994), see note 25.

18 Marijuana-Related Hospital Emergencies

1 Lee Brown, Director of National Drug Control Policy, quoted in U.S. Department of Health and Human Services Press Release, "National Drug Survey Results Released with New Youth Public Education Materials," Rockville, MD (12 September 1995).

2 Donna Shalala, Secretary of Health and Human Services, "Say 'No' to Legalization of Marijuana," *Wall Street Journal* (18 August 1995), p. A10.

3 Charles Shuster, Director of National Institute on Drug Abuse, quoted in Drug Enforcement Administration, *Drug Legalization: Myths and Misconceptions,* Wash-

ington, DC: U.S. Department of Justice (1994), p. 5.

4   Substance Abuse and Mental Health Services Administration, *Annual Emergency Room Data 1993*, Statistical Series, Series I, Number 13-A, Rockville, MD: U.S. Department of Health and Human Services (1996a); Substance Abuse and Mental Health Services Administration, *Preliminary Estimates from the Drug Abuse Warning Network*, Advance Report Number 17, Rockville, MD: U.S. Department of Health and Human Services (1996b).

5   Roberts, C.D., "Data Quality of the Drug Abuse Warning Network," *American Journal of Drug and Alcohol Abuse* 22: 389-401 (1996).

6   Substance Abuse and Mental Health Services Administration, *Preliminary Estimates from the 1995 National Household Survey on Drug Abuse*, Rockville, MD: U.S. Department of Health and Human Services (1996).

7   Substance Abuse and Mental Health Services Administration (1996a), see note 4, p.34.

8   Substance Abuse and Mental Health Services Administration, *Annual Medical Examiner Data 1994*, Statistical Series, Series I, Number 14-B, Rockville, MD: U.S. Department of Health and Human Services (1996).

19   *The Potency of Marijuana*

1   Melinda Henneberger, "Pot Surges Back, But It's, Like, a Whole New World," *New York Times* (6 February 1994), p. E18.

2   Lee Brown, Director of National Drug Control Policy, quoted in "Interview with Lee Brown," *Dallas Morning News* (21 May 1995).

3   Drug Enforcement Administration, *U.S. Drug Threat Assessment, 1993*, Washington, DC: U.S. Department of Justice (1993), p. 63.

4   Mark A.R. Kleiman, *Marijuana: Costs of Abuse, Costs of Control*, Westport, CT: Greenwood Press (1989), p. 29.

5   William Bennett, Director of National Drug Control Policy, remarks at Conference of Mayors (23 April 1990).

6   Tartaglino, A., Subcommittee Hearings to Investigate the Administrations of the Internal Security Act and other Internal Security Laws, Senate Judiciary Committee, *Marihuana-Hashish Epidemic and its Impact on United States Security*, Washington, DC: U.S. Government Printing Office (1974); DuPont, R., interview in *Science* 129 (1976), p. 647; Cohen, S., "Marihuana: A New Ball Game?" *Drug Abuse and Alcoholism Newsletter* 8,4 (1979); Maugh, T.H., "Marihuana: New Support for Immune and Reproductive Hazards," *Science* 190: 865-67 (1975).

7   Drug Enforcement Administration, *Drug Legalization: Myths and Misconceptions*, Washington, DC: U.S. Department of Justice (1994), p. 4.

8   MacDonald, D.I., *Drugs, Drinking and Adolescents*, Chicago: Year Book Medical Publishers (1984), p. 57.

9   *Potency Monitoring Project, Quarterly Reports*, University of Mississippi: Research Institute of Pharmaceutical Sciences (1974 to 1996).

10 Perez-Reyes, M. et al., "A Comparison of the Pharmacological Activity of Delta-9-Tetrahydrocannabinol and Its Monohydroxylated Metabolites in Man," *Experientia* 29: 1009-10 (1973); Avico, R. et al., "Variations of Tetrahydrocannabinol Content in Cannabis Plants to Distinguish the Fibre-Type from Drug-Type Plants," *Bulletin on Narcotics* 37: 61-65 (1985).

11 Chait, L.D. et al., "Discriminative Stimulus and Subjective Effects of Smoked Marijuana in Humans," *Psychopharmacology* 94: 206-12 (1988); Jones, R.T., "Marijuana-Induced 'High': Influence of Expectation, Setting and Previous Drug Experience," *Pharmacological Reviews* 23: 359-69 (1971); Hochman, J.S. and Brill, N.Q., "Marijuana Intoxication: Pharmacological and Psychological Effects," *Diseases of the Nervous System* 32: 676-79 (1971).

12 Warner, R., *Invisible Hand: The Marijuana Business*, New York: William Morrow (1986); Novak, W., *High Culture: Marijuana in the Lives of Americans*, New York: Alfred A. Knopf (1981); Goldman, A., *Grass Roots: Marijuana in America Today*, New York: Harper & Row (1979).

13 Mikuriya, T.H. and Aldrich, A.R., "Cannabis 1988: Old Drug, New Dangers; The Potency Question," *Journal of Psychoactive Drugs* 20: 47-55 (1988); Lerner, M. and Zeffert, J.T., "Determination of Tetrahydrocannabinol and Related Compounds," *Bulletin on Narcotics* 20: 53-54 (1968); Ritzlin, R.S. et al., "Delta-9-Tetrahydrocannabinol Levels in Street Samples of Marijuana and Hashish: Correlation to User Reactions," *Clinical Toxicology* 15: 45-53 (1979); Starks, M., *Marijuana Potency*, Berkeley: And/Or Press (1977); Perry, D., "Street Drug Analysis and Drug Use Trends, Part II, 1969-1976," *PharmChem Newsletter* 6, 4 (1977).

14 "Summary of Street Drug Results, 1973," *PharmChem Newsletter* 3, 3 (1974); Mikuriya and Aldrich (1988), see note 13.

15 Messinger, T.A., "A Decade of Drug Analysis Results: 1973-1983," *PharmChem Newsletter* 13, 2 (1984); Perry (1977), see note 13.

16 ElSohly, M.A. et al., "Constituents of *Cannabis Sativa* L. XXIV: The Potency of Confiscated Marijuana, Hashish, and Hash Oil Over a Ten-Year Period," *Journal of Forensic Sciences* 29: 500-14 (1984).

17 Nahas, G.G., *Marihuana: Deceptive Weed*, New York: Raven Press (1973); National Commission on Marihuana and Drug Abuse, *Marihuana: A Signal of Misunderstanding*, Washington, DC: U.S. Government Printing Office (1972); Sloman, L., *Reefer Madness: Marijuana in America*, New York: Grove Press, Inc. (1979); Langer, J.H., "Drugs of Abuse," *Drug Enforcement Magazine* 2, 2: 27 (1975); Goldman (1979), see note 12.

18 Turner, C. et al., "Constituents of *Cannabis Sativa* L. IV: Stability of Cannabinoids in Stored Plant Material," *Journal of Pharmaceutical Sciences* 62: 1601-05 (1973).

19 Mikuriya and Aldrich (1988), see note 13.

20 Pear, R., "155 Indicted as Two-Year Federal Drug Inquiry Ends," *New York Times* (13 March 1981), p. A12; Warner (1986), see note 12; Kleiman (1980), see note 4.

21 Tartaglino (1974), see note 6.

22 Drug Policy Office, *Federal Strategy for Prevention of Drug Abuse and Drug Trafficking,* Washington, DC: The White House (1982).

23 "How Much Marijuana do Americans Really Smoke," *Forensic Drug Abuse Advisor* 7, 1: 7-8 (1995).

24 *Potency Monitoring Project, Report #46,* University of Mississippi: Research Institute of Pharmaceutical Sciences (1993).

25 Department of Health and Human Services, "Marijuana and the Cannabinoids," pp. 131-44 in *Drug Abuse and Drug Abuse Research,* Third Triennial Report to Congress from the Secretary (1991).

26 Perez-Reyes, M. et al., "Comparison of Effects of Marijuana Cigarettes of Three Different Potencies," *Clinical Pharmacology and Therapeutics* 31: 617-24 (1982); Cappell, H. et al., "Alcohol and Marihuana: A Comparison of Effects on a Temporally Controlled Operant in Humans," *Journal of Pharmacology and Experimental Therapeutics* 182: 195-202 (1972); Chait, L.D., "Delta-9-Tetrahydrocannabinol Content and Human Marijuana Self- Administration," *Psychopharmacology* 98: 51-55 (1989).

27 Heishman, S.J. et al., "Effects of Tetrahydrocannabinol Content on Marijuana Smoking Behavior, Subjective Reports, and Performance," *Pharmacology Biochemistry and Behavior* 34: 173-79 (1989); Perez-Reyes, M., "Pharmacodynamics of Certain Drugs of Abuse," pp. 287-311 in Barnett, G. and Chiang, C.N. (eds), *Pharmacokinetics and Pharmacodynamics of Psychoactive Drugs,* Foster City, CA: Biomedical Publications (1985); Perez-Reyes, M., "Marijuana Smoking: Factors that Influence the Bioavailablity of Tetrahydrocannabinol," pp. 42-62 in Chiang, N.C. and Hawks, R.L. (eds), *Research Findings on Smoking of Abused Substances,* Rockville, MD: National Institute on Drug Abuse (1990).

28 Chait, L.D. and Zacny, J.P., "Reinforcing and Subjective Effects of Oral Delta-9-THC and Smoked Marijuana in Humans," *Psychopharmacology* 107: 255-62 (1992); Kelly, T.H. et al., "Effects of Delta-9-THC on Marijuana Smoking, Dose Choice, and Verbal Report of Drug Liking," *Journal of Experimental Analysis of Behavior* 61: 203-11 (1994); Wu, H. et al, "Effects of Smoked Marijuana of Varying Potency on Ventilatory Drive and Metabolic Rate," *American Review of Respiratory Disease* 146: 716-21 (1992); Chait, L.D. et al., "A Cumulative Dosing Procedure for Administering Marijuana Smoke to Humans," *Pharmacology Biochemistry and Behavior* 29: 553-57 (1988); Higgins, S.T. and Stitzer, M.L., "Acute Marijuana Effects on Social Conversation," *Psychopharmacology* 89: 234-38 (1986); Cappell, H. et al. (1972), see note 26; Heishman et al. (1989), see note 27.

29 Herning, R.I. et al., "Tetrahydrocannabinol Content and Differences in Marijuana Smoking Behavior," *Psychopharmacology* 90: 160-62 (1986).

30 Chait (1989), see note 26.

31 Oviedo, A. et al., "Chronic Cannabinoid Administration Alters Cannabinoid Receptor Binding in Rat Brain: A Quantitative Autoradiographic Study," *Brain Research* 616: 293-302 (1993).

32 Ritzlin et al. (1979), see note 13.

33 Calahan, D. and Room, R., *Problem Drinking Among American Men,* New Brunswick, NJ: Rutgers Center of Alcohol Studies (1974); Swift, G.C. and Tiplady, D., "The Effects of Age on the Response to Caffeine," *Psychopharmacology* 94: 29-31 (1988).

34 Johnston, L.D. et al., *National Survey Results on Drug Use from the Monitoring the Future Study, 1975-1995, Volume I: Secondary School Students,* Rockville, MD: U.S. Department of Health and Human Services (1996), p. 198.

35 Rosenthal, E., *Marijuana Growing Tips,* Berkeley, CA: And/Or Books (1986); Frank, M., *Marijuana Growers' Insiders Guide,* Los Angeles: Red Eye Press (1988).

20   *Preventing Marijuana Use*

1   Center on Addiction and Substance Abuse, *National Survey of American Attitudes on Substance Abuse,* New York (1995), p. 28.

2   Lee Brown, Director of National Drug Control Policy, remarks at *National Conference on Marijuana Use: Prevention, Treatment, and Research,* sponsored by the National Institute on Drug Abuse, Arlington, VA (July 1995).

3   Joseph A. Califano, "Don't Stop This War," *Washington Post* (26 May 1996), p. C7.

4   Donna Shalala, quoted in "Marijuana: A Recurring Problem," *Prevention Pipeline* 8, 5 (1995), p. 2.

5   James Burke, Partnership for a Drug-Free America, remarks on MS-NBC with Tom Brokaw (3 September 1996).

6   Mathea Falco, *The Making of a Drug-Free America: Programs That Work,* New York: Times Books (1992), p. 202.

7   Drug Policy Office, *Federal Strategy for Prevention of Drug Abuse and Drug Trafficking,* Washington, DC: The White House (1982).

8   Baum, D., *Smoke and Mirrors: The War on Drugs and the Politics of Failure,* Boston: Little, Brown and Company (1996).

9   National Institute on Justice, "The DARE Program: A Review of Prevalence, User Satisfaction, and Effectiveness," *National Institute of Justice Update,* Washington, DC: U.S. Department of Justice (1994); Bureau of Justice Statistics, *An Introduction to DARE: Drug Abuse Resistance Education,* second edition, Washington, DC: U.S. Department of Justice (1992).

10 U.S. Department of Education and U.S. Department of Health and Human

Services, *Report to Congress and the White House on the Nature and Effectiveness of Federal, State, and Local Drug Prevention/Education Programs*, Washington, DC: U.S. Government Printing Office (1987); U.S. Department of Education, *Drug Prevention Curricula: A Guide to Selection and Implementation*, Washington, DC: U.S. Government Printing Office (1988).

11   Interview with Thomas A. Hedrick, Partnership for a Drug-Free America, *The Facts About Tobacco, Alcohol and Other Drugs* 4, 2: 1 (1995).

12   Center for Substance Abuse Prevention, *Young Teens: Who They Are and How to Communicate with Them About Alcohol and Other Drugs*, Rockville, MD: U.S. Department of Health and Human Services (1991).

13   University of Michigan Press Release, "The Rise in Drug Use Among American Teens Continues in 1996," Ann Arbor: News and Information Services (19 December 1996).

14   University of Michigan (1996), see note 13.

15   Johnston, L.D. et al., *National Survey Results on Drug Use from the Monitoring the Future Study, 1975-1995, Volume I: Secondary School Students*, Rockville, MD: U.S. Department of Health and Human Services (1996).

16   Shedler, J. and Block, J., "Adolescent Drug Use and Psychological Health," *American Psychologist* 45: 612-30 (1990).

17   Johnston et al. (1996), see note 15.

18   Block, J. et al., "Longitudinally Foretelling Drug Usage in Adolescence: Early Childhood Personality and Environmental Precursors," *Child Development* 59: 336-55 (1988); Robins, L.N. and McEvoy, L., "Conduct Problems as Predictors of Substance Abuse," pp. 182-204 in Robins, L.N. and Rutter, M. (eds), *Straight and Devious Pathways From Childhood to Adulthood*, Cambridge: Cambridge University Press (1990); Donovan, J.E. et al., "Syndrome of Problem Behavior in Adolescence: A Replication," *Journal of Consulting and Clinical Psychology* 56: 762-65 (1988); Scheier, L.M. and Newcombe, M.D., "Psychosocial Predictors of Drug Use Initiation and Escalation: An Expansion of the Multiple Risk Factors Hypothesis Using Longitudinal Data," *Contemporary Drug Problems* 18: 31-73 (1991); Farrell, A.D. et al., "Relationship Between Drug Use and Other Problem Behaviors in Urban Adolescents," *Journal of Consulting and Clinical Psychology* 60: 705-12 (1992); Kandel, D.P. and Davies, M., "High School Students Who Use Crack and Other Drugs," *Archives of General Psychiatry* 53: 71-80 (1996); Shedler and Block (1990), see note 16.

19   Shalala, D., *Reality Check: Q & A*, Rockville, MD: Center for Substance Abuse Prevention (1996).

20   Remarks at *National Conference on Marijuana Use* (July 1995), see note 2.

21   Alan Leschner, quoted in Swan, N., "Marijuana, Other Drug Use Among Teens Continues to Rise," *NIDA Notes* 10, 2 (1995), p. 2.

22   Senate Judiciary Committee Hearings, *Teenage Drug Use* (4 September 1996).

23   Quoted in Suro, R., "U.S., Private Sector Would Split $3 Million Cost," *Washington Post* (13 February 1997), p. A1.

24   Flay, B.R. and Sobel, J.L., "The Role of Mass Media in Preventing Adolescent Substance Abuse," pp. 5-35 in Glynn, T.J. et al. (eds), *Preventing Adolescent Drug Abuse: Intervention Strategies*, Rockville, MD: National Institute on Drug Abuse (1983).

25   Black, G.S., *Changing Attitudes Toward Drug Use*, Rochester, NY: Gordon S. Black Corporation (1988).

26   National Institute on Drug Abuse, "National Ad Campaign 'Unsells' Drugs," *NIDA Notes* 3, 2: 4 (1988); Partnership for a Drug-Free America, *1995 Partnership Attitude Tracking Survey*, New York (1996).

27   Brecher, E.M., *Licit and Illicit Drugs*, Boston: Little, Brown and Company (1972).

28   Bass, L., "Public Perceptions of Marijuana: Knowledge, Attitudes, and Norms," paper presented at *National Conference on Marijuana Use: Prevention, Treatment, and Research*, sponsored by the National Institute on Drug Abuse, Arlington, VA (July 1995); Brown, L., remarks at *National Conference on Marijuana Use* (July 1995); Burke, J.E., Partnership for a Drug-Free America Press Release (12 December 1994); Drug Enforcement Administration, *Marijuana Blunts*, Washington, DC: U.S. Department of Justice (1994); Califano, J.A., "Forward," pp. 2-4 in Center on Addiction and Substance Abuse, *National Survey of American Attitudes on Substance Abuse*, New York (1995); Guttman, M., "The New Pot Culture," *USA Weekend* (16 February 1996), pp. 4-7. ·

29   Bonnie, R.J. and Whitebread, C.N., *The Marihuana Conviction: A History of Maihuana Prohibition in the United States*, Charlottesville: University of Virginia Press (1974); National Commission on Marihuana and Drug Abuse, *Marihuana: A Signal of Misunderstanding*, Washington, DC: U.S. Government Printing Office (1972).

30   Braucht, G.N. et al., "Drug Education: A Review of Goals, Approaches and Effectiveness, and a Paradigm for Evaluation," *Quarterly Journal of Studies of Alcohol* 34: 1279-92 (1973); Boldt, R.F. et al., "A Survey and Assessment of the Current Status of Drug-Related Instructional Programs in Secondary and Elementary Institutions," pp. 455-547 in National Commission on Marihuana and Drug Abuse, *Drug Use in America: Problem in Perspective, Volume 2*, Washington, DC: U.S. Government Printing Office (1973); Swisher, J. and Hoffman, A., "Information: The Irrelevent Variable in Drug Education," pp. 49-62 in Corder, B. et al. (eds), *Drug Abuse Prevention*, Dubuque, IA: W.C. Brown Company (1975); Blum, R. et al., *Drug Education: Results and Recommendations*, Lexington, MA: Lexington Books (1976); Berberian, R.M. et al., "The Effectiveness of Drug Education Programs: A Critical Review," *Health Education Monographs* 4: 377-98 (1976); Goodstadt, M.S., "Drug Education—A Turn On Or a Turn Off?," *Journal of Drug Education* 10: 89-99 (1980); Schaps, E. et al., "A Review of 127 Drug Abuse Prevention Programs," *Journal of Drug Issues* 11: 17-34

(1981); Moskowitz, J.M., "Evaluation of a Substance Abuse Prevention Program for Junior High School Students," *International Journal of the Addictions* 19: 419-30 (1984); Bangert-Drowns, R.L., "The Effects of School-Based Substance Abuse Education—A Meta-Analysis," *Journal of Drug Education* 18: 243-64 (1988); Tobler, N.S., "Meta-Analysis of 143 Adolescent Drug Prevention Programs: Quantitative Outcome Results of Program Participants Compared to a Control or Comparison Group," *Journal of Drug Issues* 16: 537-67 (1986).

31   DeJong, W., *Arresting the Demand For Drugs: Police and School Partnerships to Prevent Drug Abuse*, Washington, DC: National Institute of Justice (1987); Botvin, G.J., "Principles of Prevention," pp. 19-44 in Coombs, R.H. and Ziedonis, D.M. (eds), *Handbook on Drug Abuse Prevention: A Comprehensive Strategy to Prevent the Abuse of Alcohol and Other Drugs*, Boston: Allyn and Bacon (1995); Ellickson, P.L., "Schools," pp. 93-120 in Coombs, R.H. and Ziedonis, D.M. (eds), *Handbook on Drug Abuse Prevention: A Comprehensive Strategy to Prevent the Abuse of Alcohol and Other Drugs*, Boston: Allyn and Bacon (1995); Falco (1992), see note 6.

32   U.S. Department of Education (1988), see note 10.

33   Pentz, M.A. et al., "A Multicommunity Trial for Primary Prevention of Adolescent Drug Abuse: Effects on Drug Use Prevalence," *Journal of the American Medical Association* 261: 3259-66 (1989); Johnson, C.A. et al., "Relative Effectiveness of Comprehensive Community Programming for Drug Abuse Prevention With High-Risk and Low-Risk Adolescents," *Journal of Consulting and Clinical Psychology* 58: 447-56 (1990).

34   Flay, B.R. et al., "Effects of Program Implementation on Adolescent Drug Use Behavior," *Evaluation Review* 14: 416-49 (1990); Ellickson, P.L. and Bell, R.M., "Drug Prevention in Junior High: A Multi-Cite Longitudinal Test," *Science* 247: 1299-1305 (1990); Ellickson, P.L. et al., "Preventing Adolescent Drug Use: Long-Term Results of a Junior High Program," *American Journal of Public Health* 83: 856-61 (1993); Botvin, G.J. et al., "Long-Term Follow-Up of a Randomized Drug Abuse Prevention Trial in a White Middle-Class Population," *Journal of the American Medical Association* 273: 1106-12 (1995); Hansen, W.B. et al., "Affective and Social Influences Approaches to the Prevention of Multiple Substance Abuse among Seventh Grade Students: Results from Project SMART," *Preventative Medicine* 17: 135-54 (1988).

35   Wysong, E. et al., "Truth and Dare: Tracking Drug Education to Graduation and as Symbolic Politics," *Social Problems* 41: 448-72 (1994); Ennett, S.T. et al., "How Effective Is Drug Abuse Resistance Training? A Meta-Analysis of Project DARE Outcome Evaluations," *American Journal of Public Health* 84: 1394-1401 (1994); Rosenbaum, D.P. et al., "Cops in the Classroom: A Longitudinal Evaluation of Drug Abuse Resistance Education (DARE)," *Journal of Research in Crime and Delinquency* 31: 3-31 (1994); Dukes, R.L. et al., "Three-Year Follow-Up of Drug Abuse Resistance Training (D.A.R.E.)," *Evaluation Review* 20: 49-66 (1996).

36 Brown, J.H. et al., "Students and Substances: Social Power in Drug Education," *Educational Evaluation and Policy Analysis* 19: 65-82 (1997).

37 Johnston et al. (1996), see note 15.

38 National Commission on Drug-Free Schools, *Toward a Drug-Free Generation: A Nation's Responsibility*, Washington, DC: U.S. Department of Education (1990).

39 Brown et al. (1997), see note 36.

40 U.S. Department of Education (1988), see note 10, p. 13.

41 United States General Accounting Office, *Drug Abuse Prevention: Federal Efforts to Identify Exemplary Programs Need Stronger Design*, Washington, DC: United States General Accounting Office (1991).

42 Saunders, B., "Illicit Drugs and Harm Reduction Education," *Addiction Research* 2: i-iii (1995); Goodstadt, M.S., *Drug Education*, Washington, DC: U.S. Department of Justice (1988); Moskowitz, J.M., "The Primary Prevention of Alcohol Problems: A Critical Review of the Research Literature," *Journal of Studies on Alcohol* 50: 54-88 (1989); Polich, J.M. et al., *Strategies for Controlling Adolescent Drug Use*, Santa Monica, CA: Rand Corporation (1984); Cohen, J., "Drug Education, Politics, Propaganda and Censorship," *International Journal of Drug Policy* 7: 153-57 (1996); Rosenbaum, M., *Kids, Drugs, and Drug Education: A Harm Reduction Approach*, San Francisco: National Council on Crime and Delinquency (1996); Engs, R.C. and Fors, S.W., "Drug Abuse Hysteria: The Challenge of Keeping Perspective," *Journal of School Health* 58: 26-28 (1988); Duncan, D.F., "Drug Abuse Prevention in Post-Legalization America: What Could It Be Like?," *Journal of Primary Prevention* 12: 317-22 (1992); Brown, J.H., "Drug Education and Democracy [In]Action," *Multidisciplinary Association for Psychedelic Studies* 7, 1: 28-34 (1997); Nadelmann, E.A., "Stop Kidding About Drug-Free Kids," *Los Angeles Times* (3 January 1997).

43 National Institute on Drug Abuse, *Doing Drug Education: The Role of the School Teacher*, Rockville, MD (1975).

44 National Institute on Drug Abuse, *Let's Talk About Drug Abuse: Some Questions and Answers*, Rockville, MD: U.S. Department of Health, Education, and Welfare (1979); National Institute on Drug Abuse, *This Side Up: Making Decisions About Drugs*, Rockville, MD: U.S. Department of Health, Education, and Welfare (1977).

45 Swisher, J.D., "Prevention Issues," pp. 423-35 in DuPont, R.L. et al. (eds), *Handbook on Drug Abuse*, Rockville, MD: National Institute on Drug Abuse (1979); Abrams, A. et al. (eds), *Accountability in Drug Education: A Model for Evaluation*, Washington, DC: Drug Abuse Council (1973); Bushy, J., *Drug Education: Goals, Approaches, Evaluation*, Arlington, VA: Educational Research Service (1975); Girdana, D. and Girdana, D., *Drug Education: Content and Methods*, Reading, MA: Addison-Wesley (1972); Edwards, G., *Reaching Out*, New York: Holt, Rhinehard and Winston (1971); Cornacchio, H., *Drugs in the Classroom: A Conceptual Model*

for School Programs, St. Louis: C.V. Mosby (1973); Dohner, V.A., "Alternatives to Drugs," *Journal of Drug Education* 2: 3-22 (1972).

46 Drug Policy Office, *Federal Strategy for Prevention of Drug Abuse and Drug Trafficking*, Washington, DC: The White House (1982).

47 U.S. Department of Education, *What Works: Schools Without Drugs*, Washington, DC (1986).

48 Lindblad, R.A., "A Review of the Concerned Parent Movement in the United States of America," *Bulletin on Narcotics* 35, 3: 41-52 (1983); Booth, W., "War Breaks Out Over an Agency," *Science* 211: 648-50 (1988); Jaffe, J.H., "Footnotes in the Evolution of the American National Response: Some Little Known Aspects of the First American Strategy for Drug Abuse and Drug Trafficking Prevention," *British Journal of Addiction* 82: 587-600 (1987).

49 Cohen, J., "Achieving a Reduction in Drug-Related Harm Through Education," pp. 65-76 in Heather, N. et al., *Psychoactive Drugs and Harm Reduction: From Faith to Science*, London: Whurr (1993); Staples, P., "Reduction of Alcohol- and Drug-Related Harm in Australia: A Government Minister's Perspective," pp. 49-54 in Heather, N. et al., *Psychoactive Drugs and Harm Reduction: From Faith to Science*, London: Whurr (1993); Marshall, I.H. and Marshall, C.E., "Drug Prevention in the Netherlands—A Low Key Approach," pp. 205-32 in Leuw, E. and Marshall, I.H. (eds), *Between Prohibition and Legalization: The Dutch Experiment in Drug Policy*, Amsterdam: Kugler Publications (1994).

50 Lifeline, 101-103 Oldham Street, Manchester, England M4 1LW.

51 McDermott, P. et al., "Ecstasy in the United Kingdom: Recreational Drug Use and Subcultural Change," pp. 230-44 in Heather, N. et al. (eds), *Psychoactive Drugs and Harm Reduction: From Faith to Science*, London: Whurr (1993); Fromberg, E., "A Harm Reduction Educational Strategy Toward Ecstasy," pp. 146-153 in O'Hare, P.A. et al. (eds), *The Reduction of Drug-Related Harm*, New York: Routledge (1992).

52 Netherlands Institute on Alcohol and Drugs, "Cannabis Policy Fact Sheet," *Netherlands Alcohol and Drug Report* 1 (1995).

53 Jacobs, J.B., *Drunk Driving: An American Dilemma*, Chicago: University of Chicago Press (1989).

54 Cohen, J. and Kay, J., *Taking Drugs Seriously: A Parent's Guide to Young People's Drug Use*, Great Britain: Thorsons (1994); Miller, M. and Burbank, S., *Teach Your Children Well: A Rational Guide to Family Drug Education*, Mosier, OR: Mothers Against Misuse and Abuse (1995); De Miranda, J., "Do Our Drug Prevention Messages Underestimate Kids?" *Alcoholism and Drug Abuse Weekly* (17 February 1997); Anonymous, "The Rite of Passage: A Family's Perspective on the Use of MDMA," *Multidisciplinary Association for Psychedelic Studies* 7, 1: 40-45 (1997); Anonymous, "Stumbling on His Stash," *Multidisciplinary Association for Psychedelic Studies* 7, 1: 37-39 (1997); Beam, A., "Getting Real About Drugs," *Boston Globe* (25 November 1991).

55   Center on Addiction and Substance Abuse, *National Survey of American Attitudes on Substance Abuse,* New York (1995); Center on Addiction and Substance Abuse, *National Survey of American Attitudes on Substance Abuse II: Teens and Their Parents,* New York (1996).

Conclusion

1   Advisory Committee on Drug Dependence, *Cannabis,* London: Her Majesty's Stationery Office (1969).

2   Canadian Government Commission of Inquiry, *The Non-Medical Use of Drugs,* Ottawa, Canada: Information Canada (1970).

3   National Commission on Marihuana and Drug Abuse, *Marihuana: A Signal of Misunderstanding,* Washington, DC: U.S. Government Printing Office (1972).

4   Werkgroep Verdovende Middelen, *Background and Risks of Drug Use,* The Hague: Staatsuigeverij (1972).

5   Senate Standing Committee on Social Welfare, *Drug Problems in Australia—An Intoxicated Society,* Canberra: Australian Government Publishing Service (1977).

6   National Research Council, *An Analysis of Marijuana Policy,* Washington, DC: National Academy Press (1982).

7   McDonald, D. et al., *Legislative Options for Cannabis in Australia,* Report on the National Task Force on Cannabis, Canberra: Australian Government Publishing Service (1994).

8   Ministry of Health, Welfare and Sport, *Drugs Policy in the Netherlands: Continuity and Change,* The Netherlands (1995).

9   National Commission on Marihuana and Drug Abuse, "Marihuana Use in American Society," pp.249-339 in *Marihuana: A Signal of Misunderstanding, Appendix I,* Washington, DC: U.S. Government Printing Office (1972).

10   National Commission on Marihuana and Drug Abuse, "Enforcement Behavior at the State Level," pp. 612-728 in *Marihuana: A Signal of Misunderstanding, Apendix II,* Washington, DC: U.S. Government Printing Office (1972).

11   National Commission on Marihuana and Drug Abuse, "A Nationwide Study of Beliefs, Information and Experiences," pp. 855-968 in *Marihuana: A Signal of Misunderstanding, Apendix II,* Washington, DC; U.S. Government Printing Office (1972).

12   National Commission on Marihuana and Drug Abuse, "Opinion Within the Criminal Justice System," pp. 782-852 in *Marihuana: A Signal of Misunderstanding, Apendix II,* Washington, DC: U.S. Government Printing Office (1972)

13   Subcommittee Hearings to Investigate Juvenile Delinquency, Senate Judiciary Committee, *Marijuana Decriminalization,* Washington, DC: U.S. Government Printing Office (1975).

14   New York Academy of Medicine, Committee on Public Health, "Marihuana

and Drug Abuse," *Bulletin of the New York Academy of Medicine* 49: 77-80 (1973).

15 Quoted in Baum, D., *Smoke and Mirrors: The War on Drugs and the Politics of Failure*, Boston: Little, Brown and Company (1996), p. 92.

16 Subcommittee Hearings to Investigate Juvenile Delinquency, Senate Judiciary Committee (1975), see note 13, p. 6.

17 Quoted in DiChiara, A. and Galliher, J.F., "Dissonance and Contradictions in the Origins of Marihuana Decriminalization," *Law and Society Review* 28: 41-77 (1994), p. 58.

18 Quoted in *Marihuana and Health in Perspective, Summary and Comments* and Fischer, B., "Canadian Cannabis Policy: The Impact of Criminalization, the Current Reality and Future Policy Options," pp. 227-42 in Bollinger, L. (ed), *Cannabis Science: From Prohibition to Human Right*, New York: Peter Lang (1997).

19 Quoted in DiChiara and Galliher (1994), see note 17, p.55.

20 Quoted in DiChiara and Galliher (1994), see note 17, p.53.

22 Quoted in DiChiara and Galliher (1994), see note 17, p.52.

23 Quoted in DiChiara and Galliher (1994), see note 17, p.51.

24 President's Advisory Commission on Narcotics and Drug Abuse, *Final Report*, Washington, DC: U.S. Government Printing Office (1963).

25 President's Commission on Law Enforcement and the Administration of Justice, *Task Force Report on Narcotics and Drug Abuse*, Washington, DC: U.S. Government Printing Office (1967).

26 National Institute of Law Enforcement and Criminal Justice, *Marijuana: A Study of State Policies and Penalties*, Washington, DC: U.S. Department of Justice (1977).

27 DiChiara and Galliher (1994), see note 17.

28 Subcommittee Hearings to Investigate the Administration of the Internal Security Act and Other Internal Security Laws, *Marihuana-Hashish Epidemic and Its Impact on United States Security*, Washington, DC: U.S. Government Printing Office (1974).

29 Slaughter, J.B., "Marijuana Prohibition in the United States: History and Analysis of a Failed Policy," *Columbia Journal of Law and Social Problems* 21: 417-74 (1988).

30 Johnston, L.D. et al., *National Survey Results on Drug Use from the Monitoring the Future Study, 1975-1995, Volume I, Secondary School Students*, Rockville, MD: U.S. Department of Health and Human Services (1996).

31 Cook, M.H. and Newman, C., *This Side Up*, Rockville, MD: National Institute on Drug Abuse (1977); National Institute on Drug Abuse, *Drug Abuse Prevention for Your Family*, Rockville, MD (1977).

32 Manatt, M., *Parents, Peers and Pot*, Rockville, MD: National Institute on Drug Abuse (1979); Manatt, M., *Parents, Peers and Pot II*, Rockville, MD: National

Institute on Drug Abuse (1983); Mann, P. *Marijuana Alert*, New York: McGraw-Hill Book Company (1985); National Institute on Drug Abuse, "Celebrating Parent Power in Georgia," *Prevention Resources* 3, 3-4 (1978).

33   National Institute on Drug Abuse, "Prevention at the Grassroots," *Prevention Resources* 6, 1 (1982).

34   National Institute on Drug Abuse, *State of the Art Report on the Parent Movement*, Rockville, MD (1981).

35   Lindblad, R.A., "A Review of the Concerned Parent Movement in the United States of America," *Bulletin on Narcotics* 35, 3: 41-52 (1983); Jaffe, J.H., "Footnotes in the Evolution of the American National Response: Some Little Known Aspects of the First American Strategy for Drug Abuse and Drug Trafficking Prevention,' *British Journal of Addiction* 82: 587-600 (1987).

36   DuPont, R.L., *Getting Tough on Gateway Drugs*, Washington, DC: American Psychiatric Press (1984).

37   Manatt (1979), see note 32.

38   Baum (1996), see note 15.

39   Mann, P., *Marijuana Update*, Pleasantville, NY: Reader's Digest (1982), pp. 3, 11, 17.

40   Mann (1985), see note 32.

41   The American Council on Marijuana was later renamed the American Council on Marijuana and Other Psychoactive Drugs, and then the American Council for Drug Education.

42   For example, Heath, R.G., *Marijuana and the Brain*, Rockville, MD: American Council on Marijuana and Other Psychoactive Drugs (1981); Tashkin, D.P. and Cohen, S., *Marijuana Smoking and Its Effects on the Lungs*, Rockville, MD: American Council on Marijuana and Other Psychoactive Drugs (1981); Turner, C.E., *The Marijuana Controversy*, Rockville, MD: American Council on Marijuana and Other Psychoactive Drugs (1981); Moskowitz, H. and Petersen, R., *Marijuana and Driving*, Rockville, MD: American Council on Marijuana and Other Psychoactive Drugs (1982); Smith, C.G. and Asch, R.H., *Marijuana and Reproduction*, Rockville, MD: American Council on Marijuana and Other Psychoactive Drugs (1982).

43   Russell, G.K., *Marihuana Today: A Compilation of Medical Findings for the Layman*, New York: The Myrin Institute (1978).

44   Nahas, G.G., *Marihuana—Deceptive Weed*, New York: Raven Press (1973); Nahas, G.G., *Keep Off the Grass*, New York: Reader's Digest Press (1976).

45   Nahas (1976), see note 44, pp. 152, 163.

46   "Reagan Warns Against Easier 'Pot' Penalties," *Los Angeles Times* (5 December 1974), p. 32.

47   Drug Policy Office, *Federal Strategy for Prevention of Drug Abuse and Drug Traffick-*

ing, Washington, DC: The White House (1982).

48 "Discussion Highlights," pp. 100-108 in National Institute on Drug Abuse, *Marijuana and Youth: Clincal Observations on Motivation and Learning,* Rockville, MD (1982), p. 101.

49 "Highlights of Final Discussion," pp. 109-120 in National Institute on Drug Abuse, *Marijuana and Youth: Clincal Observations on Motivation and Learning,* Rockville, MD (1982), pp. 114-15.

50 National Institute on Drug Abuse, *Marijuana and Health,* Ninth Report to the U.S. Congress from the Secretary of Health and Human Services (1982).

51 National Institute on Drug Abuse, *Marijuana and Health,* Eighth Annual Report to the U.S. Congress from the Secretary of Health, Education, and Welfare (1980).

52 Kleiman, M.A.R., *Marijuana: Costs of Abuse, Costs of Control,* New York: Greenwood Press (1989); Reuter, P., "On the Consequences of Toughness," pp. 138-164 in Kraus, M.B. and Lazear, E.P., *Searching for Alternatives: Drug Control Policy in the United States,* Stanford: Hoover Institution Press (1991); Baum (1996), see note 15.

53 Gordon, D.R., *The Return of the Dangerous Classes: Drug Prohibition and Policy Politics,* New York: W.W. Norton & Company (1994); Trebach, A.S., *The Great Drug War,* New York: Macmillan Publishing Company (1987).

54 Federal Bureau of Investigation, *Uniform Crime Reports,* Washington, DC: U.S. Department of Justice (1991-1995).

55 Marijuana Policy Project, *"Smoke a Joint, Lose Your License": July 1995 Status Report,* Washington, DC (1995).

56 Marijuana Policy Project, "MPP Analyzes States' Medicinal Marijuana Laws," *Marijuana Policy Report* 2, 3: 1-6 (1996); Wren, C.S., "Votes on Marijuana are Stirring Debate," *New York Times* (17 November 1996), p. 16.

57 Drug Enforcement Administration, *Drug Legalization: Myths and Misconceptions,* Washington, DC: U.S. Department of Justice (1994); Barry McCaffrey, Director of National Drug Control Policy, Senate Judiciary Committee Hearings, *Teenage Drug Use* (4 September 1996); Office of National Drug Control Policy, *The Administration's Response to the Passage of California Proposition 215 and Arizona Proposition 200,* Washington, DC: The White House (30 December 1996); "Doctors Given Federal Threat on Marijuana: U.S. Acts to Overcome States' Easing of Law," *New York Times* (31 December 1996), p. 1.

58 Office of National Drug Control Policy, *National Drug Control Strategy,* Washington, DC (1989), p. 47.

59 U.S. Department of Education, *What Works: Schools Without Drugs,* Washington, DC (1992); Office of National Drug Control Policy (1989), see note 58.

60 American Management Association, *1994 Survey on Workplace Drug Testing and*

Drug Abuse Policies, New York (1994).

61 Booth, W., "Florida County Sets Drug Tests for Welfare Clients," *Washington Post* (17 September 1996), p. A3.

62 Boodman, S.G., "Testing Your Children for Drugs," *Washington Post Health* (25 February 1997), p. 12.

63 Glass, S., "Don't You D.A.R.E.," *New Republic* (3 March 1997), pp. 18-28.

64 Substance Abuse and Mental Health Services Administration, *National Household Survey on Drug Abuse: Main Findings 1994*, Rockville, MD: U.S. Department of Health and Human Services (1996); Johnson et al. (1996), see note 30.

65 For example, Center on Addiction and Substance Abuse, *Cigarettes, Alcohol, Marijuana: Gateways to Illicit Drug Use*, New York (1994); Center on Addiction and Substance Abuse, *National Survey of American Attitudes on Substance Abuse*, New York (1995); Center on Addiction and Substance Abuse, *National Survey of American Attitudes on Substance Abuse II: Teens and Their Parents*, New York (1996).

66 Leshner, A.I., "Marijuana Initiative Features Scientifically Accurate Messages," *NIDA Notes* 10, 4: 3 (1995).

67 Partnership for a Drug-Free America Press Release, "With Potential Marijuana Crisis Re-Emerging, Partnership Launches Massive Advertising Blitz on Marijuana," New York (23 January 1995).

68 Hadi, N., "The Reality Check Campaign," *Prevention Pipeline* 9, 4: 5-6 (1996).

69 Quoted in "NIDA Conference Advances HHS Secretary's Marijuana Initiative," *NIDA Notes* 10, 6: 5 (1995).

70 Ministry of Health, Welfare and Sport (1995), see note 8.

71 Bollinger, L., "German Drug Law in Action," pp. 153-68 in Bollinger, L. (ed), *Cannabis Science: From Prohibition to Human Right*, Frankfurt: Peter Lang (1997); Arnao, G., "Anti-Prohibitionism: Prospects For the Future," pp. 107-203 in *Questioning Prohibition: 1994 International Report on Drugs*, Brussels: International Antiprohibitionist League (1994); Radical Anti-Prohibitionist Co-Ordination, "The Cora and the Italian Referendum on Drugs," pp. 151-52 in *Questioning Prohibition: 1994 International Report on Drugs*, Brussels: International Antiprohibitionist League (1994); McDonald et al. (1994), see note 7.

72 McDonald et al. (1994), see note 7.

73 Bonnie, R.J., "America's Drug Policy: Time for Another Commission?" *Contemporary Drug Problems* 20: 395-408 (1993).

74 National Commission on Drug-Free Schools, *Toward a Drug-Free Generation: A Nation's Responsibility*, Washington, DC: U.S. Department of Education (1990); Office of National Drug Control Policy, *National Drug Control Strategy*, Washington, DC: The White House (1995); U.S. Department of Health and Human Services Press Release, "Marijuana and Tobacco Use Still Rising Among 8th

and 10th Graders," Rockville, MD (19 December 1996).

75 Center on Addiction and Substance Abuse, *Legalization: Panacea or Pandora's Box*, New York (1995); Gorman, T.J., *The Myths of Drug Legalization*, Santa Clarita, CA: California Narcotics Officers' Association (1994); Drug Enforcement Administration (1994), see note 57.

76 Adlaf, E. et al., *The Ontario Student Drug Use Survey: 1975-1995*, Toronto: Addiction Research Foundation (1995); Donnelly, N. and Hall, W., *Patterns of Cannabis Use in Austrailia*, Canberra: Australian Government Publishing Service (1994); Harrison, L.D., "More Cannabis in Europe? Perspectives from the USA," paper presented at the Conference on Drug Use and Drug Policy, European Research Group on Drug Issues and Drug Policy, Amsterdam (September 1996).

77 Single, E., "The Impact of Marijuana Decriminalization: An Update," *Journal of Public Health Policy* 10: 456-66 (1989); Johnston, L.D. et al., *Marijuana Decriminalization: The Impact on Youth, 1975-1980*, Monitoring the Future, Occasional Paper 13, Ann Arbor: University of Michigan (1981); Saveland, W. and Bray, D.F., "Trends in Cannabis Use Among American States with Different and Changing Legal Regimes, 1972-77," *Contemporary Drug Problems* 10: 335-61 (1981).

78 Belden & Russonello, "American Voters' Opinions on the Use and Legalization of Marijuana," national random poll conducted for the American Civil Liberties Union, New York (1995).

79 Bureau of Justice Statistics, *Sourcebook of Criminal Justice Statistics 1994*, Washington, DC: U.S. Department of Justice (1994), p. 197; Partnership for a Drug-Free America, *1995 Partnership Attitude Tacking Study*, New York (1996); Center on Addiction and Substance Abuse (1995), see note 65; Center on Addiction and Substance Abuse (1996), see note 65; Belden & Russonello (1995), see note 78.

80 Johnston et al. (1996), see note 30.

81 Bureau of Justice Statistics, *Sourcebook of Criminal Justice Statistics 1995*, Washington, DC: U.S. Department of Justice (1995), p. 219.

82 The Field Institute, poll of California voters' support for Proposition 215 (1996); Center on Addiction and Substance Abuse Press Release, "Majority of Californians Support Marijuana for Terminally Ill But Reject Other Provisions" (28 October 1996); Lake Research, Inc., national random poll conducted for the Lindesmith Center, New York (1997); Belden & Russonello (1995), see note 78.

83 Center on Substance Abuse Prevention, "Marijuana Issues: Meeting Summary," Rockville, MD: U.S. Department of Health and Human Services (April 1995); Center on Addiction and Substance Abuse (1995), see note 65; Center on Addiction and Substance Abuse (1996), see note 65; Partnership for a Drug-Free America (1996), see note 79.

84 Substance Abuse and Mental Health Services Administration (1996), see note 64.

Index